"Porte Crayon": The Life of
David Hunter Strother

"Porte Crayon," David Hunter Strother, behind one of the most famous American beards at mid-century. ". . . people know him on Broadway by the sketches he has made of his glorious beard in Harper's. . . ." (Photograph courtesy of Emily Strother Kreuttner.)

"Porte Crayon": The Life of David Hunter Strother

By

Cecil D. Eby, Jr.

Chapel Hill

The University of North Carolina Press

To

my father

Preface

THIS book treats the life and work of one of the most popular American writers of the mid-nineteenth century, David Hunter Strother ("Porte Crayon"), whose accomplishments as an artist, writer, soldier and diplomat comprise one of the most versatile careers in American history. From painting and illustration, Strother at the age of thirty-seven turned to writing; at forty-five he entered the Union army and rose to the rank of brigadier general; at sixty-three he was appointed consul general to Mexico. Like other Virginians before him, Strother had a wide range of interests which gave him access to American personalities as different as Washington Irving and Walt Whitman, Winfield Scott and Ulysses S. Grant, Robert E. Lee and Abraham Lincoln, and a host of others. As "Porte Crayon," he became one of the most widely read and highly paid writers in the United States. To the pages of *Harper's New Monthly Magazine,* he brought a talent that both molded and reflected the popular taste in literature from 1853 to 1879. His fifty-five articles in that magazine, all of them illustrated by his own woodcut drawings, are a link between the two traditions of literature in the South—the genteel romanticism of the sentimental novelists and the earthy realism of the frontier humorists. As a soldier, Strother guided the first successful Union campaign in the Shenandoah Valley and thereby incurred the enmity of a generation of his fellow Virginians. But it was with his pen

rather than his sword that General Strother made his more en-
during mark.

A biography of David Hunter Strother is long overdue. The
need for an accurate life was first felt in the early 1900's when
Daniel Bedinger Lucas was preparing a biographical sketch for
inclusion in *A Library of Southern Literature,* and this need is
even more pressing today, at a time when Southern literature
and history are undergoing serious and critical re-examination.
No other writer or artist described the Old South better or in
more realistic detail than did Porte Crayon; moreover, he
practiced the two arts in happy combination, presenting Southern
scenes not only in words but also in pictures. In recent years
the reprinting of his essays and drawings in newspapers, magazines, and books has touched off a revival of interest in Strother's work. Grandchildren are rediscovering the literature of
their grandparents and are finding in it amusement and instruction lost for a generation. Perhaps the most significant
contribution to this reawakening has been made by The University of North Carolina Press, which in 1959 published *The
Old South Illustrated,* a partial collection of Strother's best graphic and literary work. The enthusiastic reception of that volume
has proved that Porte Crayon can still win readers, and it is
hoped that this biography will introduce to the republic of
letters and to the general public a gifted writer-artist who has
been unaccountably neglected.

Biographers of most literary figures must justify a further
study of their subject. Since existing accounts of David Strother
are few and inaccurate, I have no such problem. However,
the dearth of materials about him is in itself a problem, for the
biographer must assume that the reader knows little or nothing
about either the man or his work. Not only, therefore, must
the biographer provide a portrait of the man himself, but also
he must place the man in the large canvas of American (and
Southern) culture of the nineteenth century. David Strother
was not a radical or an innovator. We are interested in him not
because he changed the course of history but because he reflected it. Like Howells and Simms, Strother was a writer who
was at once close to, yet superior to, the main currents of his

age. I have attempted to place him against the background of his era without, however, forgetting that my primary purpose is biographical, not sociological.

At the outset I confess to deliberate failure in providing a convenient pigeonhole in which to put Porte Crayon. He was, in his own words, an "aesthetic outlaw" who belonged to no coterie and abided not long within any system, though he borrowed from many. Although he was born, lived, and died in the Valley of Virginia, he was often vigorous in the denunciation of "Virginianism." He always kept one foot in the North and the other in the South, and when loyalty was often a matter of geography, Strother persisted in making up his own mind. Among American writers, he respected Herman Melville most, perhaps because both men refused to oversimplify the complex nature of human existence. Both, too, were travelers "tormented with an everlasting itch for things remote"; but while Melville was compelled, Strother was just curious. Yet for a generation Strother's travel essays in *Harper's* were deservedly popular, and gratified his readers' curiosity as well as his own.

This biography grew from a dissertation in American literature at the University of Pennsylvania, but the present work is the result of an almost total revision. On the recommendation of the publisher, I have waged a vigorous, but not entirely victorious, war upon the footnotes of the dissertation. Generally, footnotes obtrude whenever necessary, not whenever possible.

A few words are required about my quotations from Strother's more than thirty manuscript journals, which minutely chronicle his activities from 1861 to 1888. Considerations of space and readability have dictated the omission of footnotes when quoting from these journals, none of which are in the public domain. Since my dissertation is available to scholars and since that work contains most of the quotations contained in this, anyone who is concerned with the particular date of quoted materials can readily find it. Therefore, unless an unfootnoted quotation is juxtaposed with others which make its source readily clear, the reader may assume that it has been extracted from one of Strother's journals. All such quotations have been reproduced with fidelity to the original source. The customary *"sic"* mark has been omitted, as being required, if at all, often enough to "shred" certain of the journal passages.

It is to be noted here that the journals treating the Civil War years will soon be published by the University of North Carolina Press. They not only add to our information about Strother but also bear upon important personalities and issues of the age.

In the writing of this book, my greatest debt is to Mr. David H. Strother of Milwaukee, the grandson of Porte Crayon and the owner of most of the family papers. Without his unfailing interest and generosity, no biography could have been written at all. I wish to thank Dr. Thomas Haviland of the University of Pennsylvania, the supervisor of my dissertation, for his continued guidance and patience. Any serious investigator of Western Virginia history must, almost inevitably, meet Mr. Boyd B. Stutler of Charleston, whose fund of knowledge is as vast as his willingness to share it; to him I acknowledge my indebtedness. Moreover, I thank a generous group of West Virginia historians including Mr. Thornton Perry of Charles Town, Mr. Charles Shetler of Morgantown, and Mr. Charles Carpenter of Grafton.

The following have also provided me with valuable assistance and information utilized in writing this book: Mr. F. P. Voegele of Lincoln, Michigan; Mr. Francis Haber of Baltimore; Mrs. Louise Shepard of Falls Church, Virginia, and Mrs. Emily Kreuttner of North Tarrytown, New York, both of them granddaughters of Porte Crayon; Miss Katherine M. Hunter and Mr. Fred Newbraugh of Berkeley Springs, West Virginia; Dr. A. D. Kenamond of Shepherdstown, West Virginia; Dr. Thomas M. Hunter of Pottsville, Pennsylvania; Mr. Delf Norona of Moundsville, West Virginia; Mr. Charles Bohner of Wilmington, Delaware; Mr. Stuart Brown of Berryville, Virginia; Dr. Jay L. Curtis and Dr. Joseph Kraus of Harrisonburg, Virginia; Mr. Chester Goolrick of Lexington, Virginia; Mr. Curtis Carroll Davis of Baltimore; Mr. and Mrs. Travis Coe and Miss Winnie Eby of Charles Town, West Virginia; Mr. Edwin K. Tolan of Washington, Pennsylvania; Mr. Howard J. Shannon of Jamaica, New York; Miss Emily Shepherd of Charleston, Illinois; and the late Mr. Harry E. Pratt of Springfield, Illinois.

For their assistance I am also grateful to the librarians and staff of the following: the University of Pennsylvania, West Virginia University, the University of North Carolina, the University of Virginia, Princeton University, the University of Maine, the Woman's College of the University of North Carolina, the National Archives, the West Virginia Archives, the Library of Congress, the New York Public Library, Duke University, the Peabody Institute, High Point College, and Madison College.

Last, but by no means least, I wish to thank my wife Patricia for many services in the preparation of this book, and the editorial staff of the University of North Carolina Press for their advice in my work on this biography as well as on *The Old South Illustrated* which preceded it.

Contents

List of Illustrations

"Porte Crayon": The Life of
David Hunter Strother

Chapter I

The Early Years, 1816-1832

A T the dawn of the nineteenth century, the village of Martinsburg at the northern end of the Valley of Virginia was
something more than a trading center for the Blue Ridge country.
The county seat of Berkeley, Martinsburg could boast two hundred houses and nearly twelve hundred inhabitants, and the
double columns of aristocratic-looking Lombardy poplars along
Queen Street were a source of civic pride. It was the first place
of any size encountered in Virginia by the Pennsylvania emigrants streaming across the nearby Potomac River en route to the
cheap lands to the southwest. Their heavy wagons and dusty cattle were a familiar sight for Martinsburgers throughout the
National Period, and no less than eight taverns did a thriving
business on the main street. Few emigrants stayed on in Berkeley
County, for even at this early date the land was occupied. The
soil of the north Valley was unusually rich for Virginia, the
crops were abundant, the water supply was remarkable, and a
flourishing group of farmers had acquired what passed for
wealth in this tramontane section of the state. With wealth had
come leisure, and a "coffee house where almost all the papers in
the United States are read"[1] served as a meeting place for local
gentry in town for business or pleasure.

Martinsburg owed its prosperity to the two principal roads
which intersected the town. The "Great Road," which later became the Valley Turnpike, conducted the emigrants to Staunton;

1. F. Vernon Aler, *History of Martinsburg* (Hagerstown, Md., 1888), p. 275.

the other connected Washington City with its favorite spa, Bath
or Berkeley Springs, at the sparsely settled northern end of the
county. The original settlers of Martinsburg had come along one
or the other, the Germans and Scots-Irish from the north and the
English from the south. These racial streams had converged
in Berkeley County, those from Pennsylvania supplying the mer-
cantile and industrial energy, and that from older Virginia the
social and cultural tone. Berkeley County early became a micro-
cosm of nineteenth-century America, a melting pot into which
were poured quite different national groups. Social and economic stratification was less evident here than in Virginia east
of the Blue Ridge. Cut off from Richmond by the mountains,
Berkeley men learned to rely upon Georgetown and Baltimore
for trade and to look to Washington for advantageous legisla-
tion. They took the Baltimore newspapers and paid little heed to
Richmond, except during election years.

During the first quarter of the century, the clerk of the
Berkeley County court was Colonel David Hunter, known
through the region as a man of substance, of aristocratic bearing,
and of uncompromising Federalist politics. His assistant clerk
was John Strother, a veteran of the War of 1812 who had married one of the Colonel's daughters in 1815. In a rented stone
house on Burke Street, David Hunter Strother was born at ten
o'clock in the morning of September 26, 1816. He was the first
of eight children born to John and Elizabeth Hunter Strother
and the only male child to reach maturity.[2] John Strother (1792-
1862) had grown up on his father's farm, "Park Forest," near
Charles Town but had shown little interest in agriculture. After
his father's death in 1807, he had been placed as an apprentice
clerk in the Berkeley courthouse and had been virtually adopted
by Colonel David Hunter. John was largely a self-made and self-
taught man. He studied Latin and history during leisure

2. David and Emily (1820-1904) were the only children to survive infancy.
The Strother family Bible lists the names of six male children who died. For a
genealogical account of the descendants of David and Emily, see John Bailey
Calvert Nicklin, "The Strother Family," *Tyler's Quarterly Historical and Genea-
logical Magazine,* XL (October, 1929), 113-40; (January, 1930), 182-99; and
(April, 1930), 251-65.

moments at the courthouse, emulated the manners of the Colonel's children—with whom he lived—and became a lieutenant in the local regiment of militia. When the War of 1812 broke out, he resigned his Virginia commission, joined the regular army of the United States,[3] and served with distinction on the Canadian frontier at the ill-fated Battle of Crystler's Farm. At the war's end, he returned to his post at the courthouse, married Elizabeth Hunter, and showed himself a rising man in Berkeley affairs. By the 1820's he was a property owner, a lieutenant colonel in the 67th Regiment of Virginia militia, and a power in local politics. In the same decade the "courthouse clique" made him clerk of the circuit court, an appointment which placed him first in line for succession to the county clerkship when Colonel Hunter retired or died. Not even political rivals ever questioned the integrity of John Strother. He had a will of iron and the character of a gentleman, two qualities highly esteemed in northern Virginia.

Elizabeth Hunter Strother was related to a distinguished line of Virginia families which included the Hunters, the Pendletons, the Dandridges, and the Cookes. "Cousins count in Virginia," wrote John P. Kennedy, "and have great privileges," and through his mother David Strother could count as cousins such literary notables as John Esten Cooke, Philip Pendleton Cooke, John Pendleton Kennedy, and Philip Pendleton Kennedy. From his mother he doubtless drew his respect for tradition and his veneration of the Virginia past. Elizabeth Strother was not an exciting parent, but she was remembered by her son as "a pious and devoted parent, a model housewife, endowed with a lively fancy and conversational powers, . . . the delight of the society in which she moved."

Because death was such a frequent visitor among the Strother children, the parents were solicitous about the health of young Dave. They had reason to be, for he was a small and feeble child, racked with fevers and at first unable to enter into the round of active outdoor sports expected of most Virginia youths. Twice each month his mother took him to her church, the Presbyterian;

3. *Calendar of Virginia State Papers,* X, p. 223. There is a short biographical sketch of John Strother in Aler, pp. 143-44.

on the alternate Sundays his father conducted him to his, the Episcopalian. Confused by this, the boy became indifferent and finally lost all interest in sectarian religion. Although he attended the Martinsburg Academy in the same class with Phil Cooke (who was born in the same year), he received his most valuable instruction at home under the guidance of his father. Colonel John taught him how to draw pictures, and read him tales of border fury and martial glory from the books of Sir Walter Scott, who became his favorite author. Dave spent his leisure time illustrating these readings by sketches, said to have been fanciful and imaginative. Some of his earliest recollections were of fireside tales in which his father told of stooping to kiss the soil of Virginia before departing for the Canadian War, and of carrying off the body of a dead kinsman after the Battle of Crystler's Farm. The dust and grime of the big ledgers at the courthouse became synonymous with the tedium as well as the drama of the Virginia past, and veterans of the Revolutionary War still tottered about the streets of Martinsburg. Major Henry Bedinger, a tall, white-bearded old man, had been with the march of Daniel Morgan's militiamen to Cambridge in 1775. Old "Shopestall," a Hessian prisoner who had been taken at Saratoga and who drew a government pension, used to be hauled through the streets as a hero during the Fourth of July processions, at least until he fell, dead-drunk, in the cart. Limping Peter Cook was a familiar figure; he had lost his foot in St. Clair's battle by his failure to tell a dead Indian from a live one. Many could still remember eccentric General Charles Lee, who had lived at "Prato Rio" after his disgrace at Monmouth, although most Berkeley Countians knew more about Lee's pack of dogs than about the Virginian-hating General himself. At least one authenic frontiersman remained, John Myers of Meadow Branch. "Hunter" or "Wolf" Myers lived in the nearby mountains and made the trip to town every other week during winter with loads of venison, bear, and wild turkeys. Six feet, four inches, in height, Myers was an awesome character who stood "halfway between savage and civilized life."[4] He was a principal character in John Esten Cooke's first novel, *Leather-stocking and Silk: Hunter*

4. Aler, *History of Martinsburg*, p. 127.

John Myers and His Times (1854), and he exerted a strong influence upon Dave Strother as well. If a boy wanted to find heroes, he needed to look no further than the courthouse square.

There was no dearth of visits among kinfolk. Dave often saw John P. Kennedy, who came up from Baltimore every summer for a visit with his mother. Some said that "Swallow Barn" was really "The Bower," the Dandridge home over on the Opequon River, and it probably was. Phil Cooke, who shared Dave's artistic sensitivity, was a playmate, and Dave occasionally drew illustrations for Phil's verse.[5] His favorite playground was "Locust Grove," the home of his Aunt Catherine Crane (his father's sister) near Charles Town. His cousins Joe and Smith Crane taught him how to shoot wild fowl in the cattail marsh and rambled with him through the crumbling ruins of St. George's Chapel, an edifice so old that it was already a gothic landmark. Although his father's relatives were not so distinguished and prominent as his mother's, he found them more easygoing and openly generous. They remained his closest friends for a lifetime. But perhaps his most interesting relative was grandfather Hunter, an entertaining raconteur and a widely traveled man. The old patriarch particularly liked to storm about the English pickpockets who had plagued him on a business trip to England in the 1780's. One story in particular Dave never forgot. Colonel Hunter learned to keep his hands at all times in his pockets to protect his guineas. One day in Sheffield he joined a crowd to hear the Prince of Wales speak and, having some money with him, he buried his hands deeply in his pockets. When the Prince had concluded, the crowd snatched off their hats and cheered wildly, but the American who valued his change more than the royal blood kept his hands on guard until a fellow behind him knocked off his hat with a "you must be a damn'd American not to salute the prince!" Instantly he grabbed at his falling hat, caught it, and on revisiting his pockets found them both emptied! There may have been exaggeration in the Colonel's story, but it delighted his grandson. Colonel Hunter enjoyed a good story, and young Dave was encouraged to search for similar ones; the result was a rich vein

5. John D. Allen, *Philip Pendleton Cooke* (Chapel Hill, N. C., 1942), p. 11.

from which to mine when writing his own tales thirty years later.

Although John Strother encouraged his son's artistic talent, he nevertheless was disappointed that the boy would not be able to enter West Point some day and take up a military life. Dave had shy and secluded habits, and was given to amusements which his robust fellows thought were effeminate. But proof of his talent for drawing was revealed in the aftermath of a fire which gutted the Strother house on an icy night in November of 1825. Except for two leather buckets hanging on the walls of each house, there was no fire-fighting apparatus in Martinsburg, so that the Strothers lost nearly everything they owned. In the annals of the town the holocaust is chiefly memorable for the fact that the trustees shortly thereafter voted to purchase a fire engine,[6] but it has also given rise to a legend of such tenacity that it is probably founded in fact. Tradition says that Dave Strother, then a boy of nine, drew a picture of the fire which was so accurate in its details that the likenesses of the spectators were distinctly recognizable.[7] Whatever the merits of this drawing might have been, it doubtless made John Strother realize that he had a potential artist on his hands. Perhaps he felt that his son was largely unfit for anything else; at any rate, in an era which championed material success as the highest of human aspirations, it is gratifying to find that Colonel John tolerated, even encouraged, his son's nascent interest in art, which promised dubious rewards in the 1820's.

At the death of Colonel David Hunter in 1829, John Strother was promptly elevated to the vacant clerkship, which at that time was not an elective office. The event was of far-reaching importance for his family. With his financial situation improved, he was able to do something for his son's art. Dave was sent to study under Pietro Ancora at the Pennsylvania Academy

6. J. E. Norris (ed.), *History of the Lower Shenandoah Valley* (Chicago, 1890), p. 274.

7. Daniel B. Lucas in *A Library of Southern Literature* (Atlanta, 1908-1923), p. 5131, gives Strother's age at the time as three; also see Ella May Turner, *Stories and Verse of West Virginia* (Hagerstown, Md., 1923), p. 60. There are still people in Martinsburg who claim to have seen this picture, but it cannot be found.

of Fine Arts in Philadelphia, then the leading institution of its kind in America. Little, however, is known of Dave's studies there. Ancora had ill luck with his pupils, it seems, for the most outstanding painter to come under his charge, John Neagle, remained with him only for a quarter until removed by his father and apprenticed to a grocer.[8] Dave's tutelage probably did not last much longer, for by the late fall of 1829 he was again back in Martinsburg. Apparently he had little interest in the laborious copying from old masters—the standard method of teaching art at that time. He was always bored too easily to become concerned with technical perfection of his craft, and he doubtless felt that there were far better subjects for his coarse but spirited caricature on the streets of Martinsburg and in his father's books. But his short study in Philadelphia enlarged his vision of the world and acquainted him with the republic of the arts; moreover, it set him off from his Martinsburg contemporaries as a youth of greater promise.

At about this time an attack of measles miraculously invigorated his physique and radically altered his temperament and personality. With improving health, he developed such a reckless and headstrong spirit that he became the source of anxiety and wonder to his parents and friends. His personality now became as volatile and aggressive as it had formerly been passive and retiring. Books and drawing materials were thrown aside for guns and horses. The introverted amusements of the fireside were forgotten as he threw himself into the turbulent currents of boyhood with a boldness that foreshadowed leadership, for either good or evil. The deviltry of thirteen submerged years exploded in a series of pranks that were conversational topics in the town of Martinsburg for the next fifty years. Berkeley County chroniclers were certain to put one of Dave Strother's exploits into their books.

At one time he instigated a number of companions to assist him in capturing a small jackass, and carrying it up the winding stairs, into

8. William Dunlap, *A History of the Rise and Progress of the Arts of Design in the United States* (Boston, 1918), p. 165. A brief mention of Ancora may be found in J. Thomas Scharf and Thompson Westcott, *History of Philadelphia, 1609-1884* (Philadelphia, 1884), II, 1052.

the steeple of the old court-house, and tying it to the bell . . . . The ringing of the bell and the braying of the ass made melody in the air, not much resembling the Trinity chimes, and the good citizens, startled from their sleep, and but partially dressed, stood about in gaping wonder, not able to account for the phenomenon. It was not until morning that any could be found to brave the evil spirits and ascend to investigate, and it took all day for the city fathers to devise ways and means to lower the animal.[9]

With two companions he hiked to Bath, and on the Potomac pirated the ferry boat, leaving the irate boatman stamping on the other shore vowing he'd have their heads. With his Crane cousins he paid a visit to Charles Town, mustered a company of town roughs, broke up a meeting of the genteel debating society at the academy, and concluded the evening by nearly setting a tavern afire after throwing a shovelful of hot coals into a pot of whiskey.

Dave also had a hand in half a dozen gunpowder plots. Although he was always a poor shot, he did distinguish himself, in a manner of speaking, with firearms. Martinsburg was startled awake one Christmas evening by an explosion in the market place. Citizens found that the old whipping post, a vestigial token from another era, had been blown to pieces by a heavy charge of gunpowder. The culprit was never found, but even half a century later Dave was mentioned in connection with the memorable explosion. After the Nat Turner uprising in the early 1830's, the county clerk's house became an arsenal for use during any future slave insurrection. The location of this armory proved to be unwise. One day Dave caught a young cousin meddling with the guns and, to frighten him, took down one of the supposedly unloaded pieces, made the cousin kneel down, and twice snapped the gun at his head. While Dave was cocking for the third time, the boy bolted from the room. Carelessly Dave pointed the gun at the window, pulled the trigger, and blew out the window frame! To such heights had his reputation for mischief grown that in 1832 he was accused of having attempt-

9. [H. H. Hardesty] *Historical Hand-Atlas,* Special Berkeley and Jefferson County Edition (Chicago, 1883), p. 14. Aler's history mentions the jackass incident, but no names are given.

ed to assassinate his father's political rival, Harrison Waite. After a particularly bitter election, Waite, the Democratic candidate, had defeated Colonel John for the clerkship. One day the successful candidate was standing by the stove in the grocery store across from the Strother house when a musket was fired from Dave's garret window. The ball ricocheted off the stove within an inch or two of Waite's head and buried itself in a bale of cloth on a shelf. The thunderstruck observers saw smoke drifting from the Strother window and concluded that Dave had taken a shot at Waite. Fortunately, the accused was at school and an explanation was found: a Negro servant had been tampering with a loaded carbine and it had gone off in his hands.

Colonel John Strother must have viewed his son's strange metamorphosis with alarm and bewilderment. Here was conduct not fitting any artist he had ever heard about. However, he soon realized that Dave's reckless energy could be directed toward the long-cherished ambition of West Point and a military career. Hadn't the boy already organized a volunteer company among the academy boys and brazenly elected himself captain of it? Colonel John failed to understand that his political influence in Berkeley County had been broken forever by the rise to power of the Democrats during the Age of Jackson. His own political defeat was the first sign of changing times in Martinsburg. The patricians were out, and the Democrats could hardly be expected to sponsor the son of Berkeley's outspoken opponent of the common-man ideology. Dave's application was turned down in 1832, but the Colonel and his son determined to try again the following year. In the meantime, it was necessary to find some other activity which would stimulate the boy constructively, for already Dave had developed a recklessness that threatened to destroy every positive quality he had. It was decided that he should enter college in the fall and await the overthrow of the Democrats in the next election.

At this time there were two David Strothers: one was the mirror of his former self, an artistic and solitary youth searching for an inward inspiration; the other was the mirror of his father, a tumultuous boy wishing to find his place in the world as a man of action. This conflict between imagination and action, between ideality and reality, was never entirely resolved. It explains in part the erratic path of his later life, when in the midst of leisure he yearned for action, and in the midst of action he pined for leisure. His early, protected years had served their purpose— they had given him an unusually reflective mind, and sensibilities which could convert natural impressions into literary and artistic forms. But the abruptness of his physical transformation had its effect as well—it gave him an inordinate desire for boldness and recklessness. In his reaction against control of any kind, he forced himself to become left-handed, solely because he could not tolerate the natural tyranny of his right hand! It was this split in his character which produced the two David Strothers— one an artist and the other a soldier. Martinsburg nurtured both, each in a different way. Like his cousin Phil Cooke, David had read voraciously in works of the past, but of greater value was his saturation in the active drama of Berkeley County's present.

Chapter II

The Artist as a Young Man, 1832-1840

COLONEL John Strother had little enough faith in the politics of Thomas Jefferson and perhaps less in his university at Charlottesville, which was chiefly remarkable in the 1830's for the dissolute character of its student body.[1] Knowing that his son's high spirits would not be curbed in such an environment, the Colonel looked elsewhere and settled on Jefferson College in Canonsburg, Pennsylvania. This institution afforded the benefits of a religious as well as academic education, and it had graduated a number of distinguished Berkeley men. Its political principles were suitably Whiggish and pro-Union. Therefore, in the early fall of 1832, Dave took the western stage up the National Road for Canonsburg. He was admitted to sophomore standing and began what proved to be his last year of formal education.

The choice of colleges was lamentably unwise. He found the sectarian narrowness of the place confining and the academic program stultifying. It might be noted that his sojourn in

1. The experiences of Poe are too well known to bear repeating here. Because of the growing rift between the eastern and western counties, the University of Virginia was never popular west of the Blue Ridge. My examination of the annual catalogues of the University prior to 1860 reveals less than a half-dozen students from Berkeley County. One historian has said that there were twice as many residents of western Virginia in Ohio and Pennsylvania colleges as were in institutions of eastern Virginia. See Charles H. Ambler, *Sectionalism in Virginia from 1776 to 1861* (Chicago, 1910), p. 275.

Canonsburg was so short that he never learned how to spell the
name of the town correctly—until his last years he persisted in
writing "Cannonsburg." The college itself was probably neither
better nor worse than most classical schools of its time. It was
reputed to be the first college west of the mountains, a place
where, said a contemporary pamphlet, "heroic hexameters were
sung almost in the hearing of the war whoop of the savage."[2]
Although Dave took little interest in the studies—Latin, Greek,
German, algebra, Grecian antiquities, elocution, and composition
—the many references to college acquaintances scattered through
his private journals in later years show that he enjoyed the social
activities there. Perhaps the strongest impression he made upon
his colleagues was as an ingenious prankster; many years later
a Presbyterian minister inquired through a mutual friend for
news of David Strother, having followed his career ever since
the night Dave bedeviled him by putting a dozen eggs and
a turtle in his bed. The reason for his withdrawal from college
is unrecorded. The alumni rolls attribute to him the B. A.
degree in 1835 and the M. A. degree (honorary) in 1845, but
the official records are contradicted by his own testimony, which
Strother wrote in third-person many years later: "having little
taste for the prescribed curriculum and less for college discipline,
his unprofitable career there terminated in less than a year."[3]
As late as the Civil War, Strotherian escapades were remembered
in Canonsburg, so it is probable that the college authorities did
not regret the young man's resignation from school after the
spring term. Perhaps they rightly suspected that the wild Virginian had a hand in the stealing of the clapper from the college
bell that tolled the students to their classes. At any rate, while
Strother never revealed any animosity toward Jefferson College,
he regarded a classical education with scant respect and in later

2. James Veech, *The Annual Oration before the Alumni of Jefferson College*
(Canonsburg, Pa., 1835).

3. Mr. Edwin E. Tolan, Librarian at Washington and Jefferson College,
writes me that Strother was listed as a sophomore in the catalogue published in
July, 1833, but that his name does not appear in subsequent catalogues. The
minutes of the trustees for 1845 do not state why he was granted the honorary
degree of M. A. in that year. Mr. Tolan assumes that "in granting the honorary M. A. degree he would automatically be granted an honorary B.A."
Letter to the author, February 6, 1959.

years refused to subject his own son to such an impractical program. In *Virginia Illustrated* he summarized his college career:

One of our hero's early misfortunes was that he had been sent to college. Being naturally of an erratic and wayward disposition, he forsook the beaten track of learning, discarded the presented programme for the sophomore year, and diligently perfected himself in the mysteries of "old sledge" and the fiddle. At the end of the year his Euclid and Graeca Majora smelt as fresh as on the day they left the book-store, while he had sawed through innumerable strings of cat-gut, and thumbed to pieces pack and pack of Crehore's Cards, with a perseverance which some persons might say worthy of a better cause.

In his manuscript version of the same work, Strother praised the rigid discipline of the military colleges, which he contrasted with the laxity of the classical institutes. Doubtless thinking of his wasted year at Jefferson, he wrote: "What premature vices are acquired by the freedom from sound restraint, what bubble of conceits are engendered from the smattering of the classics, with which the young hopeful returns home to delight the sisters and astound the negroes, and puzzle the old-time pate of Papa as to whether his son is a genius or a puppy." Probably his most valuable experience during the year at Canonsburg was a visit to the bustling river town of Wheeling, the gateway to the Mississippi and the Western frontier. Here Dave caught the fever of exploration, which he gratified five years later by his own trek into the West.

Returning to Martinsburg in the spring of 1833, Dave again took up the unfinished business of the West Point cadetship, but without success. Three years in succession, he had marched afoot with rifle and knapsack down to Washington to visit the offices of the Secretary of War, Lewis Cass. Promises and vacillation had marked each interview, and Dave's desperate efforts to obtain an appointment recall those of Edgar Allen Poe only a few years before. At the final interview with Cass in 1834 or 1835, the Secretary by an expression of impatience made it clear that party politics had more to do with cadetships than patriotic zeal. Stung by Cass's cynicism, Strother rose to his feet and proclaimed with a spirit worthy of his father, "I at length under-

stand, sir, that I am denied the privilege of serving my country in
arms, because my Father is not a subservient partizan of the
Party in power. I am prouder of the disability, than I should
have been of your appointment. Good morning, sir." This
was the young man's first political disillusionment—by no means
his last—and from it he learned to distrust politics and politicians.[4]

The three years during which he had waited for the cadetship he considered the most wasteful of his life. While his contemporaries were making their marks in the world—Phil Cooke,
for example, had already published poems in the *Knickerbocker
Magazine*—Dave had only increased his idle time. For a while
he worked as a sub-clerk at the courthouse and made desultory
efforts at the study of law, medicine, and engineering, none of
which had any strong appeal for him. He frequented the weekly
cockfights in Martinsburg and took in most of the horse races at
the half-dozen courses scattered through the upper Valley. His
own riding was widely admired, but he never came up to Captain Jack Hurst, who could ride a horse when too drunk to walk.
Dave joined the militia, was elected fourth lieutenant, thought
he should have been first lieutenant, and resigned indignantly.
There were plenty of pretty girls in and about Martinsburg, and
Dave was in and out of love with a dozen of them. He pains-
takingly polished his "impromptu" verses, rendered "The Devil's
Dream" on his fiddle at picnics, and generally "wasted in non-
sense a stock of energy which if worked in harness might have
carried me far in an honourable career."

Since boyhood, Dave had shown an unusual interest in
narratives of travel, particularly when these treated remote and

4. Ironically, three generations of Strothers have been turned away from
West Point. David and his son John were unable to obtain appointments.
John's son, David H. Strother II, obtained an appointment but was rejected
for faulty vision. The Class of 1836 at West Point, consisting of forty-five
graduates, included Generals Montgomery Meigs (whose son campaigned with
Strother in 1864) and Thomas W. Sherman. Only five graduates of this class
held ranks in the Union Army higher than that of David Strother; as a civilian
soldier he made a better record than most of those who would have been his
classmates. Fisher Lewis, the successful candidate from Strother's district, retired from the army two years after receiving his commission and never fired
a shot for either side during the Civil War.

unfamiliar regions. During his academy days his strongest
subjects had been geography and natural history, and he was
nearly infallible in "naming the countries where bears, lions,
tigers, elephants, and boa constrictors are to be found; or the
seas in which sharks, whales, and sea serpents most abounded."[5]
He had developed an intellectual curiosity which made him always want to follow a creek to its source or to find out what was
on the other side of a mountain. Except for his trips to Philadelphia and to Canonsburg, Strother had never traveled outside
the northern Shenandoah Valley, but in 1835 he undertook his
first extensive tour—a five-hundred-mile hike up to the Natural
Bridge and across the Blue Ridge into the Virginia Piedmont.
This trip was the grand climax to his restless youth, and the
numerous references to it scattered in his published work show
how much he was influenced by it. Fortunately there is a fragmentary manuscript—the earliest extant writing of David Strother—which contains an account of the journey as far south as
Rockingham County. Although this fragment breaks off without warning and often is little more than the chronicle of an
exuberant boy with a ravenous appetite, it does foreshadow one
element of Strother's later style—an ability to turn the laugh upon
his own flamboyant romanticism. The manuscript catches the
spirit of adventure and the picaresque affection for fellow travelers on the road. Dave's subsequent path after the first four
days can be reconstructed in part from scattered references in
Virginia Illustrated, which treats another Valley excursion eighteen years later.

For Strother and his companion, James Ranson (Jim Rawlins
in *Virginia Illustrated*), the morning of October 7 dawned especially bright, because the tour "started twenty times in imagination" had become an actuality. With rifle and knapsacks, they
left Martinsburg and the clerk's office far behind, capering and
singing along the turnpike for Winchester. There in Lord
Fairfax's stately old town, the wayfarers shocked sedate diners at
Sauck's Hotel by glutting appetites whetted by their twenty-
mile hike. "We licked up the gravy and finally like our great
ancestors of Britain who sheathed their swords for lack of argu-

5. "The Young Virginians," *Riverside Magazine,* II (August, 1868), 373.

ment, we stopped for lack of meat." While they found the towns of the upper Valley "miserable" or "inconsiderable" in comparison with Martinsburg, the mountains were magnificent and their appetites were never better. Even in this early manuscript Strother showed a bemused self-appraisal which counteracted the boyish ebullience of his narrative: "Perhaps my reader (particularly if he has eaten a hearty dinner) may be wearied with these frequent descriptions of dinners and suppers but he must be thrown in the same situation to know how intimately they are connected with the reminiscences of a pedestrian traveler." On the evening of the fourth day, the hikers reached the neighborhood of Weyer's Cave, a hundred miles from Martinsburg, and with night closing in and the Shenandoah River unforded, they were undecided what to do. Impetuously Strother leaped into the current and edged over to a rock in the middle of the river. When he reached it, he found himself unable to move in either direction. The manuscript leaves him—and the reader—suspended there, but its conclusion contains no false heroics. "Here was I again at a stand, the water around the rock was as nearly as I could measure about six feet deep and what may appear singular I could not possibly tell where and how I got there. The wind howled and the river roared. This is really quite romantic thought I—if I was certain of getting out of it safely. It was rather cold for romance and I had got my breeches wet which grieved me considerably."[6] How Dave retrieved himself is unknown, but we know that twice again on this trip he risked his life with reckless daring. Perhaps envious of the fame of James Piper, who twenty years before had become the only man in history to scale the Natural Bridge,[7] Strother climbed out upon a rotten stump hanging over the abyss, an escapade which he recalled in horror in 1853. Moreover, he near-

6. This manuscript fragment is undated. Although in *Virginia Illustrated* Strother says this trip was made in 1834, after a conversation with James Ranson in later years he was assured it was 1835.

7. A whole literature has grown up around Piper's feat, the most important element of which is William A. Caruthers, "Climbing the Natural Bridge," *Knickerbocker Magazine,* XII (July, 1838). For others and a mention of Strother, see Curtis Carroll Davis, "The First Climber of the Natural Bridge: A Minor American Epic," *Journal of Southern History,* XVI (August, 1950), 277-90.

ly lost his life in a "bottomless" sinkhole nearby. Despite the entreaties of friend Ranson, whose enumeration of the attendant dangers only served to kindle Dave's enthusiasm, he was lowered into the cave with a fearlessness worthy of a Scott hero or a St. George. "Here was a dragon worthy of my daring." The ropes supporting him unraveled and he spun giddily around in the blackness, his grip weakening with each revolution. Only in the nick of time was he hauled to safety. Looking back on his hairbreadth escape, he commented philosophically, "Boys must slay their dragons, and nations must have their wars. If their hands and heads ache for it, so much the better; they are both likely to be more rational, at least for some time afterwards."[8]

Other adventures are recounted in *Virginia Illustrated*. The two friends climbed the Peaks of Otter, and from the cone-like peak Strother looked for the first time into the Piedmont and Tidewater. At the nearby hotel, Jim consumed twenty-two biscuits in one sitting, a feat that the proprietress remembered clearly eighteen years later. At Lynchburg they engaged passage on a tobacco barge and floated toward Richmond in much the same careless way that Huck Finn and Jim drifted down the Mississippi. The barge was manned solely by Negroes. Caleb, the first mate, proved to be an excellent caterer for the boys; he would pocket their cash and steal whatever food they wanted— fighting cocks, an old gander, a bag of sweet potatoes, or a hatful of eggs. He was a man of one song, which he sang over and over.

> I went to see Jinny when my work was done,
>   And she put de hoe-cake on, my love,
>   And Jinny put de hoe-cake on;
> But master he saunt and called me away,
>   'Fore Jinny got de hoe-cake done, my love,
>   'Fore Jinny got her hoe-cake done!

This ballad had twenty-four verses to it, all precisely alike. When Caleb got to the third verse, Uncle Adam, the captain, stood it

8. Strother's exploit is recounted in *Virginia Illustrated,* pp. 187-94. Re-visiting the region after the war, Strother found that the sinkhole was still known locally as "Strother's Cave."

no longer; he yanked the banjo from his mate's hands and rapped him over the head with it. "You fool nigger, hush up dat! I'se been 'noyed 'bout dat hoe-cake for three years; don't want to hear no more 'bout it!" At twilight the barges would pull into a silent cove under the overhanging sycamores, fires would be lighted along the shore, and the whiskey jug would be passed from hand to hand. "Ah! cousin," said Porte Crayon in *Virginia Illustrated,* "of all the aimless, vagabond adventures of my boyhood, none has left so lively and agreeable an impression on my imagination as that old time boating on the James."[9]

The boys returned to Martinsburg filled with tales of their adventures. For the present, Dave's wanderlust had been satisfied, but the Valley trip acted as a spice to tantalize him to continue his explorations further afield. His impressions, particularly of magnificent landscape and of humorous characters, probably exerted in the long run a greater influence upon his later life than any amount of plodding application at West Point or some other college. However, for his father, impressions were at best intangible and hardly an excuse for ignoring a more urgent problem, the proper choice of a career. Accordingly, Dave once again determined to become an artist.

An important influence upon him at this time was John Gadsby Chapman, who as a portrait painter in Winchester during the 1820's had been a familiar figure among the gentry of the north Valley. Chapman had gone on to New York to become one of the celebrated painters of his time; he was an honorary member of the National Academy of Design in 1832 and a National Academician in 1836.[10] It was doubtless he who sensed Strother's talented but undisciplined style and recommended formal study with one of his New York colleagues, Samuel F. B. Morse. Although Dave was primarily interested in sketching, oil painting was the principal medium for success in the fine arts, and Morse, who was president of the

9. *Ibid.,* pp. 231-33. George William Bagby's "Canal Reminiscences" treats a similar area in a similar manner several years later.

10. Eliot Clark, *History of the National Academy of Design* (New York, 1954), p. 250. Chapman's paintings were praised highly by Mrs. Frances Trollope. "The Baptism of Pocahontas" now hangs in the rotunda of the Capitol in Washington.

National Academy of Design, was esteemed the best painter of the age. Therefore, in the fall of 1836, Strother left Martinsburg for the second time to prepare himself for a career in art.

At this time the type of American painting most in demand was the portrait, a highly pragmatic form. The portrait painter served the same function as the later daguerreotypist or photographer: he preserved for posterity the likenesses of affluent business men and their families. The state of Amercian portrait painting resembled the condition of literature in the late Middle Ages. There were two types of painting: the larger one was formal portraiture, patronized by the cultivated and wealthy minority; the other was genre art, depicting in an informal way the activities of rustic folk who were not financially able to encourage painting. Sometimes a particularly lucky and strikingly original painter like Thomas Cole, who about this time became the leader of the Hudson River School, could succeed by a new departure, but generally it was a painter of portraits like Thomas Sully who gathered the rewards and the fame during the National Period. The prevalent aesthetic credo was a hallowed deference to the methods and subjects of the old European masters, held in awesome veneration. Not only did the American artist have little economic security, but he was also hedged by, and judged by, the outdated conventions of the Italian Renaissance. The dictatorship of European values was as strong in art as it was in literature, and the leadership of Samuel Morse in attempting to free the American spirit from aesthetic servitude recalls similar attempts of Emerson. By the 1850's patrons of art had learned to accept native scenes and landscape, but at the time of Strother's study with Morse, portrait painting was virtually the only door open to the aspiring artist. As it happened, formal portraiture was the kind of work which Strother was least interested in and least fitted to do.

Strother, however, could not have chosen a better man under whom to study. As president of the National Academy from 1826 to 1845, Morse was the leader of avant-garde American painting. Throughout his long presidency, he was the champion of artistic freedom and the enemy of aesthetic conventionality. He was opposed by two formidable enemies: the public press, which derided non-utilitarian art in an age of "progress," and the older New York Academy of Fine Arts, which opposed innovation as a matter of hidebound principle and refused to tolerate Morse's questioning of traditional themes and modes. Indicative of public scorn is this newspaper attack (which is one of many, and which Morse was compelled to answer): "We are not prepared to see the American system, as it is called, extended to literature and the arts. It would be the worst possible policy for the artists. Painting and sculpture are not among the necessaries of life. Much as they improve and adorn society, a taste for them is not even the necessary accompaniment of a high degree of civilization."[11] Public apathy at length forced many artists to enter other fields in order to earn a living—Morse's experiments with daguerreotypy and telegraphy are well known. While an artist like Sully, who is said to have painted two thousand commissioned portraits, found rewards in art, most American artists were not so fortunate. Mrs. Frances Trollope wrote what might have served as the epitaph for the American artist in the 1830's: "With regard to the fine arts . . . the wonder is that any man can be found with courage enough to devote himself to a profession in which he has so little chance of finding a maintenance. The trade of a carpenter opens an infinitely better prospect."[12]

In the fall of 1835, a ponderous building in neo-gothic style had been erected at the northern end of Washington Square to house the University of the City of New York (now New York University), which since its founding three years before had been forced to share Clinton Hall with the National Academy. Morse was installed as its professor of fine arts, the first position of its kind at an American college, but his position was more honorary than remunerative; he received no salary, only the fees from his students—a meager fifty dollars per quarter apiece. For two years, from 1836 to 1838, Strother lived with his instructor and three other pupils in the nearly empty, church-like build-

11. Quoted, *ibid.*, p. 27.

12. Frances Trollope, *Domestic Manners of the Americans*, ed. Donald Smalley (New York, 1949), p. 326.

ing.[13] Although Morse was immersed in his telegraphic experiments, for which he had rented additional rooms on the third floor, Strother found him a sincere and thorough art teacher. "Morse," he said, "was a faithful teacher, and took as much interest in our progress—more indeed than—we did ourselves."[14] What Morse thought of Strother's art is unknown, but by his own admission Dave knew that he made little progress in the use of oils, although his "spirited sketches in Crayon elicited compliments from the Professor and the respect of his fellow students." If one takes a Strother painting and places it beside one of his pen or pencil sketches, the estimate is seen to be correct. He never learned to use color as an organic principle of composition. Rather he employed it as a child might—to decorate a drawing which already had a distinctive form of its own. Morse did teach him how to paint a tolerable portrait, but Dave found that while he could capture a face he failed to add anything beyond the veritable impression. He always had to compose quickly, with a flash dependent more upon intuition than upon careful discipline. Otherwise he lost interest in his subject. His flood of travel sketches in *Harper's Monthly* twenty years later shows a facility for seizing upon a scene virtually on the run and completing it rapidly before becoming bogged in the tedium of revision and re-drawing. Such a faculty was wholly unsuitable for a successful portrait painter, who must be precise and cautious if anything. Had Strother been born a decade later, he might have become a fine genre painter like William Sidney Mount or George Caleb Bingham, both of whom exploited the local color and folk scenes that Strother loved, but he was trapped in an era of portraiture.

During his first winter and spring in New York, he made nine paintings, four of which were portraits. He attended the lectures at Clinton Hall sponsored by the National Academy, as well as meetings of improptu sketching clubs which would

13. Strother was not a regularly enrolled student at the University; at least there is no record of his name upon the roster of alumni. Letter from G. H. Carlock, Assistant Secretary of the Alumni Federation of New York University, to the author, January 22, 1957.

14. Edward Lind Morse, *Samuel F. B. Morse: His Letters and Journals* (Boston, 1914), II, 162.

give a prize for the best or most amusing sketch prompted by a platitude like "Too Late" or "Too Soon." Perhaps Strother's work was included in the reference of a contemporary newspaper to the "brilliant productions of the school of artists congregated under the roof of New York University";[15] certainly he was one of the earliest artists of Washington Square, which gave rise to the Greenwich Village of a later New York.

His activities as a portraitist were far more extensive during his summer vacation in Martinsburg in 1837 than they had been during the previous winter in New York. In rapid succession, he did fourteen paintings, for which we hope that he obtained encouraging fees. Returning to New York again in the fall, he lagged. Three Scotsmen, perhaps desiring portraits for inconsiderable fees, gave him something to do, but the Virginian was restless and stifled. His imagination took him back to Hunter John Myers, who represented a life freed from emasculated drudgery, a life in which a man must battle nature rather than the muddle of his own intellect. As Strother painted Myers' portrait from memory, he thought of his own escape from the city, of fleeing from the idle pursuit of art, of putting his feet toward the Western horizon where the frontier still remained. Also from memory, he painted that lovely Virginia mountain, Peaks of Otter, a work that was placed in the annual exhibition of the National Academy of Design for 1838.[16]

About this time Morse jarred Strother's aesthetic aspirations as effectively as Lewis Cass had shaken his political idealism. The second quarter's payment to the Professor was overdue, and the remittance from Colonel John had not yet arrived. A financial panic swept the country, and Morse not only had financial worries but also he had received the disappointing news that he would not be one of the painters chosen to complete the historical series in the rotunda of the Capitol. Perhaps at the nadir of his life, Morse called upon Strother.

15. Carleton Mabee, *American Leonardo: A Life of Samuel F. B. Morse* (New York, 1943), p. 181.

16. *National Academy of Design, Exhibition Record, 1826-1860* (New York, 1943), II, 143.

"Well, Strother, my boy, how are we off for money?"

"Why, Professor," I answered, "I am sorry to say I have been disappointed; but I expect a remittance next week."

"Next week!" he repeated sadly. "I shall be dead by that time."

"Dead, Sir?"

"Yes, dead by starvation."

I was distressed and astonished. I said hurriedly—"Would ten dollars be of any service?"

"Ten dollars would save my life; that is all it would do."

I paid the money, all that I had, and we dined together. It was a modest meal but good, and, after he had finished, he said—

"This is my first meal for twenty-four hours. Strother, don't be an artist. It means beggary. Your life depends upon people who know nothing of your art and care nothing for you. A house dog lives better and the very sensitiveness that stimulates an artist to work keeps him alive to suffering."[17]

Such advice, coming from the foremost painter of the age, impressed Strother deeply. It was both a warning and a summary of the condition of the fine arts in America. He became increasingly aware of the prevailing public disregard for the arts as a mere trifling diversion—nothing more. At approximately the same time a New York writer, Charles Fenno Hoffman, expressed a similar view with respect to literature: "a literary man is a sort of a Pariah in our money-making community unless he gets to the comfortable eminence of reputation."[18] Even with a reputation, Morse was an outcast. Success was the criterion for artist, writer, and businessman; America could waste little time or sympathy upon a failure.

In the late spring of 1838, Strother left New York, his instruction in the craft of portrait manufacture at an end. In the same year, Morse left for Europe, not as a painter but as an inventer looking into telegraphic developments abroad. The same promptings, disaffection with the state of the arts in America, carried both master and pupil far away from New York—

17. Morse, *Morse: His Letters and Journals*, II, 162-63. The editor erroneously says this dialogue occurred in 1841. The original source of it is John R. Chapin, "Random Recollections of a Veteran Illustrator," *Quarterly Illustrator* (January, February, and March, 1895), pp. 107-8.

18. Quoted in Stanley Williams, *The Life of Washington Irving* (New York, 1935), II, 31.

Morse to the older culture of Europe and Strother to the ragged frontier of the Ohio Valley.

Strother spent the summer in Martinsburg where, in a flurry of activity, he did ten portraits. October found him in Wheeling, Virginia, making preparations for his trip down the Ohio. From this place his earliest extant letter—to a college friend who had just lost the election to the Maryland legislature as a Whig candidate from Allegany County—was dated. He offered condolences but lacked sympathy for the political hopes of his friend: "I felt vexed at the failure of the Whig Party but on your own account I doubt not but you will be quite as happy as if you had gained the election."[19] He sent along a hastily drawn picture, the subject of which was symbolic of his own trek into the West, "a young aristocrat who had escaped from the nursery and gone a-fishing." Thus commenced a tour of greater scope and duration than his Valley jaunt three years before, and one which was supported by his own resources. The West was opportunity, and Dave intended to search for it, whether it took the form of painting river-town worthies or following outlets as yet unseen. While the trip did not substantially fatten his purse or provide him with the raw materials for creating a great indigenous American art, it did gratify his instinct for adventure and did extend his appreciation for the boundless and wild scenes of American life.

American enthusiasm for the West had been fired by the books of Timothy Flint and James Hall, both of whom had acquired reputations as early as 1832. As the East became more comfortable, the West became more romanticized. Its supposed Rousseauvian simplicity and directness became more appealing to the civilized Easterner. Enjoying the West meant enjoying natural scenery and rough contrasts, because except for Cincinnati there was nothing remotely suggesting culture west of Pittsburgh. The West was acquiring its own mythology and folklore, but the traveler was usually impressed by hugeness rather than by richness. William C. Preston, a Virginian aristocrat, had found that his four-thousand-mile horseback journey

19. Letter from Strother to Hansom Pigman, October 13 [1838], in the Gratz Collection, Historical Society of Pennsylvania. Pigman was defeated by less than a hundred votes; see *Baltimore American*, October 8, 1838.

through the Western country some years before "gave occasion for much musing and reveries . . . while my body was hardened and my mind habituated to self-independence."[20] Strother, too, learned from his experience, and his travels gave him a first-hand knowledge of the gigantic latent power of the Republic. He marveled at the "floating palaces on the Western waters"[21] and his imagination was stirred by the seemingly endless panorama of untouched wooded river banks. Apparently the West marveled at Strother, too. In Louisville there was nearly a scrap with a boatman who mistook Dave's long artistic ringlets for those of a girl—a girl in pantaloons!

Like Preston, Strother had been amply provided with introductions to myriads of cousins—Virginians of good family who had sought greater opportunity in the less-populated frontier country. He went directly to one, the Reverend William Matthews of Madison, Indiana, and in this small river town he helped pay his way by painting two family portraits and several landscapes of the Ohio River. He spent the winter in Louisville—then a booming city of twenty thousand which had doubled its population in two decades—and painted eight standard portraits, three designs—one based on John P. Kennedy's *Rob of the Bowl*—and a flag on silk for the Louisville Guards. In Kentucky, even painting was done Western-style, for here Dave executed one of the largest canvases of his career, a six-by-five-foot potrait of the Douglas family; perhaps he demanded payment by the square foot. He spent the summer of 1839 with cousins in Carmi, Illinois, from which he made a trip to the Mammoth Cave and claimed the discovery of the eyeless fish there. After a trip in the late fall to St. Louis, Strother seriously considered remaining in the West, if we can trust the romantic retrospection in his autobiography: "He at length became so enamoured of this untrammeled life that he thought frequently of taking his rifle and seeking a lodge with the hunters

20. Minnie C. Yarborough (ed.), *The Reminiscences of William C. Preston* (Chapel Hill, N.C., 1933), p. 11. There is no record that Preston and Strother ever met, but their impressions of travel both in Europe and in the West coincide remarkably.

21. "Pen and Ink Sketches of an Artist, IV," *Gazette* (Martinsburg), July 8, 1841.

and trappers beyond the confines of civilization. Apprehending
the possibility of such a result, his father lured him homeward,
with the suggestion of a trip to Europe." His identification with
Hunter John Myers is unmistakable; Strother saw himself cast
in the role of a single man subduing the wilderness. But like
many Americans of his day who talked about reducing the
complexities of life to the single integer, survival, his talk was
stronger than his determination. By the winter of 1839-40, he
was again back in Martinsburg.

In the next twelve months Strother did forty-one paintings—
nearly one each week! These, if sold even at the average price for
the time, twenty dollars, must have brought a modest supply of
ready cash to assist his father in financing the European tour.
At no other period of his life did Strother work so rapidly. Having exhausted the available subjects—and perhaps the patience—
of the Martinsburg gentry, he moved during the spring to nearby Shepherdstown, perhaps the most historic old town in the
Valley. Here he found a congenial friend in Alexander Boteler,
the former roommate of Philip Cooke at Princeton, and an
author as well as an occasional painter.[22] Another intimate at
this time was Henry Bedinger, a contributor of poetry to the
Southern Literary Messenger, who twelve years later became
Strother's companion on the mountain expedition which marked
the first entry of "Porte Crayon" on the American literary scene.
Provincial society was by no means dull in Shepherdstown,
which perched on a bluff above the twisting Potomac like a
Rhine village and was an inspiring place for an artist. His diversional paintings at this time showed a marked change. An
increasing number treated landscape and folk subjects. Such
works as "Moonlight," "Scene in Indiana," "Picnic Party Landscape," and the ever-recurring "Peaks of Otter," indicate that
Strother was allowing himself greater flights of fancy in the
manner of the genre school. Often humor tinted the paintings

22. Alexander P. Boteler (1815-92) represented the district in Congress in
1859 and during the Civil War was the designer of the Confederate seal. He
was the author of *My Ride to the Barbecue,* a minor classic of Southern humor.
Strother was later his second in a projected duel. For a biographical sketch, see
Millard Bushong, *A History of Jefferson County, West Virginia* (Charles Town,
W. Va., 1941), pp. 279-80.

in a way that suggested his later woodcuts for *Harper's Maga-zine*. This was seldom biting but rather was mild satire direct-ed at fashionable people in unguarded moments.

Preparations for the European tour occupied his attention during the late summer and early fall of 1840. The Grand Tour would not be made in the grand style. Strother would, he promised his father, travel as a student and a painter. He would walk—if necessary—from place to place like the genial Gold-smith. Colonel John borrowed a sum of money and in early November Dave set out for New York on the first leg of his pil-grimage to that Mecca of the American artist—Europe.

Chapter III

Europe and the Grand Tour, 1840-1843

NEVER had there been a more romantic young man of twenty-four than David Strother was on the morning of the sixteenth of November, 1840, as the *Ville de Lyon* pulled out of North River on its run to Havre. Looking back, he could see the steeples of New York growing dim in the distance and "castles seemed mingled with the mass of buildings beyond them." Looking ahead into the future, his imagination, kindled by readings from Scott, Moore, and Byron, took a fanciful turn. Humorously he wrote in his journal: "What adventures were to be mine? Our stately vessel would be wrecked and I of course would float ashore upon a spar, my body would be found by some Haidee and restored to life and sensibility. On my arrival a new revolution would break out and I would lead the fiery populace to victory, then having recovered from my slight but honorable wound, I would narrowly escape death in the frozen passes of Switzerland, then as a prisoner of banditti . . . or the happy lover of some fair countess I figured in Italy." Imagination was a fine companion, but there was also the principal but less exciting business to be attended to, the careful study of the great art treasures of Europe. In New York, John G. Chapman, himself a seasoned and worldly European traveler, had outlined an ambitious program of studies for his protégé. With self-conscious pains, Dave had inscribed in French the older man's detailed and pedantic itinerary. Three cities must receive the greatest attention: Rome, Florence, and Venice. The painters to be studied carefully were Raphael, Michelangelo, Veronese, Tintoretto, and Titian. Chapman knew his Italy and even recommended such out-of-the-way spots as the church of St. Elmo near Naples. Preparations also included a strong antidote for the "pox," which Strother duly jotted in his notebook. Whether Europe welcomed him with opportunities for study or for love, he planned to make the most of them.

More can be learned about Strother's journeys in Europe than about any other period of his life prior to his years with *Harper's Magazine* in the 1850's. Materials available for following his activities are of three types: his journal, thirteen articles published in the Martinsburg *Gazette* during this time, and letters to his father. Using these, one can reconstruct a portrait of David Strother which is a mixture of ardent romanticism and sardonic humor. Although he followed Irving to the shrines of Europe, Strother tempered ebullience with salty dashes of irony; moreover, one looks almost in vain through his later literary work for references to and influences of his travels abroad. Most travelers were willing to admit that the natural beauty of America could rival that of Europe, but their writing nevertheless reveals an almost slavish deference to the venerable shrines of the Old World. Strother, however, was rather unusual for an American traveler in Europe, for his judgments were for the most part objective and independent. He compared Europe with America rather than the reverse. His writings are filled with judicious commentaries upon the splendors of Europe, but they contain few traces of the irascible expatriated zeal with which many of his contemporaries damned all things west of Land's End.

There was nothing in the Hunter-Strother constitution which could have promised immunity from seasickness. Colonel Hunter after his voyage to England half a century before had sworn that had he not been formally engaged, nothing could ever have induced him to return by ship to America again. His grandson fared no better. On the second day out he succumbed without further struggle and on the tenth day of the passage was shocked when the stewardess guessed his age to be thirty-five!

"'Good Heavens, woman!'" he exclaimed. "'Hand me the looking glass.' I was horror stricken at the apparition therein reflected. I really believe the good woman intended to flatter me when she made the guess." His condition was so miserable on the eighteenth day that when an English brig was sighted in distress and without provisions, Strother could feel no sympathy with those who wanted eatables when at sea. Later, however, his condition improved, and on the twenty-first he climbed the mizzentop to gaze for the first time at a foreign shore. Brought up from youth as a vehement Anglophobe, he found his emotions strangely mixed during his two-hour observation of the English coast. Bitter feeling engendered by the War of 1812 wrestled with the body of English literature that he had grown to love. In his journal he wrote: "From childhood I had nourished a habitual hostility towards England and English. But now a glimpse of her distant shore filled me with unaccountable and delightful emotion. My eyes filled with tears and in an audible voice I repeated, 'England, England.' Was it the instinctive yearnings of the heart toward kindred blood, the depths of the soul? Or the magic chord of our common literature which vibrated?" In his first letter home Strother dared not mention his burst of feeling to Colonel John; furthermore, at some unknown later time Strother himself scratched in the margin of his journal the anticlimatic observation, "As I never experienced it afterward, I suppose it was nothing but the excitement of seeing a new country."

On the seventh of December, as the ship neared the French coast, the passengers saw an unusual phenomenon. The whole line of the horizon was like a mass of fire. "The stupendous cliffs of flame, which towered above the deep green sea and relieved the leaden sky, almost black toward the horizon, seemed more like enchantment that reality. No one on board had ever seen it before." Nor would anyone ever see it again, for the brilliant glow was the light from countless bonfires along the mainland, kindled in order to celebrate the triumphal return of Napoleon I to his country for re-burial. The effect was splendid and memorable for a Virginian imbued with longing for military glory; the fires which guided the body of Napoleon to port also seemed lighted for the American just beginning his career.

At Harvre, Strother was struck at once by the differences between the Old World and the New. His first inclination was to stoop and kiss Mother Earth, which during his illness he had never expected to see again, but "her face looked strange to me; old and withered in comparison with the blooming land I had left."[1] For one who had only a month before been "popping squirrels in the beech forests of Kentucky," the transition to a strange culture was abrupt. "Like a somnambulist I followed my friends into a cafe where I sweetened my coffee with a lump of salt and intending to enliven my bread and butter with grated sausage, introduced a spoonful of ground pepper into my mouth." There was an undercurrent of disappointment at the tame natural setting of France. As his diligence rolled toward Paris, Strother noted the lack of ruggedness in the landscape, which contrasted sharply with the back country of western Virginia: "I do not think I saw a tree of natural growth on the whole route. They were all arranged in ranks, like platoons of soldiers; or on long double rows, like lean sickly boarding school misses taking their walk; or in fanciful groups like opera singers on the stage; nothing wild or natural."[2] This was a far cry from the usual stereotyped first impression of *la belle France.* He ventured such appraisals without concern for *how* he ought to react, but rather exerted his independence of judgment in a manner which Emerson would have applauded. Sometimes his comparisons were humorous. Shortly after his arrival in Paris, he ordered half a cord of wood for his chilly apartment on the Rue Lafitte. In a city where wood was doled out by the pound, the concierge was staggered by the request, but recovering from his surprise, mildly suggested a trifling fifty pounds. Strother, accustomed to the abundance of America, shouted in dismay. " 'What, do they sell wood by the pound!' exclaimed I. To one just from the banks of the Ohio the idea was ludicrous enough. . . . My garcon told me it was the custom of the venders to soak

1. *Gazette* (Martinsburg), February 25, 1841.
2. *Ibid.*

it in the Seine to make it weigh well, and, said he, 'If it makes little heat, it sings very well fine music.' "

From mid-December of 1840 until late March of 1841, Strother remained in Paris. He was disappointed with the city, for so well had he pored over guide books and engravings back in Martinsburg that there was little to surprise him. The art treasures of the Louvre displeased him, for he noted that many of the pictures were hung solely for their antiquity, not for their merit. His independent criticisms of the Old Masters would have delighted Professor Morse, whose own paintings had been neglected by fellow Americans largely because they were executed by a non-European. "I don't know when this rage for antique pictures commenced," Strother wrote in his journal, "but I know that many of the most celebrated paintings have been dragged from closets and garrets where they had been bestowed as rubbish." He might have added that the ones not hung in the Louvre were sold at outrageous prices to gullible American *nouveaux riches*. In Europe as elsewhere, Strother stood slightly aside from the crowd and made up his own mind; he detested cultural despotism, which compelled acceptance of certain prescribed forms and the rejection of others. Years later, he confirmed his earlier aesthetic independence: "These absolutists, tyrants, autocrats of the barroom and art galleries rule by reason of the ignorance of their subjects and their tyranny deprives the world of much happiness, much innocent pleasure, for who dares to enjoy a picture condemned by the art dogmatist, or what ambitious youth will not turn his stomach endeavoring to swallow the whiskey provided by the swash guzzler autocrat, except some poor aesthetic outlaw like myself who can't help enjoying what is lovely."

However, his independence did not prevent him from enjoying the round of activities available to the art student in Paris. He was pleased with the frank and jolly camaraderie of his fellow students. He enrolled at an *atelier de dessein,* where, after the crabbed seriousness of study in New York, talent rather than wealth or social position was the single requisite for the aspiring artist. The obsession with success—bred into the subconscious of American art students—was apparently a malady unknown in

Paris. He had never before had such a friend as one Bisson, who feasted (in affluent days) upon a roasted apple and whose shoes were only bundles of rags. Strother was amazed at the devil-take-all attitude of this starving student, whose talent for mischief, humor, and art belied his abject poverty. It was no wonder that in this atmosphere Strother became for a time a Bohemian. To Colonel John he wrote (with greater seriousness than the facts wholly warrant) that he was avoiding American company. "Of all the servile apes of fashion, folleries, and frivolities of European aristocracy there are none more slavish than our independent Republicans . . . . The French, Italians, and Germans are more to my taste and more than all as these are not ashamed of economy and do not think poverty a disgrace."[3]

The highlight of Strother's sojourn in Paris was the funeral procession of Napoleon, perhaps the greatest parade of the century. His account, read back in Martinsburg in the columns of the *Gazette,* was a mixture of satire and romanticism.[4] A Virginian whose conception of martial splendor had been formed by the drunken brawls which passed for provincial militia musters could not fail to be awed by the grand procession of 120,000 brilliantly arrayed soldiers preceding the gilded car of the former emperor. As he watched regiment after regiment of flashing helmets pass, the broad avenue glittering with armed men, Strother felt the universal glory of war, a feeling which he still had twenty years later during the Civil War: "But still they come, and thousand upon thousand the iron masses rolled on. Such a thought would make a coward brave. I ceased to wonder at the mad rage which induces men in battle to rush on certain death, or the noble phrenzy which inspires kings to waste their domains and risk their lives and thrones in the magnificent game of war." Suddenly the distant peal of cannon announced that the coffin of Napoleon had entered the city. Finally the hearse, decked in purple and gold and followed by the remnants of the original Imperial Guard—now only several hundred

---

3. Letter from David Strother to John Strother, September 7, 1841. Among the family papers.

4. *Gazette* (Martinsburg), February 25, 1841.

withered and limping old men—moved abreast of him. Strother's flamboyant imagination, inspired perhaps by tales of the French Revolution, visualized the exulting crowd breaking through the police cordon, tearing the horses from their traces, and pulling the carriage with their own arms to Napoleon's grave. Instead, he witnessed with disgust an apathetic crowd more impressed by the gold trappings than the presence of their emperor. The whole pageant "seemed to be regarded more as something to amuse the people than a tribute of respect to the ashes of Napoleon. There was more of moral sublimity in such a meeting as the Baltimore Convention, by far, than this." The misty-eyed Virginian found that the grandeur of the past suffered from the tawdriness of the present. He heard the hawkers crying their wares, "les petits Napoléons pour trois sous," and looked with repugnance at the little figurines of the emperor which had their bellies filled with eau de cologne. It was ironical, he thought, that an American could identify himself with the magnificent drama of the moment while Frenchmen apparently could not. This was not the kind of transcendent patriotism taught by Sir Walter Scott and Colonel John Strother. With a shock he realized that here, indeed, was nothing save a gigantic and horrible apathy.

Strother's check list of paintings tells us that he was busy until the first of March copying "les etudes et desseins en abondance." His three months in Paris removed some of the back-country roughness. He never forgot the performances of Madame Grisi, nor the gay masquerades which "would be characterised precisely *comme il faut* with us—in Paris it is another thing."[5] His journal often records humorous situations in which the writer is not averse to depicting himself in the role of the country bumpkin confronting the newness of the city. At the Royal Academy of Music, he mistook for pickpockets the hordes of ticket sellers who mobbed him, struggled to escape from them, and held firmly to his watch and purse. "At length my hat fell off and in desperation I whirled my tormentors from me, and stamping fiercely on the pave, shouted the English shibboleth, *God Damn,* at the top of my voice. At this my enemies gave back and

5. *Gazette* (Martinsburg), July 8, 1841.

seemed awestruck." Such episodes are not only interesting to read, but they also reveal aspects of foreign travel often encountered but not as often described by more serious writers in Europe. Strother, like Mark Twain, did not take himself so seriously that he forgot how to turn the laugh upon himself.

Late in March, 1841, Strother put Paris behind him as he traveled by coach through Auxerre and Lyons to Marseilles. The rumor of a possible war between the United States and Great Britain and the thought that he might be required to return home disrupted his plans for a longer sojourn in Paris. His destination was Italy, which was, acording to Chapman, the only place in Europe where an artist had any business in the first place. The trip south afforded him opportunities for comic caricature with his pen. One anecdote, worthy of Fielding or Smollett, showed his remedy for dealing with one of the banes of any traveler—importuning beggars:

One sturdy fellow who assured us he was dying of hunger strolled beside the diligence with wonderful activity and perseverance for nearly a mile clamouring most lustily all the while. The burden of his petition was a crust of bread. "Gentlemen, for a poor starving dog. A crust of bread for the love of heaven." When he was about to give up the chase, I called him to the diligence and handed him a crust of bread which I happened to have in my pocket. His astonishment at having his prayers answered so literally was extremely laughable. He returned me thanks and then kicked the bread into the road with as much contempt as Robin Roughead did the dumplings.

Travel was making Strother a realist and often a sardonic one. He was developing a sharp eye for sham and charlatans, and after a visit to Petrarch's cottage near Vaucluse his remarks anticipated the skepticism of Twain's Europe rather than reflecting the sentimentalism of Irving's. Instead of penning a eulogy about the unhappy Petrarch, Strother wryly observed that the venerable cottage "looks in marvelous good repair, and the laurel very young for their age," while the tall building towering over it was nothing more or less than a paper mill.[6] He did not belittle the overpowering Alpine scenery of the spot. The cliffs,

6. *Ibid.*

perpendicular and stark, nearly shut out the sun, and these evoked his praise in ways that the apocrypha of Petrarch did not.

From April to November Strother lived in Florence in a room on the Piazza San Croce across from the Duomo. From his window he could see the tower of Galileo in the distance "half ruinous and desolate," and in the foreground was the buzzing market place of the Piazza. Florence became his favorite European city, perhaps because it was medieval rather than classical. The associations of chivalry were bound up with feudalism; for a generation of Virginians nurtured on Scott and Froissart, decaying castles were more picturesque than Roman baths. Florence symbolized antiquity as Paris did not, and even the stair he climbed to his room took on the aura of the Middle Ages. "It is strange," he wrote in his journal, "for an American to climb stairs which were built so many years before the existence of his country was even dreamed of." Nowhere had he written of Notre Dame de Paris, but San Croce with its monuments to Machiavelli, Michelangelo, and Alfieri brought into his mind the evanescence of human life and ambition. The distance between Florence and Martinsburg was measured in centuries rather than in miles, yet paradoxically, Florence, a monument to art, was the very place where his own studies languished. He seems to have absorbed and dreamed more than he created, for his check list mentions only two paintings completed during his residence there at this time. His reaction was, however, not so surprising, for other American artists behaved similarly. Benjamin West, for example, is said to have been made seriously ill by the shock of seeing in Florence so much magnificence after the barrenness of America.[7]

In the city there was a circle of American artists which included Horatio Greenough, Hiram Powers, and S. V. Clevenger. These promptly adopted him, and he had the pleasure of seeing Greenough's controversial statue of Washington destined for the Capitol. The sculptor, who hoped to make a synthesis of American history and Roman art, had decked out General Washington in a Roman toga with an antique sword in his hand. Strother was very impressed with the conception, although eight years lat-

7. Robert Spiller, *The American in England* (New York, 1926), p. 73.

er he had radically changed his mind: "the idea of representing General Washington in the costume and position of a Heathen God, a Jupiter, etc. was unfortunate for the artist." Of the work by Powers and Clevenger, Strother had less to say, but he was particularly close to modest Clevenger, a generous and humble man whose earliest models had been the only thing at hand in his Ohio village—tombstones. On fine days there were horse races along the Arno, recalling quarter races back in Berkeley. He fell in love with Maria Rossi, his landlord's daughter, and painted her picture.[8] By way of contrast, he met Mrs. Frances Trollope, whom he characterized as "an *intellectual sow*," although he admired very much her traveling companion, Lady Bulwer. There seemed to be time for everything, except serious study.

Although Strother was not aware of it until September, he was already an author with a following of loyal readers in Berkeley County. Before he had left Martinsburg, Colonel John had extracted a promise from his son to write home faithfully and fully. The promise was kept, and the proud parent, realizing the literary merit of his son's letters, rushed off with them to his cousin Edmund Hunter, editor of the Martinsburg *Gazette,* in whose columns they were printed.[9] When Dave first learned that his private letters were being read by every idle eye, he wrote with indignation to his father:

I should have been considerably mortified had I not reflected that it was only in the Martinsburg Gazette and at any rate nobody will remember anything about it by the time I get back . . . but to say the least of it, it is the greenest piece of stuff I ever saw in print,

8. Veiled references in his journal suggest that Maria Rossi gave birth to a child of Strother on June 14, 1842. The name of the child cannot be ascertained, but it is apparently referred to as "scholarum—la parola per identificare il figlio." At about this time he wrote a fictionalized half-page story in his journal about a visit to an orphanage to see his child, whose mother was named "Rosa." After Strother left Europe, Maria Rossi married an Italian whose surname was Fineschi, according to a reference in Strother's journal for November 20, 1885. If this hypothesis is valid, and Strother did have an illegitimate child, the secret was closely kept. It is doubtful that any members of his family ever knew about it.

9. Edmund Hunter, a graduate of Jefferson College, was a Martinsburg legislator, lawyer, and journalist. See F. Vernon Aler, *History of Martinsburg* (Hagerstown, Md., 1888), pp. 190-93.

excepting probably some of those quarrels in the Virginia Free Press. I wrote with that childish sort of freedom, because I thought that certainly there was more good sense among you than to let it go into the paper. However, it is not a matter of much importance, and if some things that I have written since are not published I shall consider myself fortunate.[10]

Despite his apparent anger, further letters continued to appear in the newspaper, and with the passing of time Strother thought more highly of his "green stuff." Thirty years later in his autobiography, he recalled them as "a series of letters of travel which were published in a country newspaper and attracted some general notice for their purity of style and graphic power"! In any case, the "pirated" letters, serialized under the title, "Pen and Ink Sketches of an Artist," have the distinction of being the first published work of David Strother, and they show an eye for striking observation and a skill in conveying a sense of scene. Certainly they are much better than the fragments of short stories which clutter his journal. The best of the latter treats a thirteenth-century Florentine nobleman, Bonndelmonte, who is involved in a bloody vendetta. This fiery lord behaves like a latter-day Byron playing in a third-rate melodrama. Apparently with utter seriousness, Strother described his hero this way: "Raven locks escaped from beneath his cap and fell in waves upon his neck . . . which together with a large moustache relieved his elegant features of any charge of effeminacy." This Lothario, who is in love with his enemy's daughter, rattles his sword terribly in its scabbard, and swaggers through several scenes before the manuscript breaks off just before the climax. As a piece of fiction, the story is unforgivable. The melodramatic plot, the histrionic gestures, and the pompous diction all show that the author had little ability to write a serious imaginative tale. At the crucial point, Bonndelmonte is left forever to his fate, and the reader experiences neither curiosity nor concern. Unquestionably the best writing which Strother did in Europe— or in his later career, for that matter—was based upon the actual

10. Letter from David Strother to John Strother, October 10, 1841. Among the family papers.

experiences which came before his eye, particularly those susceptible to satiric or humorous treatment.

Far more than Italy's treasures of art, Strother admired its
natural beauty. The distant ridges of the Apennines drew him
to make long excusions afoot in the same way that the Shenandoah and Ohio Valleys had drawn him earlier. In part his model
was John G. Chapman, who had "arrayed in the goatskin and
untanned shoes of a peasant wandered over the greater part of
Calabria."[11] Strother had always preferred unbeaten paths, of
which there were many in Italy. With crayon and sketch pad,
he explored obscure districts and visited towns unnamed in guide
books. He slept at times in peasant hovels, at others among antique ruins; he was a frequent visitor among the monks of La
Verna, Vallombrosa, and La Certosa. In the Italian mountaineers
he found the same qualities of honesty and independence which
he discovered among Virginia mountain men thirty years later.
Both seemed to him to have retained a self-reliance which had
been lost by dwellers on the plain. At times he satirized these
mountain folk, but always with good humor. His caricature
of a professional hunter resembles many others in his later work:

A magnificent figure entered the locando dressed in full hunter's
costume and covered with broad leathern belts and pouches, his
legs clothed in enormous swamp boots and his head with a shaggy
fur cap. His face which a painter would have chosen as a model for
a knight of Rhodes was bronzed by exposure, the lower part of it
being concealed by a superb black beard and thick curling moustache.
As he entered, he saluted us with a short bow, smashing his heavy
fowling piece, and . . . called for refreshments in a voice of the
richest bass. I continued to look at this noble manly figure with
admiration not unmixed with awe. Before the time of the French
he would have certainly figured as a chief of brigands. In these
peaceful times I supposed he had just returned from a boar hunt.
The landlord came in and recognizing him exclaimed, "Ah, Signor
Cacciatore, what luck today?" "Better," growled he complacently
and thrusting his brown arm into a game bag that would have held
a bushel, he lugged out one by one—four sparrows!

The formula is one which Strother used again and again, both
in describing his European experiences and in writing his essays

11. Henry Tuckerman, *Book of the Artists* (New York, 1867), p. 217.

for *Harper's* a decade later: building up grandly to a high point and concluding with an anticlimax. Scenes like this, drawn from life rather than from art, characterize his Florentine journal.

Early in November of 1841, Strother, in the company of four other American artists, left Florence for Rome. Originally, he had convinced the others to accompany him on foot, but the sickness of one of the party forced them to take a diligence, as he said, "with great reluctance as I never felt more inclined for a long, strong walk than at present."[12] Despite its estimated ten thousand art students, Rome was a disappointment during his residence there (until May, 1842). "For filth and fleas it certainly has no equal," he told readers of the *Gazette,* and he heretically doubted whether St. Peter's was the architectural equal of the Capitol at Washington.[13] Neat grassy walks had been laid out in the forum for curious tourists, and the Colosseum, so magnificently described by Bryon, looked "more like an unfinished contract than a ruin of two thousand years." Instead of a crumbling ruin lighted by moonlight and inhabited by solitary artists, Rome vied with Paris in its brilliance and modernity. There was a small academy consisting of six or seven painters, for the most part Americans, who exhibited their pictures occasionally for each other's edification and assisted one another financially. Their headquarters was the Cafe Greco, meeting place for expatriate artists for half a century, and it was here that Strother met the three Thomases—Cole, Rossiter, and Crawford—all of whom helped to relieve his disenchantment with the Eternal City.

Early in March, Strother's most impressive adventure in Italy began. With two other Americans, William B. Cooper of Tennessee and another known only as Kennedy, he hiked two hundred miles from Rome to Naples in ten days. They went first to Subiaco, where they learned that there were two routes they could take: the first one was usually followed, while the second was hazardous, impracticable, and infested with banditti. Dave, of course, chose the second: "As for robbers, any of us would

12. Letter from David Strother to John Strother, October 10, 1841.
13. *Gazette* (Martinsburg), October 29, 1842.

have given his best sketch to have met a gang—provided the number did not exceed three."[14]   They passed over the snow-capped peaks near Avezzano, where the customs officers were so startled to see them that they were passed without examination.   At one point they were lost in a mountain blizzard, but they found a company of muleteers and were conducted into the Kingdom of Naples.   After only one day's rest, they twice ascended Vesuvius, afoot and alone, scorning guides, horses, railways, and Englishmen.   Hovering on the brink of the uppermost cone, they peered into the heart of the volcano.   "Except for the ocean in a storm, I have not seen anything as calculated to excite great awe as a look into the aperture of Vesuvius,"[15] Strother wrote.   Awe gave way to audacity as they threw slabs of lava into the crater to encourage an eruption.   They were partially successful, for the volcano hissed and threw up clouds of sulphurous smoke, from which they flew down the slope in terror.   Even at Naples they awaited patiently the eruption they were sure would come.   "None came, however," he informed his *Gazette* readers, who would probably not have been surprised had Dave been successful in effecting this newest explosion.

Returning to Florence in May, 1842, for a final twelve months in Europe, Strother turned with greater seriousness to his art. He realized that much of his time had been wasted, so in rapid succession he produced nine paintings, some of which he sent home to Martinsburg for sale.   To his father he wrote that he had painted a jackass and hung it on his wall "in hopes that a look everyday at his Phiz will teach me the lesson I want."[16] Yet he was beginning to tire of Europe and vagabondage, for in the same letter he said, "Now two years are finished.   In tracing back the time from point to point it seems like an age, but looking back directly to home it seems but a month.   But even now there is a haze over the memory of things in America, which did not exist before last summer."   To his very great surprise he learned about this time that his father was having serious financial difficulties, and that additional help from him was out

14. *Gazette* (Martinsburg), October 6, 1842.
15. *Gazette* (Martinsburg), October 13, 1842.
16. Letter from David Strother to John Strother, November 2, 1842.   Among the family papers.

of the question. Protected and indulged as an only son, Dave was taken aback at the news, because he had never before given much thought to the matter of money. "Up to the present moment," he wrote, "I have never known anything of your affairs, either the amount of your debts or to whom you were indebted. Why have you never told me?"[17] As his realization of hardships at home grew, even the attentions of Maria Rossi—eagerly welcomed at first—could not be reciprocated with a pure conscience. He was beginning to see that the real business of life lay in the future, not in the present.

His situation was not yet critical. The Rossi family mended his rags until they would no longer stick together, after which they knit him stockings and even bought him shirts from their small store of savings.[18] But his last nine months in Europe were marked by a poverty so extreme that he began to look like his friend in Paris, Bisson. In the late fall, the arrival of some acquaintances from Rome drew him from his studies long enough to guide them to Vallambrosa and La Verna. The party included James DeVeaux and Thomas Rossiter, the latter of whom left an account of the trip.[19] With "spirits tinctured with the romantic," they followed the Arno to its source and sang along the Apennine valleys in a drenching rain until they reached the convent. There a roaring fire awaited them and from the peak could be seen the Adriatic to the east and the Mediterranean to the west. "No undertaking seemed too formidable for novices in search of the picturesque and beautiful," wrote Rossiter, and DeVeaux, whose career as artist was cut short by his death scarcely more than a year later, observed, "We shall never meet again on such terms—youth, good spirits, and light hearts to cheer us." When inclement weather moved in, the travelers were forced to return to Florence. For Strother, the end of his European sojourn was in sight. His circle of friends was vanishing. Some of them had wintered in Rome, consumption was riding

17. Letter from David Strother to John Strother, November 5, 1842. Among the family papers.

18. Letter from John Strother to his daughter Emily, April 20, 1843. In the possession of Boyd Stutler, Charleston, W. Va.

19. Robert Gibbes, *A Memoir of James DeVeaux of Charleston, S.C.* (Columbia, S.C., 1846) p. 229. This book contains many references to Strother and other American artists in Italy.

Clevenger to death, and Kennedy departed for America with only three dollars in his pocket.

Lack of money prevented Strother from following the footsteps of Byron to Greece and Turkey, a trip he earnestly wished to make. More than ever his thoughts flew westward, and he was gripped with the old feeling of aimlessness. One of Strother's last paintings in Florence was characteristically entitled "Ishmael."

On April 1, 1843, he began his journey home. He made a hurried survey of the art museums in Bologna and Venice, and in the latter was careful to make a pilgrimage to the rooms of his hero, the late Lord Byron. John Chapman would have been shocked at Strother's succinct evaluation of the Venetian school, "stupido e barbaro," although he admitted that the coloring was fine. Pausing at Innsbruck for a better look at the magnificent Alpine scenery, he pressed on to Paris. After nearly three years of gathering countless impressions, he took little interest in the final remaining months; at least nowhere in his journals are they discussed, and his series for the *Gazette* was never completed. There is a hint of a flying tour to England, but this cannot be verified. Even the date of his arrival in America is unknown, but presumably he was back in Martinsburg by the late summer or early fall of 1843. His notebooks and mind were filled with graphic impressions, his gaunt face was now concealed by a long and impressive-looking beard, and he had a desire to create a durable American art. But his principal task still remained: finding a place somewhere between the depressing level of commercial life and the lofty, and rather precarious, eminence of art. From Europe he had obtained a wider horizon, which was both an asset and a handicap. He would henceforth be more aware of the multiplicity of life than his contemporaries and by this awareness more susceptible to disappointment. Although he thought nothing of it at the time, he had served his literary apprenticeship through his sketches for the *Gazette*. The most ironical result of his study abroad was that he had gone to learn how to paint but had inadvertently learned how to write. Yet this was a matter which did not enter his head for nearly ten years.

Chapter IV

The Artist, 1843-1853

WRITING to James Fenimore Cooper, Samuel Morse perhaps summarized the feelings of the American artist returning from Europe: "You will certainly have the blues when you first arrive, but the longer you stay abroad the more severe will be the disease."[1] Certainly David Strother had an extreme case of this malady. In a culture which prized economic realities and eschewed artistic fancies, the artist had to adapt or be damned. Strother was not yet ready for either. He was twenty-seven years of age, had talent and cultivation beyond his years, but was as far from obtaining the fruits of his profession as he had been eight years ago in New York. Art seemed to be outside the main currents of American life. In Europe, exiled, he had not suffered from want of companions; in America, he found that he was at best regarded as an eccentric but harmless misfit. Philip Cooke at about this time was learning that to live by writing poetry was impossible, and he was forced to take up law in order to survive. Someone once said to Cooke earnestly, "I wouldn't waste time on a damned thing like poetry; you might make yourself, with all your sense and judgment, a useful man in settling disputes and difficulties."[2] Poetry and painting were praiseworthy adornments for a gentleman, but few Americans would have considered either as an excuse for not earning a

1. Carleton Mabee, *The American Leonardo: A Life of Samuel F. B. Morse* (New York, 1943), p. 157.
2. Quoted in Jay Hubbell, *The South in American Literature* (Durham, N.C., 1954), p. 504.

living. Strother's problems of adjustment were no greater than those faced by countless artists before him, but they were nevertheless very real problems. His decline from serious painter to dilettante, if we may call it that, was brought about by the prevailing indifference to art and the artist.

More than anything else, Strother feared failure. Of what value was confidence in oneself if that confidence was not shared by others? Success had seemed much easier to achieve in Italy, where he was surrounded by kindred spirits, than in the crabbed atmosphere of Berkeley County. In his journal there appears a fragmentary character sketch which can be dated from this period and which is a revelation of his state of mind. The central character, S., is a man of promise who commences life with education and money but who soon sinks into an abysmal dissipation. Having exhausted his credit in the city, he removes to a country town, where through boredom he takes to drink. His face becomes bloated, his clothes wear out, and he becomes a sponge. As he sinks in public estimation, he talks of the past and boasts of the figure he had once cut in the great world. In a short time he is made the butt of barroom jokes, and a wag calculates that he must be one hundred and fifty years old to have done all the things he has claimed. From the town sot, he graduates to the town bore, "whose only resource is to tack himself to strangers to find a listener and a dram." Such figures were all too common in Virginia towns, and Strother dreaded the prospect of becoming a man who lived in the exaggerated glories of his past and who accomplished nothing.

In many respects, Strother was temperamentally unsuited for an artist's career. He did not have the plodding perseverance by which many artists compensated for their want of genius. Years later, he analyzed his deficiences in painting and sketching. "I believe I have been limited by some mechanical incapacity, some feebleness of hand or nerve, which no study nor effort has ever sufficed to overcome . . . . Added to these mechanical deficiences there has always been a sort of mental imperfection, or carelessness, or lack of concentration in my work." He was never able to decide whether he was essentially a man of action or an artist. Although in his later years, after having acquired some fame in both areas, he lived with this dilemma without trying to resolve it, the period from 1843 to 1853 was the most disturbing of his life because of his failure to understand himself.

Strother spent the first year after his return from Europe in Martinsburg, where he painted only nine portraits and several genre pieces. This activity soon died out as he entered a phase of profound pessimism and cynicism. The town had been "painted out," and even the beloved mountains were a reminder that art could not hope to vie with nature. His emotional disturbance had become so critical by the winter of 1844-45 that a change became urgent. With a sense of desperation rather than of anticipation, Dave went down to Baltimore, where he arrived on November 4. One of his father's oldest friends was John Pendleton Kennedy, who was always ready to entertain and to encourage his many Virginia cousins, especially one as cultivated and well-traveled as David.[3]   Although he arrived too late to see the famous Delphian Club in its glory, he found a lifelong friend in the author of *Swallow Barn* and *Horseshoe Robinson*.[4]   Baltimore, called "The Social Athens of America" by N. P. Willis, the authority in such matters, was always the favorite city of Berkeley County people, but it was almost entirely bourgeois in its taste and outlook.   Even the magnificent parties of Madame Jerome Bonaparte and other Baltimore acquaintances served only to make Strother more painfully aware of the unbridgeable gap between the powerful and the artistic. By January he had reached what seemed to be the nadir of his existence.   Overcome by the futility of life, he wrote in his journal: "I am in my 29th year—have seen much of the world, have

3. David Strother and John P. Kennedy were first cousins once removed. Strother's grandfather, David Hunter, and Kennedy's father had married daughters of Philip Pendleton of Martinsburg.   Kennedy's mother and his two brothers, Andrew and Philip ("Pent"), lived in or near Martinsburg.   The friendship of John P. Kennedy and John Strother antedated the War of 1812.

4. The heyday of the Delphian Club was between 1816 and 1825.   Among its members were Francis Scott Key, Rembrandt Peale, and Hugh Henry Brackenridge.   See Annie L. Sioussat, *Old Baltimore* (New York, 1931), p. 221.   For a discussion of the David Strother—John Kennedy relationship, see Henry Tuckerman, *The Life of John Pendleton Kennedy* (New York, 1871), pp. 160, 319, 324, 363, 383, and 488.

travelled considerably, have tasted all the pleasures of life and have drained them to the dregs. I have succeeded tolerably well in my profession and am a person of some consideration . . . but I have no ambition, none at all . . . . My life is a dreariness to me. I work, I eat, I drink and laugh mechanically. Nothing excites me. I am dreadfully lonely." He reflected bitterly upon the fate of Correggio, who spent his life in poverty and died from carrying home a sum paid to him in coppers for one of his greatest works. Painting was temporarily abandoned, for his check list reveals only the single word, "Nothing," for the Baltimore period. However, he did find a patron in John P. Kennedy, who bought one of Strothers' completed works and no doubt helped to arrange for the sale of others.[5] Some of Strother's genre pictures were exhibited at the Maryland Historical Society a few years later. It is probable that these were sold some time during the spring of 1845.[6]

It is ironical that the two writers who most depressed him, Voltaire and Volney, were indirectly responsible for his recovery from the slough of despond into which he had fallen. Voltaire's cynicism with respect to man's purpose in life and his doubts about the perfectibility of mankind negated Strother's Byronic sort of individualism. There was at least negative comfort in the realization that his own confusion was but the reflection of deeper frustration dwelling in all men in all ages. In his journal he wrote, "We plan, we resolve, we imagine that we are shaping our own course but after all we have little to do with it. Chance, destiny, or providence like the wind with unresisting cloud, drives us whither it liketh and we know it not." His speculations show that he was transcending the almost incapacitating egocentric sentiments which he had derived from romantic writers, and that he was searching for a more pragmatic point of view. Volney taught him to question the permanence of the civilizations

5. At Kennedy's death this painting, "The Painter's Atelier," was willed to Strother. It has since disappeared.

6. His paintings were exhibited at the Society in 1848, 1849, and 1858. They were owned by O. A. Gill and were entitled "The Greek Boy," "Old Uncle Ned," and "Sam Bates and Sally Jones." *Catalogue of Paintings, Engravings, Etc. at the Picture Gallery of the Maryland Historical Society* (Baltimore, 1848), and the catalogues printed under the same title for 1849 and 1858.

through which man obtained his notions of human progress. Human institutions are as frail as human beings. Absolute truth is unknowable and man's comprehension is infinitesimal. Because man is compelled by life to act, he necessarily seizes upon convenient generalizations and rationalizes them into what he thinks are absolute principles. The effect of these cogitations permitted Strother a wider course of action than heretofore. If human endeavor was futile—or its results inscrutable— then the idealism of the artist or thinker might be as purposeless as the materialism of the businessman. The artist could accept the practical objectives of his age without compromising his art, because a compromise is meaningful only in relation to an absolute value, which does not really exist. There can be no doubt that Strother was evolving a personal theory of relativism, and was losing his former conviction of the artist as some special and sanctified seer apart from the world. Although he retained a love of the beautiful until the end of his life, he felt now that life rather than art was the most important of man's pursuits.

An unpublished short story written during the Baltimore period dramatized his changing attitude toward the artist. The protagonist, Henry, is a painter of twenty-six, who is "at present serious, sentimental in the extreme, with traces of a rich vein of waggery." Falling asleep in his studio before a large blank canvas, he dreams that he has painted, with unusual facility and speed, a masterpiece, the subject of which is his beloved Matilda, daughter of the rich burgher who has commissioned him to do the portrait. Exultant, Henry cries, "It will be bought by the king and placed in the Louvre . . . . A man who has painted such a picture is worthy of any woman." Descending the stairs, he is amazed to find that even his landlady treats him with respect, and in the streets he notes that all his acquaintances, having heard of the picture, salute him deferentially. At the home of Matilda, Henry finds that she is anxiously awaiting him and is changed from an affected coquette to a dove-like female filled with love. A knock at the door awakens the artist to the reality—a gloomy room and his curt landlandy who has brought him two letters. The first is from a merchant canceling his agreement to sit for a portrait because Henry's fee of thirty dollars is exorbitant; the gentleman can get a "much larger one done by Mr. N— for twelve dollars." Henry disposes of the unfinished canvas with a kick, his boot passing through the nose of the merchant. The next letter is an invitation to Matilda's wedding with a friendly note from her. Her fiance, C—, is ordered away on a naval cruise and insists upon being married at once. As a final indignity, Matilda hints that C— may purchase her portrait "if he thinks it is a good one." Henry rages, starts to destroy the painting with a palette knife, but reconsiders: " 'Insult me in this way. Purchase it ? Damn his navy buttons, nobody appreciates the arts here.' The glow of anger in Henry's face began to subside into thoughtfulness. 'Thirty dollars. By George, I'll sell it to him. . . . Thirty dollars will come in very well at present and as for Miss M—, she may go to——, anywhere she chooses.' "

In this story, both painters and patrons are handled roughly; the worlds of art and commerce are satirized. Strother could now get far enough away from his own ego to laugh at the sentimentality of his protagonist, who, despite his romantic ardor, is willing to unbend for money. The naval officer, a man of action rather than sensibility, is the successful competitor. Such a man, Strother seemed to say, is better equipped to win the honors of the age or the love of a woman. A similar conflict, dreaming versus action, was used as a subplot for his series, "The Mountains," which appeared in *Harper's Magazine* thirty years later. Lawrence Laureate, the name which Strother gives himself, is on a mountain expedition in West Virginia with Major Martial, a grizzled veteran of the Mexican War. With their party is Rhoda Dendron, a charming widow, who is attracted to both the poet and the soldier. Although Laureate has the advantage over his rival in youth and intellectual accomplishments, his shy and introspective manner leaves him in the background. Once, having fallen asleep by a mountain stream, he is awakened by Rhoda, who asks, "Still dreaming away the precious hours and opportunities of life?"[7] Laureate sees that he must choose whether "to wear the cowl or gird on spur and sword and enter the lists of action." He chooses the

7. "The Mountains, VI," *Harper's New Monthly Magazine,* XLVI (November, 1872), p. 802.

second and enters into a man's life. In quick succession, Laureate tames a skittish horse, rescues a lost companion, and wins a mountain tournament, performing each deed with courage and prowess. These accomplishments, along with the poetry, of course, win Rhoda's love. In this, as in the earlier story, Strother pits the artist against the soldier—each reflecting a different side of his own temperament. While Henry loses because he cannot adapt to the world as it is, Laureate wins because he defeats the major on his own ground, the field of action.

As his winter in Baltimore drew to its close, Strother turned again to art, but he was now realistically prepared to adapt it to a more utilitarian goal than formerly. His experience with Morse and Kennedy's sad tale of Edgar Allan Poe were sufficient to make him accept the fact that the dedicated artist was at best an anomaly in American life. In the nick of time, he learned to readjust his vision to the world as it was, for it is doubtful that Strother would have found either satisfaction or success in the field of painting. This, he knew, must forever after be only an avocation.

In late spring of 1845, Strother left Baltimore, and in the fall of that year he was urged by John G. Chapman to come to New York in order to learn the craft of preparing wood blocks for the engraver. The age of illustrated books was just beginning, and Strother could not have selected a better time to enter this new vocation. According to a historian of American wood engraving, prior to 1843 there were few calls for woodcuts other than those illustrating some new inventions or counterfeiting the labels of French perfumes.[8] But shortly thereafter, publishers began to put an occasional illustrative frontispiece in their books. This practice, begun as an adornment, quickly became so popular that it became an important requirement of publishing. Under the leadership of the House of Harper in the latter years of the decade, American wood engraving came of age.

Strother could not have found a better teacher this side of the Atlantic, for Chapman, a designer as well as an engraver, was the dean of early American wood engravers. The illuminated

8. W. J. Linton, *The History of Wood-Engraving in America* (London, 1882), pp. 20-22.

Bible published by Harper in 1846 contained no fewer than fourteen hundred designs by Chapman, and his wood cuts in *The American Drawing Book,* published a year later, have been called "as clean and firm as if engraved on steel."[9] There were two steps in preparing the block for the printer, drawing it and cutting it. A seasoned piece of boxwood, planed to the thickness of the necessary type, was rubbed with pumice stone and water to provide a good basis for the drawing, made directly upon the block. With lead pencil or India ink the artist made his design and then gave the block to the engraver. Before the actual engraving, the block was covered with a smooth piece of translucent paper which was pasted over the drawing. Then, with a gouge the engraver cut the block bit by bit, the paper indicating where he had not worked. Strother seems to have learned only the first step; at least no illustration has been found which bears his name followed by the engraver's mark, *sc* (sculpsit). However, he found plenty of opportunities to draw upon the wood block, a technique which he learned during his first winter.

From the illustration of Sunday-school books and works for the American Tract Society, Strother moved to an association with an early apostle of literary mass production, S. G. Goodrich, better known as "Peter Parley." Goodrich, who had conceived the crusader's notion of purging the nursery of wickedness by making children's tales reasonable and truthful, was the author of over 170 volumes, some of which went through many editions.[10] Strother was one of many artists who worked for him during the winter of 1845-46, but it is impossible to determine which illustrations are his. Certainly the quality of the work is not high, and all of the myriads of drawings are equally undistinguished. One of the most ambitious of the Goodrich books was *A Pictorial History of the Western World* (1850), and within its profusely illustrated pages a number of designs—particularly those of Virginia scenes—suggest that Strother may have been the artist. The experience Strother gained was invaluable, because from it he would develop a skill which would assist his

9. *Ibid.,* p. 26.

10. Strother is not mentioned in Goodrich's autobiography, which does, however, contain relevant material about the illustrating trade. See S. G. Goodrich, *Recollections of a Lifetime* (New York, 1857).

rise a few years later as a contributor to *Harper's Magazine*. He would be able to place his drawings directly upon the block, eliminate the middleman, and thereby save his publisher money and his engraver time in making a suitable cut for the printer.

From the anonymity of the Goodrich literary factory, Strother made a significant step early in 1847 when his name for the first time appeared upon the title page of a book he had illustrated. *Illustrated Life of General Winfield Scott,* published by A. S. Barnes, was a timely volume, for the General's armies were pushing across Mexico and the General was being groomed for the Whig nomination to the presidency. The fact that no author's name appeared on the title page, only "Illustrated by D. H. Strother," has sometimes resulted in his being catalogued as its author, but it is doubtful that he had a hand in the writing. The little volume is a mediocre one, the drawings crude if lively. Whatever its merits as a biography, it does show that Strother now commanded enough respect to be mentioned as its illustrator. This fact alone must have been of enormous importance to the self-respect of an artist who only two years before had been plagued by a sense of failure.

When John Pendleton Kennedy was preparing his second edition of *Swallow Barn,* he requested Strother to make up twenty illustrations of Negro and Old Dominion scenes for the book. They agreed that the profits from their collaboration would be divided equally and that Strother would arrange for an engraver to cut the blocks, Kennedy already having found that Putnam's would publish the book. On March 8, 1851, Kennedy wrote to Strother, "Suppose therefore that we start *on* or *after* the first of April. We shall break ground on our enterprise —*entamer la Swallowbarniade.*"[11] To illustrate a novel of the famous Kennedy would have turned the head of an artist of greater fame, but the collaboration was advantageous to both. *Swallow Barn* had been, acording to Kennedy, old-fashioned when it had first appeared twenty years before, and Strother's especial gift for drawing the Southern Negro brought to it an unmistakable vitality. Henry Tuckerman, a historian of art and later Ken-

11. Letter from Kennedy to Strother, March 8, 1851. In the Kennedy Collection of the Peabody Institute, Baltimore.

nedy's biographer, summarized the merits of the drawings: "The illustrations by Strother are excellent, and suggest the artistic treatment in which the author excelled by furnishing such graphic pictures of real life, to the ready pencil of one to whom Virginia was as favorite and familiar a theme as to himself."[12] The financial returns were modest: the edition netted $360, of which Strother obtained his promised one-half.[13] The book was received very favorably. John Esten Cooke wrote Strother a letter of congratulation from Richmond, telling him of the popularity of the drawings there. Strother replied as follows: "I feel it as a compliment that my illustrations of Swallow Barn should be appreciated in Richmond. The drawings have at least the merit of originality and although badly executed & very badly printed have met with commendation from several quarters— quite as much as I expected & more than probably they deserved."[14] There is no doubt that Strother was becoming one of the most important designers in New York. In fact James Chapin, a veteran draftsman, nearly half a century later recalled Strother's name as one of three or four of the leaders in the field.[15]

During his winters in New York from 1846 to 1848, Strother became acquainted with members of the later Knickerbocker school and others of the New York group of writers, including William C. Bryant, James K. Paulding, and Fitz-Greene Halleck. Indirectly, he could boast a relationship with one of the Salamagundi group, for the "Patroon," old Gouverneur Kemble, whose mansion across the Hudson had been the original of "Cockloft Hall," was one of his closest friends during the New York years. General Winfield Scott had called Kemble "the most perfect gentleman in the United States,"[16] and Strother con-

12. Tuckerman, *Life of Kennedy,* p. 160.

13. Journal of John P. Kennedy, September 10, 1852. In the Kennedy Collection of the Peabody Institute.

14. Letter from Strother to Cooke, December 12, 1851. In the John Esten Cooke papers of the Duke University Library.

15. James Chapin, "Random Recollections of a Veteran Illustrator," *Quarterly Illustrator* (January, February, and March, 1895), p. 107.

16. James G. Wilson (ed.), *The Memorial History of the City of New York* (New York, 1893), III, 218. This work discusses Gouverneur Kemble and "Cockloft Hall" rather fully.

curred in this estimate; the Kemble hospitality extended even to the next generation of Strothers.[17] John Chapman had always been an enthusiast for sketch clubs, and in 1847 under his guiding hand the Century Club was organized from one of them. Among the charter members of the Century Club were the Kembles, Thomas Rossiter (whom Strother had known in Italy), and Asher Durand, a painter whose work Dave particularly admired. Chapman doubtless took his protégé to the club rooms on Broadway, and Strother extended his familiarity with the artistic and literary circles comprising New York's cultural life in the late forties. The pessimism characterizing his Baltimore years was largely dispelled by an increasing self-confidence. Much of the older rebelliousness had now disappeared. Perhaps, too, some of his early vigor and imagination had rubbed off, but he had acquired an assurance in his craft that now only waited to be used for more important things. Having illustrated books, Strother was ready to write his own.

Although Strother had been assimilated by a New York coterie which he both respected and liked, he had by no means cut away the roots which attached him to the Valley of Virginia. Martinsburg was still his home, and he was never very long away from it. He spent his summers at Berkeley Springs (or Bath, its official name), a popular spa about twenty-five miles northwest of Martinsburg. Here Colonel John Strother had opened a boarding house in 1833, a short time after he had been ousted from the clerkship of Berkeley County. That year was propitious, because a cholera epidemic in 1832 had driven residents of the eastern seaboard to all of the Virginia springs in unprecedented numbers. John Strother's boarding house thrived, and he soon was renting several houses to accommodate his guests. Bath had been a fashionable watering place since before the Revolutionary War, and when the trunk line of the Baltimore and Ohio Railroad was completed to Sir John's Run, two miles away, the spa became more desirable and accessible than ever. It was the only spa in Virginia which ever boasted a theatre, and it provided a place where "many a Southerner had

17. Strother's son John was a frequent week-end visitor at the Kembles during his years at Peekskill Military School in the mid-eighties.

learned his spa manners"[18] before the warmer waters of White
Sulphur and Hot Springs put the town on a falling tide at
mid-century. John Strother ran his temperance houses and
purchased lots, until in 1845 or 1846 he was able to construct a
large hotel, with accommodations for three hundred people,
which eclipsed its rivals in size, services, and reputation.[19]
This edifice, known variously as Strother's Hotel and the Pavilion Hotel promised the traveler bathing accommodations
"more extensive and varied than can be found at any other establishment in the United States."[20] Its proprietor was admirably
endowed with the intellectual and social graces which a good
hotelkeeper must have: he was hospitable without being familiar;
he was conscious of rank without being obsequious; and he was
impeccable in character.

A list of the celebrities entertained at Strother's Hotel before
the Civil War would include generals, statesmen, exiled royalty,
presidents, and writers. Sometimes Colonel John's politics got
him into trouble, as, for example, during the visit of President
James Knox Polk in the summer of 1848. Polk arrived un-
heralded on a Saturday, stopped at the hotel, bathed ("I . . . could
not discover that it was in any respects superior to a bath taken
any where else"[21]), and spent an agreeable day. Early on Sunday
morning, poison was poured into his ear by a local Democrat,
who warned the President that "Strother was a violent Federalist
and very vindictive." Two stage routes connected Berkeley
Springs with the Baltimore and Ohio Railroad: one went to
Sir John's Run, three miles distant, and the other to Hancock, six miles away over a notoriously bumpy road. When
Polk tried to engage a seat for Monday on the Sir John's stage,
he was told by the Colonel that all were occupied and that he
must travel on the Hancock stage. The President bitterly wrote
in his journal: "Strother pretends to belong to the mock aris-

18. Percival Reniers, *The Springs of Virginia* (Chapel Hill, N.C., 1941), p.
41.
19. The Pavilion Hotel is discussed in detail in Katherine M. Hunter, *Pavilion
vs. Pavilion, or Polk's Choice* (privately printed monograph, 1953).
20. *Enterprise* (Bath), May 14, 1857. Advertisement.
21. The visit of Polk to Berkeley Springs is described in Milo Quaife (ed.),
The Diary of James K. Polk (Chicago, 1910), IV, 99-101.

tocracy, but must be a low-bred man, and I attribute the bad
treatment I have received to his vindictiveness in politics." Colonel John must have amused himself with the democratic principle of "first come, first served"; in any event, the President of
the United States had to take the Hancock carriage!

It was to Berkeley Springs that Dave retired nearly every
summer after 1845; in time the village replaced Martinsburg as
his real home. The town was an ideal place for an artist. It was
situated in the hollow of a deeply wooded gorge with a mountain spur rising about five hundred feet directly above the springs.
On all sides was woodland, and a ride of a mile or so took the
traveler into virgin forests. There were striking social contrasts,
which provided fine subjects for caricature. On Saturdays during
the summer, nabobs, fops, and mountaineers gathered on the
square to hear the band concerts in the hotel yard. Dave assisted
his father in the management of the hotel, where he observed
and drew the three aristocracies of wealth, birth, and talent.
Among these he found congenial and cultivated society, but he
remained rustic enough to appreciate the rawness of the natives.
In Berkeley Springs bear steak was washed down with the best
champagne, distances were sometimes measured by the number
of "barks of a dog," and a legal suit involving the sale of "snake-
bitten beef" was not uncommon. The village was a delightfully
incongruous mixture of the civilization of the plain and the
frontier of the mountains, and here David Strother spent the best
years of his life. In such an atmosphere, lassitude triumphed
over ambition. The winters in New York ceased, as he settled
down to enjoy rural pleasures.

On May 15, 1849, David Strother married Ann Doyne Wolff,
the daughter of a Martinsburg saddler. His wife was a girl of
nineteen, while he was thiry-two. Very little is known of Ann
Strother, for the journals of her husband contain no references
to her, nor have any letters come down through the family.
According to family tradition, the marriage was not encouraged
by Dave's parents; perhaps they had expected greater things than
his marriage to an obscure, yet respectable, young woman. Ann
was flighty, lovable, and emotional. The character, Minnie
May, in *Virginia Illustrated* was no doubt modeled upon her:

Minnie is not accomplished, as the world goes, for she can't sing except a little in concert, and is equally unskillful in fitting a dress or compounding a pudding. If she reads much she seems little the wiser for it, for most probably romances and poetry received the principal part of her attention . . . . Unpretending and child-like in her manners, she has a quick and original wit, and reads character by intuition. To this power . . . she owes the unbounded influence she exercises over every one about her. Even Porte's proverbial obstinacy is not proof against it. He flounders and fumes like a bumble-bee stuck fast in molasses.

Theirs was undoubtedly a love match, and from her he drew the sympathetic companionship of a lovely woman until her death ten years later. The birth of their daughter Emily on March 21, 1850, was another bond between Strother and Virginia.

Although Strother had traveled through the West and had lived in the North, strange to say he knew little of Virginia except the Blue Ridge region. In late October of 1849 he made a tour into the Tidewater of his state, and was led to contrast life along the Potomac with that in the most hallowed of holy places, the lower James. His observations, recorded in his journal, consist of a lively blend of upcountry awe and cosmopolitan satire, and show that he was aware the Old Dominion had fallen from its early grandeur. He was both a Virginian and an outsider; his account shows a veneration for the Virginia past, but he could not overlook the decadence of the Virginia present. Traveling first to Washington, Strother stopped off for a look at the art in the rotunda of the Capitol, where his estimate of Trumbull's painting of the Declaration of Independence showed his very Southern loyalties. "The countenances of the Northern men," he wrote, "had a prim puritanical expression, as did also their attitudes. The Southerners on the contrary had jovial generous faces, easy in their attitudes and of pleasing countenances." At his first presidential levee, he found appealing the simple cordiality of his distant kinsman, Zachary Taylor, but confessed that "nothing in his manner, conversation, or history warrant greatness."

From Washington he took the steamer down the Potomac to Norfolk and went overland to Williamsburg, entering a strange-

ly appealing and leisurely world which at first fulfilled his antic-
ipations of the best Virginia tradition. There were huge break-
fasts running the gamut of edibles from oysters to roast wild
duck, supervised by the most amiable of landlords who sat at
the head of the table and muttered like grace, "My ham, sah,
was a failure, sah, a failure, sah—that black rascal, sah." He
called upon Nathaniel Beverley Tucker, a Virginia firebrand
who, as author of the vitriolic novel, *The Partisan Leader,* was
convinced that war between North and South was inevitable.
Tucker, then a professor of law at William and Mary College, which had but seventeen students that year because of a
faculty feud, proved to be one of the most urbane and hospitable
men whom Strother had ever known. When repeated invita-
tions to remain overnight were rejected, Tucker surreptitiously
had a servant remove all of Strother's belongings from Hanes-
ford's City Hotel to his own home so that the younger man
would have to partake of his hospitality.[22] Although Dave did
not wholly concur with Tucker's view that "the Virginian is a
Virginian everywhere," he nevertheless was deeply impressed by
the intelligence and courtly graces of the man who had shaken
hands with John Hancock and George Washington. Strother had
met a public figure who was the epitome of decadent Virginia,
a man who represented both the aristocratic confidence of the old
tradition and the stubborn belligerence of the new. Compared
with such an evening, side trips to Jamestown and Yorktown,
both desolate and seedy, were anticlimaxes suggesting far less
powerfully the golden period when American history was
made largely by Virginians.

The dilapidation of Williamsburg was deeply impressed upon
Strother's mind. He noted that only the foundation and walls
remained of the former state house, and that cattle and pigs
grazed in the weed-matted streets of the once grand city, and
he was made livid with rage when two roughnecks came into his
hotel one evening and deliberately annoyed him by blowing tin

22. This visit to Williamsburg became the subject for one of his last articles,
"A Visit to the Shrines of Old Virginia," *Lippincott's Magazine,* XXIII (April,
1879), 393-407. An edited version of Strother's manuscript has been published
under the title, " 'Porte Crayon' in the Tidewater," *Virginia Magazine of History,* LXVII (October, 1959), 438-49.

whistles in his ear. After a dinner party at nearby "Brandon," he saw that economic stagnation had lower Virginia in its grip. As he was being rowed across the river, his host hailed a sloop at anchor, which proved to be from Maine with a cargo of lime, selling at 12½ cents per bushel. His host bought the entire cargo at once, and Strother was struck at once with the economic fallacy at the heart of the slave system: "So, they can burn lime in Maine and deliver it on the James River in Virginia cheaper than we can make it at home with all facilities, wood, limestone, and labour just at hand . . . . There must be something wrong in our system of labour or why is theirs so much more efficient that they can thus undersell us with the immense disadvantage of this distant transportation added?" Here, eight years before Hinton Helper's *The Impending Crisis of the South,* was an indictment of slavery upon the grounds of its economic wastefulness rather than its morality. Having come from a lavish dinner waited upon by flocks of slaves, Strother could see that even Virginia hospitality, so lauded and so famous, was an anachronism. The Virginian, pluming himself upon his generosity, was the victim of an inefficiency which was making him a pauper. In the dramatic juxtaposition of the aristocratic planter and the sloop captain, Strother saw the America which had been and the America which would be. Charmed though he was by the Virginia Tidewater, Strother could not ignore—as his cousin John Esten Cooke ignored—the inevitable economic forces which augured a change in the balance of power away from the South and towards the North and West, those areas of gigantic industrial and commercial potentiality.

As his boat ascended the river, Strother's first view of Richmond was of the state capitol, which looked pure and Grecian on its hilltop eminence. A closer view revealed the stucco and wood of which it was composed. This disenchantment was symbolic of his short visit to the city. As a Virginian, he expected to find the artistic acclaim which had been denied him in the North. With great expectations he arranged several paintings in his lodgings for an informal exhibition of his work and awaited his first visitors, who soon arrived:

Two persons came up the stairs in hot discussion; on entering, they paused a moment, saluted me kindly, and looked around without marking anything particularly. "The constitution," quoth one, "is clear on that subject, etc." Several others entered and the discussion became a hot and general dispute—the tobacco juice flew. I was in agony. Presently a mouthful struck my Madonna in the eye and coursed down her blooming cheek. I could scarcely contain myself . . . . Two mortal hours they stayed belabouring the constitution; the sound of the dinner bell dispersed them. On taking leave they expressed themselves much gratified with my paintings and expressed many kind wishes for my success.

Politics, not art, absorbed the Richmonders. Strother's account of the Tidewater tour concludes with his visit to the capitol building, where he noted that whole carloads of historical documents belonging to the historical society were lying in an unwanted heap, rotting away in a barren room. To Virginians of the forties, even the relics of the Old Dominion were only a heap of rubbish not worth the trouble of sweeping away. Without reluctance, Strother returned to Berkeley County with more than a suspicion that the glory of Virginia was no more. Sixteen years later, he returned to Richmond with a conquering army bent not upon venerating the past but upon burying it.

Strother apparently planned to remain in Berkeley Springs and Martinsburg permanently. He already owned a summer cottage at the Springs, and early in 1851 he bought the "poor house lot" on the northwest edge of Martinsburg, a property which contained one of the fine old mansions of the county, Norborne Hall.[23] This stately brick house on West Race Street—which today stands next to a fertilizer store—became his winter home until the Civil War. Although it was the setting for his nostalgic description of ante-bellum Virginia life in his series for *Riverside Magazine* in the late sixties, Norborne Hall was not the ancestral seat of the Strother family as those sketches imply.[24]

23. The Norborne Hall property, consisting of four acres, was purchased for $1800, the deed being made on March 29, 1951 (Berkeley County Court Records, Deed Book 53, p. 635). By a deed made on September 17, 1852, the property passed to Strother's sister's husband, James L. Randolph, although the property was not turned over officially until February 20, 1869 (Berkeley County Court Records, Deed Book 54, p. 439). Strother probably lived at Norborne Hall until the death of Ann Wolff Strother in 1859.

24. The Norborne Hall of this series is a composite picture of many houses

Strother's painting at this time was diversional and executed in a leisurely manner, for the hotel provided him with an ample income. Freed from the necessity of earning a living from his art, Strother selected subjects for himself rather than for patrons. He turned to homely scenes of country life about him in the manner of the genre painters. "Mill Boys," "Morgan [County] Quilting," "Scene in Harvest Field," and "Scene in Country Store" were narrative paintings with their sources in American life.[25] From 1836 to 1852, he painted approximately 175 pictures, and drew a countless number of sketches. Although he did not realize it at the time, his period of oil painting had reached its close; almost through accident he became a literary figure. It now remains to show how this gradual evolution took place and how "Porte Crayon" was born.

One of Strother's closest friends in Martinsburg at this time was Philip Pendleton Kennedy, the youngest brother of the Baltimore novelist. "Pent" was an erratic genius, a litterateur, and a brilliant wit, but his fondness for sprees and hard liquor kept him dependent upon the support of his anxious mother and his more solvent brother. For a time he studied law, but he was constitutionally unable to settle down to a practice in Martinsburg. However, he had a passionate fondness for wild scenery, and as a sportsman was known throughout the region of the upper Potomac. His single published work, *The Blackwater Chronicle* (1853), treated an expedition made in the company of David Strother and other local sportsmen to the Blackwater Falls, a virtually unexplored tract of Randolph County, in the summer of 1851.[26] This, the first Blackwater expedition, was followed by another in the summer of 1852, which Strother used as the subject for "The Virginian Canaan," his first article for *Harper's Magazine* in December, 1853. Because there were two

in which Strother had lived as a boy and also his father's birthplace, Park Forest.

25. Only "Scene in Country Store" has been found. It is owned by Strother's grandson, D. H. Strother II, of Milwaukee.

26. Kennedy used the pen name, "The Clerke of Oxenford," for his book, the full title of which is *The Blackwater Chronicle, a Narrative of an Expedition into the Land of Canaan in Randolph County, Virginia, a Country Flowing with Wild Animals, such as Panthers, Bears, Wolves, Elk, Deer, Otter, Badger, etc., etc., with Innumerable Trout—by Five Adventurous Gentlemen,*

trips to the Blackwater and because Strother illustrated both of
them, authorship of *The Blackwater Chronicle* has often been
ascribed to him.[27] The confusion is understandable, but the
manner of writing is entirely different: the style of Kennedy
is flashing, prolix, and as centrifugal as that of Laurence
Sterne; Strother's is more direct, more readable, and less literary.
Kennedy was interested in impressions; Strother in experiences.

The Virginia Canaan was a tract of wilderness in the Allegheny Mountains which had been bypassed in the settlement of
western Virginia. Although the Baltimore and Ohio Railroad
passed through Oakland, Maryland, only twenty miles away,
and trout fishermen had fished at the mouths of its numerous
streams, the Canaan country was known only to a few hunters.
At Winston's Hotel near the mouth of the Blackwater River, a
place of rendezvous for flocks of eastern fishermen during the
summer and fall, Pent and Dave first heard of the wild Canaan.
The prospect of exploring this unknown wilderness lying so
close at hand intrigued both men, who assembled a party of five
souls to examine the tract in the summer of 1851.

The Blackwater Chronicle is a curiosity of American literature. Recalling sometimes Hazlitt and at other times Sterne, its
tone is more British than American and its literary allusions run
the course of English literature. The wayfarers are, above all
else, gentlemen—veritable American Tories from the "garden
of Virginia"— led by Triptolemus Todd, Esq. (Kennedy), and
Signor Andante Strozzi, Italian artist and musician (Strother).
The latter is described, facetiously, at length. Despite his histrionic garb, he is a pillar of strength, especially when the party
becomes lost in the woods. Because Kennedy's portrait is one of

*without Any Aid of Government, and Solely by Their Own Resources in the
Summer of 1851* (New York, 1853). Strother's name appears on the title page
of this edition as its illustrator. The English edition, which was not illustrated
by Strother, is entitled *Narrative of an Expedition of Five Americans* (London,
n.d.). The German edition is entitled *Blackwater oder eine Entdeckungsreise in
das Land Canaan (Randolph-County, Virginien) im Sommer 1851* (Leipzig,
1855). Subsequent page numbers refer to the English edition.

27. The mistake has been made frequently, most egregiously in *A Library
of Southern Literature,* which includes an excerpt from *The Blackwater Chronicle*
as a sample of Strother's writing.

the few contemporary descriptions of Strother which have come down to us, it should be quoted in full:

There stands before you a slight, elastic, and somewhat gaunt gentleman, with a dark, concentrated eye, sunk deep beneath a marked and rugged brow. The expression of his face at present is particularly indicative of that sort of energy and determination of character, which is apt to make its possessor what is vulgarly called *Head-Devil* in all matters of feud, foray, or whatever enterprises that might be classed under the designation of marauding—all dare-devil achievements. The imagination of the wilderness before him, has called into play these latent qualities of his nature. The gentleman wears a beard, after the fashion of the middle ages, that has held undisturbed possession of his lower face for now some fifteen years; and with all his present surroundings, it gives him the look of a brigand as in a picture; meet him in the streets of a capital, and it would impress you with the idea that he was a practitioner of astrology, or some other occult matter—maybe some Italian philanthropist, or revolutionary conspirator—the friend of liberty all over the world, wherever liberty had a market; his disdain of a feather and all melodramatic show of appearance precludes the idea of the Hungarian, as recently impressed upon our minds. He wears a green cloth cap, with a straight projecting square visor to it, like the European military caps. An old black coat, with gray pantaloons, and a pair of tough boots with large red tops—these drawn on outside, complete his dress. He has no small wallet strapped to his back—a blanket and a great coat rolled up constitute it. Around his neck is suspended an artist's sketchbook. In his right hand is a frying pan. This is our artist, the signor Andante Strozzi . . . one in every way the very person for an expedition into the Canaan— a man who would laugh a bear in the face, and take particular pleasure in pitching a panther; one who would be about as careless of consequences in any encounter as eight of these last two named gentlemen![28]

"Head-Devil" was a fitting name for Strother at this time, and later the motley garb, grizzled beard, and military cap became

28. [Philip Kennedy] *Blackwater Chronicle,* pp. 47-48. Pent is probably wrong in saying that Strother's motley outfit owed little to the Hungarian influence. Colonel John Strother welcomed Kossuth's refugees at Berkeley Springs, and one of them, Ernest Szemeleny, dedicated a piece of music to David Strother: "A Day at Berkeley Springs," published by F. D. Benleen and William T. Mayo of New Orleans, 1853.

the hallmarks of "Porte Crayon" as readers of *Harper's* came to
know him.

Believing as they did that the wilderness had the power of
remolding man into the wild beast from which he sprang, none
of the travelers reflected Rousseau's sentiments as they struggled
through the laurel brakes of the gothic-like forest. Pent, however, noted that camping on the Blackwater revitalized their
primal senses; colds, brought from civilization, magically disappeared although the season was wet. Not only did they discover the fabled falls, but they also discovered fresh resources
within themselves. "The earth," wrote Pent, "is entirely new
to our senses; and it is all our own—an entire and absolutely
perfect fee-simple estate of inheritance in land and water, the
deed recorded in the most secret recesses of our breasts." Thousands of trout awaited the sportsmen, and the amber-tinted
waterfall attracted the artist. Pent realistically knew that the
unspoiled secrets of the Blackwater would soon be devastated by
the encroaching forces of American materialism. It would not
be long, he warned, before speculators would open up the region
and exploit it for the natural resources therein; the rape would
not be by such men as themselves but by "men with necessity at
their elbow."

The Blackwater trip had been an expedition, not a quest.
The sportsmen entered the woods not as Thoreau had—in
order to reduce life to its lowest terms—but instead in the tradition of Frank Forrester, to search for temporal enjoyment and
adventure. *The Blackwater Chronicle* is not a Southern *Walden*. It is erudite, witty, and occasionally lighted by brilliant
flashes of humor, but its principal limitation is the same one
that pervades much of Southern literature before the Civil War—
frivolousness. As a book it helped open the Allegheny Mountains for later writers in search of fresh materials, but from
beginning to end it is so reactionary that it seems out of step with
the age. Only when Kennedy foresaw the imminent changes
which threatened the whole way of life for the Southern gentleman did his book transcend the anachronistic spirit in which
it was written and sound a note of prophecy.

Chapter V

Enter "Porte Crayon," 1853-1855

DURING the late spring of 1852, Strother returned to the Blackwater with another sporting expedition, and this time he made a greater number of sketches than during the trip of the year before. The fruits of this second trip were an agreement to write for *Harper's Magazine* and the birth of "Porte Crayon." A series of fortuitous events led Strother into writing. Unquestionably his illustrations for *Swallow Barn* had given him a stature he had never before enjoyed, particularly among professional men. In the spring of 1853, he received a commission from Ele Bowen, a Philadelphia writer, to make a few small drawings on wood with descriptive literary sketches, for which he was paid seventy-five dollars, a good price.[1] In January of the same year, Barnum and Beach of New York called upon Strother for four drawings to be used in their short-lived *Illustrated American News,* the first pictorial newspaper in this country worthy of the name.[2] Although by November their enterprise had failed, they did pay Strother half of the promised one hundred dollars. His most important opportunity came in the spring of 1853. Having gone to New York to arrange for placing some of his pencil

1. "The Negro Sketches were furnished by David H. Strother, Esq., of Virginia, a gentleman widely known for his fine literary and artistic talents." Ele Bowen, *Ramblings in the Path of the Steam-Horse* (Philadelphia, 1855), p. vii.

2. W. J. Linton, *The History of Wood-Engraving in America* (London, 1882), p. 29.

sketches of plantation Negroes on exhibit at the National Academy of Design,[3] he was urged by his friend Charles Edmonds, an engraver, to show his sketch book to members of the firm of Harper and Brothers. Strother did, and Fletcher Harper, after looking through his portfolio of Blackwater drawings, commissioned him on the spot to write an account of the trip and to transfer his best sketches to wood blocks for use in the newly-lanuched *Harper's New Monthly Magazine*. An agreement was struck by which Strother became a contributor to the magazine, and the association endured for a quarter of a century.

With its five buildings on Pearl Street and six on Cliff Street, the publishing establishment of Harper and Brothers was perhaps the largest in the world. The four brothers owed their prosperity largely to their inexpensive reprints of pirated English fiction, totalling 615 different volumes.[4] Largely self-educated, they remained sympathetic to the requirements of the masses of America, who wished both entertainment and instruction in their books. The first issue of the *Monthly* had appeared in June, 1850, and though its original purpose had been to draw attention to their books, it soon grew into a wholly different thing. The magazine lacked the literary tone of *Putnam's,* had none of the tradition of *Knickerbocker,* but it became the meteor of American monthlies. Within six months, circulation had jumped to 50,000 and by the end of the fifties had reached the unprecedented total of 200,000.[5] One contemporary wrote, "There is not a village, there is scarcely a township in the land into which your work has not penetrated."[6] *Harper's Monthly* had many competitors and imitators, but none succeeded so well in Fletcher Harper's objective, "bringing within the reach of the great mass of the American people, an immense amount of useful and entertaining reading matter."[7]

3. *National Academy of Design Exhibition Record 1826-1860,* II, 143.
4. Frank Luther Mott, *A History of American Magazines,* II (Cambridge, Mass., 1938), 383.
5. J. Henry Harper, *The House of Harper* (New York and London, 1912), p. 87.
6. *Whig Review,* July, 1852, as quoted in Mott, *History of American Magazines,* 391.
7. From the "Advertisement" to the bound edition of *Harper's New Monthly Magazine,* I.

At first *Harper's* was an eclectic review, its pages given over to excerpts from British journals. However, to counteract accusations that it said too little about "the American flag and Yankee Doodle and Home Literature," the editors began to encourage contributions from native writers. There was a major problem with regard to publishing articles on American history, travel, and society: *Harper's* was evolving rapidly into an illustrated journal. It was all very well for an author from Georgia or Maine, for example, to submit a paper about some localized phase of his own state, but how could the editors obtain suitable illustrations for it? The simplest solution, of course, was to find that rare amalgam, the writer who could also illustrate, and it is no coincidence that so many of the contributors to *Harper's* in the early years were artist-authors. Benson J. Lossing, J. Ross Browne, T. Addison Richards, Brantz Mayer, and David Strother were all adept with both pen and pencil.

Historians of journalism have presented many theories to account for the tremendous popularity of *Harper's Monthly*: the English serials by Dickens, Thackeray, and Lever; Jacob Abbott's *History of Napoleon Bonaparte,* which ran through seven volumes of the magazine; and its unusual length—144 pages. The most obvious causes were its illustrations and its variety. Coincident with the increased sales was an increase in the number of drawings. The two or three woodcuts, for the most part portraits and fashion plates, of the initial issue were increased to as many as fifty, a decade later. The editors had no qualms in appealing to "all readers of average intelligence."[8] Although they hoped to reach the level of *Blackwoods* in time, their main purpose was to reach the literate many rather than the literary few. Then as now, pictorial magazines could better perform this objective than could unillustrated ones. Oblivious to the sneers of the "genteel" magazines, *Harper's* outsold them all and often forced them, to survive at all, to add the noxious illustrations. The magazine went everywhere. John Reuben Thompson complained that it had five times as many subscribers south of the Potomac as his periodical, *The Southern Literary Messenger,* and his successor, George William Bagby, put it

8. Harper, *House of Harper,* p. 87.

accurately when he wrote, "Southern patriotism never was proof against Northern newspapers and picture magazines."[9]   The age of illustrated literature had arrived, and *Harper's Magazine* led the way.

Add variety to illustration and you have the Harper formula. In the issue of January, 1855, the publishers promised that every number would contain eleven types of articles, among which were American biographies, illustrations of American life, narratives of exploration, descriptions of the Holy Land, scientific expositions, and fiction.   Here was a taste for every palate.   Although the New England writers often remained aloof, a list of the contributors during the first thirty years of *Harper's Magazine* is like a recitation of names picked from a volume of American literary history, beginning with Melville and working down to Frank Stockton.   No matter what the rival editors said, the Harpers gave their public the best as well as the fair.   The coverage was so extensive and varied that, in an address to the American Library Association (in Boston), Charles Francis Adams, Jr., said all that needs be said: "I long ago decided that, if I could have but one work for a public library, I would select a complete set of *Harper's Monthly*."[10]

In the summer of 1853, while at work on his Blackwater article, Strother heard that Washington Irving, the guest of John Pendleton Kennedy, would make a visit to Berkeley Springs.   Kennedy had invited Irving to join him in making a trip to "Cassilis," his brother's home near Charles Town, and an excursion to Berkeley Springs for a visit with his Uncle Phil Pendleton, the original of Frank Meriwether in *Swallow Barn*.[11] Late in June, Irving found himself in the Valley of Virginia; "and a glorious Valley it is," he wrote, "equal to the promised land for fertility, for superior people—choice though not cho-

9. Joseph L. King, Jr., *Dr. George William Bagby: A Study of Virginian Literature, 1850-1880*, (New York, 1927), p. 38.

10. Quoted in John Kouwenhover, "Personal and Otherwise," *Harper's Magazine*, CCI (October, 1950), 11.

11. Irving wrote in acceptance: "I should indeed like to be of your party, for I am bewitched with the South and Virginia has always been a poetical region with me." Letter from Irving to Kennedy, April 24, 1853, in the Kennedy Collection of the Peabody Institute Library.

sen."[12] Irving was charmed by Kennedy's niece Mary of "Cassilis"—enough so to return in October, and again in January to attend her wedding.[13] At Berkeley Springs, he found the weather insufferably hot but the company of Judge Pendleton, "that rare old cavalier,"[14] particularly fine. Irving remained at the Springs for ten days, and Strother amused the two venerable men of letters with his drawings of the Blackwater.[15] Irving's visit, coinciding with Strother's first real literary efforts, gave birth to the pen name, "Porte Crayon."[16] Despite their difference in age, both shared similar views: they had a penchant for tradition and antiquarianism; they looked upon literature as the avocational occupation of a gentleman; and they were perhaps more at home in the old America than in the new. As Irving had made the Hudson familiar to every American, so Strother would try to interpret the regions south of the Potomac. He would compound informal essays, descriptive pieces, character sketches, and amusing anecdotes in the Irving manner, and would supplement these by his own illustrations. The time was ripe for such an enterprise. Already execrations were being hurled North and South as the rift in sectional interests widened in the 1850's. In the midst of this heated antagonism, Strother's Virginia seemed not too far removed in spirit from Irving's New York.

12. Letter to Sarah Irving, June 22, 1853, as quoted in Curtis Chappelear, "Irving's Visit to the Valley," *Magazine of the Jefferson County Historical Society*, I (December, 1935), 14.

13. The affection of Irving for Mary Kennedy is brought out by Stanley Williams and Leonard Beach (eds.), "Washington Irving's Letters to Mary Kennedy," *American Literature*, VI (March, 1934), 44-65. She married Henry P. Cooke, a younger brother of John Esten Cooke and a cousin of David Strother.

14. Letter from Irving to Kennedy, August 31, 1854, in the Kennedy Collection.

15. Journal of John P. Kennedy, June 28, 1853, in the Kennedy Collection.

16. A historical marker at Berkeley Springs points out the house of David Strother and claims that Irving wrote part of his *Life of Washington* there; however, the designated house was not owned by Strother until 1866. David had a cottage elsewhere in the village, but it is unlikely that Irving would have done any writing on what was primarily a pleasure trip. Strother's adoption of "Crayon" might have been a pun on the surname of his cousins, the Cranes. In any case, it was not unique, for William Cox had published *Crayon Sketches* as early as 1833.

"A Visit to the Virginian Canaan" was published in the December, 1853, issue of *Harper's Magazine*. Although "Porte Crayon" was the narrator, the article was signed "by a Virginian." By good luck, its publication escaped the fire which destroyed the Harper establishment on December 10th, a holocaust that wiped out the January issue of the magazine.[17] Had Strother's manuscript and wood blocks perished, he might have scrapped the idea of writing altogether.

Strother's essay was predominantly masculine in its appeal. Its tone was humorous, its style literary. The six sportsmen, whose adventures form the narrative, are delineated in outline rather than in detail. There is first of all Mr. Penn (Philip Kennedy), who, as Strother judiciously observes, "had no command over his language. It poured forth in an irresistible torrent, carrying away the speaker himself, and overwhelming or putting to flight his audience." Next is Mr. Jones, a corpulent gentleman fond of rural sports whose "game bag was usually fuller when he went out than when he returned." Porte Crayon is then modestly introduced in third person as one whose "poor abilities were entirely inadequate to do justice either to the sublimity of the natural scenery or the preposterous absurdity of the human species on that memorable expedition." X.M.C. (ex-Member of Congress) is not a caricature of John P. Kennedy, as has been claimed, but is Strother's friend from Shepherdstown days, Henry Bedinger, soon to be made minister to Denmark.[18] Completing the roster are two unidentified characters, Mr. Dindon and Mr. Smith. The humor of the article still lives: Mr. Jones's hanging to a horse's tail on the steep incline, X.M.C.'s knocking with a rock a stubborn trout from a tree where it had landed, and Mr. Penn's magnificent cast—fancy rod as well as fly—into the Blackwater are fine episodes. Little philosophy and less politics mar the narrative, which preserves a balance between instruction (description of a new region) and amusement (satirical characterization of tender sportsmen). As would be expected,

17. The fire destroyed John Esten Cooke's *Leatherstocking and Silk* on the eve of its appearance. See Harper, *House of Harper*, pp. 95-96, and John O. Beaty, *John Esten Cooke, Virginian* (New York, 1922), p. 35.

18. Cecil D. Eby, Jr., "John Pendleton Kennedy Was Not 'X.M.C.,'" *American Literature*, XXXI (November, 1959), 332-34.

the illustrations are so well done that they almost detract from the literary portions of the work, a situation which persisted during Strother's career as a writer.

The Harpers liked the piece and subscribed for more like it. They gave the author a roving commission to travel wherever he liked in search of fresh material.[19] His articles were soon elevated to the lead-off position in the magazine, and it was not long before Strother became "the highest-paid contributor *Harper's* ever carried during the ante-bellum years."[20] He received about four or five hundred dollars for each of his contributions to *Harper's* and averaged two a year for twenty-five years. This was an extraordinary sum for the era; even at the height of his popularity Hawthorne received only one hundred dollars for a ten-page article,[21] while other writers were fortunate to obtain half this amount. Prolific as he was, John Esten Cooke, a professional novelist, had earned only thirteen thousand dollars by his pen in 1873;[22] by this date Strother had earned twenty-five thousand dollars. With the exception of William Gilmore Simms and Augusta Evans Wilson, Strother was perhaps the most successful writer, financially considered, in the ante-bellum South.

The extraordinary popularity of Porte Crayon was the result of three factors—the man, the magazine, and the moment. It has been pointed out that Strother's training prepared him for the age of illustrated literature, and that *Harper's* editorial objectives conformed to the spirit of the times. Something now must be said about the literary climate of the age. In 1850, American writing was beginning to shake off its amateur status.

19. Harper, *House of Harper,* p. 89. The financial arrangements of this roving commission are not clear, but it seems that Strother was permitted to draw on Harper and Brothers for his expenses.

20. The claim has been made perhaps half a dozen times by various authorities. The quotation is taken from William O. Stevens, *The Shenandoah and Its Byways* (New York, 1941), p. 230. While this work is popular in its style and approach, Stevens deserves mention as one of the first recent writers to rediscover and publicize the writings of Porte Crayon.

21. Randall Stewart, *Nathaniel Hawthorne: A Biography* (New Haven, 1948), p. 225.

22. Jay Hubbell, *The South in American Literature* (Durham, N. C., 1954), p. 518.

The professional writer was appearing on the horizon. Emerson and Poe had found literature of little help to their personal finances, but as the monthly magazines found a vast public, American publishers became more friendly to American writers. In 1830, only 40 per cent of the books published in the United States were written by Americans. By 1850, however, the ratio had risen to 70 per cent.[23] Whereas English literature had formerly been satisfactory for most readers (a happy condition for the publisher, because with no international copyright law no payment to the author was necessary), the public now showed signs of wanting to hear about American people and places. These, obviously, were beyond the province of English writers. One sees the change from foreign to native literature in the early volumes of *Harper's Magazine*. In its first years, it had been given such names as "Monthly Corn-Plaster" and "Buccaneer's Bag," because the editors relied so heavily upon pirating from British sources. When, however, the magazine was transformed from an eclectic foreign review into a national periodical, public approval was amply reflected by the circulation figures. What the public demanded, the publishers supplied.

How much Porte Crayon was responsible for the popularity of *Harper's* it is impossible to determine; publishers often find that overpraising one of their writers is bad business. Certainly, by the end of the decade Porte Crayon was a household word. On streets and in hotels, north and south, Strother was often recognized from his self-portraits in *Harper's*. Throughout his life, he heard innumerable accounts of his popularity. There was a soldier who carried *Virginia Illustrated* in his knapsack during a six-month campaign, and a New York packer affirmed that the same book was the first and most important one he had read. In 1870, H. M. Alden, editor of *Harper's* from 1869 to 1919, told him that his papers were of a character "which had never been furnished before or since." Strother seemed to be able to ignite a spark of literary interest in all classes of people. The nation was filled with writers whose pages were more broadly humorous; others were more elevating; still others were more

23. E. Douglas Branch, *The Sentimental Years: 1836-1860* (New York, 1934), p. 109.

informative. But Porte Crayon promised amusing anecdotes capably told, historical sketches, fine bits of natural description, sagacious philosophical reflections, and, in addition to these, an illustration on every other page. His formula, so successful for twenty-five years, called for "getting near to the popular heart and confidence by mingled humor and sentiment, then introducing a higher philosophy, original, just, and coloured with quaint humor and sarcasm."

Virginia Illustrated, a collection of his articles, is his best-known work and the only one published in book form (1857 and 1871). It consists of two unrelated parts, one of which, "A Visit to the Virginia Canaan," has been discussed. The other, "Adventures of Porte Crayon and His Cousins," is a travel narrative of a trip up the Valley of Virginia and into the Piedmont during the late fall of 1853. Whereas the first was designed for the male reader, the second made a bid for the female. Porte Crayon is accompanied not by four sturdy sportsmen but by three females. Strother ably solves the principal problem, attracting women readers without alienating the male, by combining light sentiment with sardonic wit. It is a mistake to think that the delicate requirements of the "feminine fifties" compelled him wholly to surrender to their standards. *Virginia Illustrated* is a frame story in which the unifying thread is a visit to towns, resorts, and natural features of the Old Dominion. Because a frame story usually sacrifices depth for breath, we expect (and find) that Strother's principal defect is structure. Sometimes the narrative disappears beneath the weight of a digression. At other times the narrative is too minutely told. Writing within a chronological sequence, Strother was trapped by the necessity of recounting each day's travel as it was. In real life, the events of some days are more interesting than others, and to render all of them as if they were of equal importance must result in an uneven piece of writing. Strother was well aware that the dullness of some incidents would slow down his narrative, but he was too much a realist to eliminate these portions. In justification of his painstaking realism, he wrote, "If persevering good-humor at length becomes wearisome . . . charge it up in the general account against human nature, and not to your humble and faithful servant." After all, any traveling has its duller moments. The sentimentalist might choose to forget them, but Strother did not. While the novelist is free to select and even to distort, the travel writer is not. Strother's philosophy of composition—a preference for fact rather than fiction—is a bad one for the novelist but a good one for the social historian. In the novels of John Esten Cooke, who, like Strother, wanted to be the interpreter of Virginia life, one can never be quite certain where fact leaves off and fiction begins: hence his writing must be examined from a purely literary point of view. "Not one single solitary buzzard was ever seen in Mr. Cooke's skies," wrote George W. Bagby, who waggishly concluded that buzzards must have come into existence after the Revolution.[24] In contrast, perhaps it was Strother's robust and unpretentious verity which caused Dr. Bagby to call him "our own matchless, artist-writer, Porte Crayon,—the best contributor, by long odds, that Harper can boast,"[25] a compliment even more generous when one considers that Bagby, too, was a contributor.

Something needs to be said about Strother's style, which at first sight seems sometimes to be stilted and often to be affected. At times it appears that Strother went out of his way to find a Latinate construction like "a bag plethoric with lunch" or "effervescence of enthusiasm" when a simpler one would have sufficed. Much of this usage was, of course, borrowed from the best writers of the age, for whom the spoken and the written language were wholly different things.[26] However, Strother does not always use "tinsel rhetoric" in his articles. He draws upon the speech of two national types, the Southern Negro and the Appalachian mountaineer. Moreover, Strother is one of the first American writers to make extensive use of both. Tim Longbow's outburst, "I don't like to be stumped nor yit to be called a squirrel-picker, by no set-up swell whomsomdever," is at the opposite pole from the swollen verbiage that Strother uses upon serious occasions. Yet he carefully restricted his use of

24. Kings, *Bagby: A Study of Virginian Literature*, p. 83.
25. *Ibid.*, p. 88.
26. An excellent discussion of this attitude may be found in Herbert Ross Brown, *The Sentimental Novel in America, 1780-1860* (Durham, N. C., 1940), pp. 134 ff.

dialect. Neither his readers nor his editors would have accepted the rich but coarse diction of the *Spirit of the Times*. *Harper's* may not have been highbrow, but it was genteel. Although Strother read and enjoyed the sketches of Ham Jones and Johnson Hooper before the war, and Artemus Ward and Mark Twain after it, he still did not regard them as writers of literature. His own style was the result of wide readings in English literature and the cultural milieu in which he wrote. His artful humor and playful satire prevent his style from becoming smug, as his taste prevents it from becoming coarse.

Virginia Illustrated falls within the tradition of the pictorial sketch of the 1850's. This neglected genre exploited one of the popular fetishes of the period, romantic attachment to rural solitude. The reader was moved by a desire to return to Rousseau, at least for a week end. As the increasing ugliness of the cities forced increasing numbers into the suburbs, so there grew the demand for the rural essay and the Downing villa. America was reaching a stage in its culture where the sight of a tree called forth the poet's pen as well as the woodman's axe. Strother's literature provided pastoral scenes in abundance and, what is more important, showed that they were within the reach of everyone. The writer most responsible for opening the field of pictorial art and description in the South was T. Addison Richards, a frequent contributor to *Harper's*. His engravings for *Georgia Illustrated in a Series of Views* (1842) were successful in revealing the beauty of remote localities, and Strother perhaps was moved to adapt the title for his own work. Richards' steel engravings were a novel and rich exploration of local color. Ten years later he had a lead article in *Harper's* in which he particularly recommended Virginia as a field for the pictorial artist.[27] Throughout his career as writer and artist, Richards popularized picturesque American byways, and many followed his example with sketches of Arcadian America in appealing moods and thereby prepared the public for the more concerted efforts of the local colorists two decades later.

27. T. Addison Richards, "The Landscape of the South," *Harper's New Monthly Magazine*, VI (May, 1853), 721-29.

The characters in *Virginia Illustrated* include Porte Crayon, Fanny Crayon (Strother's sister, Emily), Minnie May (his wife), Dora Dimple, and Little Mice, the gigantic Negro driver. They leave Martinsburg in October, 1853, and their travels for the ensuing five weeks are described in detail. Porte, priding himself on his bewhiskered resemblance to Captain John Smith, is a stoic of the Pyrrhonic school—except where females are concerned; his crotchety remarks, philosophic digressions, and reminiscent odds and ends alleviate the literal account of the journey itself. In him we see Strother's picture of himself. The journey includes most of the scenic wonders of the Valley of Virginia and a large number of the resorts. From Winchester, the travelers enter the secluded Fortsmouth Valley for a visit to the now-abandoned Burner's Sulphur Springs. At Weyer's Cave, farther to the south, Porte discovers that foreign travel has not dulled his appreciation of the caverns which enchanted him as a boy, but he also finds that he is unable to copy "Nature's Great Masterpiece."

When the travelers arrive at Staunton, Little Mice first becomes the comic character that enlivens so many pages of the book. Aware of the cultivated tone of that town, Porte flourishes his portfolio in order to suggest that his party is a group of literary tourists. Mice upholds the "literary" pretentions of the wayfarers by sallying forth garbed in a ruffled shirt of red calico set off by a June-bug breastpin, a copy of *Harper's* under his arm. Strother well describes the mien of the plantation Negro who attracts the attention of the town and mortifies his master: "Occasionally he paused to address a condescending question to some 'common nigger,' to salute some turbanned damsel of his own race at an opposite window, or to cast a look of ineffable satisfaction at his goodly shadow, which entirely overspread the narrow sidewalk." In the era before guilt or social protest colored every characterization of the Negro, the scene was accepted and enjoyed by readers as a familiar comedy of manners. Strother's attitude was typical of the enlightened and humane Virginian of the time. He saw the Negro as a person rather than as an abstraction. At Berkeley Springs, Strother had long been an observer of what he called the three aristocracies—wealth,

birth, and talent—and had noted that the old Negro servants
often "had more real elevation and dignity of character than
all the others." His trip into the Tidewater had shown him
something about the economic fallacy inherent in the "peculiar
institution," but it had not made him an abolitionist. He doubted, as many Negroes then doubted, whether the average Negro
would ever acquire the intellectual, social, and economic status
of the white man. Even Mice, in reply to his master's query as
to whether he would like to be white, replies without hesitation,
"Bless your soul, Mass' Porte, I'se better as I is. I'se a pretty good
nigger, but I ain't got sense enough to be white." Mice, like
other Negroes in Strother's literature, has a humble place in the
Southern hierarchy, but he is treated with humorous good-will
and human compassion wholly outside the rigid molds of the
propagandist, North or South.

Putting Staunton behind them, the travelers visit the Natural
Chimneys, a group of seven limestone pinnacles near Mt. Solon.
Porte objects to the term "Cyclopean Towers," which was also
in use, because it inappropriately mixed Old and New World
associations. Using a *double entendre,* he includes hostile European travelers like Mrs. Trollope and Captain Basil Hall in his
remark, "We doubt if the introduction of distinguished foreign-
ers is of much advantage to us in any way on this side of the
water." His attitude recalls a similar one which he had during
his travels in Europe, an obstinate application of Emerson's
insistence upon self-reliant judgments. Before they leave the
Chimneys, Porte also satirizes those Americans who feel compelled to see European associations in all native landscape. Referring to the Chimneys, he says, "Their whole appearance reminds one of the ruined stronghold of some feudal baron surrounded by its neglected moat. To those whose fancies are
more exclusively American, they look like the chimneys of a
deserted iron foundry."

As the carriage winds through the Allegheny foothills, Porte
shoots partridges from the driver's seat, and later these appear
on inn tables, along with heaps of venison, corn-dodgers and
other upland delicacies. One of the best scenes in *Virginia
Illustrated* is the crowded drovers' tavern, which in setting and

characters anticipates Mark Twain's Virginia City. Delayed by
a snowstorm, the drovers are being entertained by the tall tales
of Tim Longbow when Porte enters the bar room. Tim, mor-
tally offended when Crayon refuses to drink with him, compares
the artist's beard to the beard of a "Mexican greaser." When
Tim threatens Porte with a bull whip, a fight nearly ensues, but
tempers are quieted by the landlord. Tim continues his story
of an expedition to California, but Porte surpasses it with one
of his own, an account of a visit to the North Pole. So thoroughly does he vanquish the "bar-room Munchausen" that Tim
forgets his antagonism, doffs his hat respectfully, and offers it
to Porte as a token of defeat. Behind his pugnacious prattle,
the mountain tough has a sense of fair play and a commendable
nobility about him, which Strother attributes to his place of
birth: "although something of a swell, a bully, and a liar, Tim
was still a Virginian." As in portraying the Negro, Strother cut
away superficial differences between social types to reveal his
characters as people. *Virginia Illustrated* treats not just a single
layer of Virginia society but the aristocrat, the common man,
and the slave.

After making the rounds of the Virginia springs, the visitors
return to the Valley and proceed to the Natural Bridge, which
Strother had seen eighteen years before. Once again he reflects
on the ascent of Jim Piper, rating this cliff climber as high as
"the founder of universities and the leader of armies." From
the Bridge, the party turns east to the Peaks of Otter, which had
long symbolized for Strother his love of Virginia. Falling in
with some emigrants to the Western country, Porte shows his
distrust of Greeley's glib Western optimism in an anecdote of
Sally Jones, which Van Wyck Brooks found the most impressive
thing in *Virginia Illustrated*.[28] Sally, the "belle of the Cacapon
Valley," is as pretty and buxom a girl as ever thumped butter-
milk in a churn, but she has the misfortune to be in love with
Sam Bates, a very bashful fellow. Sam, who stands "in winter,
six feet, two inches in his stockings (in summer he didn't wear

28. Van Wyck Brooks, *The Times of Melville and Whitman* (New York,
1947), p. 55. The story of Sally Jones and Sam Bates appears in *Virginia Illustrated*, pp. 201-8.

any)" has a heart "as big as his foot" and is the owner of a flourishing wagon shop and several hundred acres of uncleared land. Humiliated in front of Sally by his inability to remove his huge foot from its stirrup, he takes out his grief frontier-fashion by chopping down several acres and retiring from society. In the meantime, Sally's father decides to leave Virginia for Missouri and holds a sale of their belongings. Painfully, Sally watches each familiar object disappear until she can stand it no longer. Mounting an inverted kettle, she offers to sell herself. "I don't want to go West, I don't want to leave Virginny; and I won't leave, if there's a man among ye that has spunk enough to ask me to stay." Fortunately Sam, hovering in the background, rushes forward to claim her and to avert an unwilling expatriation. Strother particularly appreciated this story, because loyal provincialism triumphs over aimless fortune-hunting. Whether abolitionism or manifest destiny, Strother distrusted panaceas and schemes which smelled of the pulpit or of newsprint. Theories, he thought, were apt to cause more trouble than they could cure.

Porte Crayon's conservatism was mild in comparison with that of Billy Devilbug, a Negro bootblack whom he meets at a wayside tavern. Billy has only contempt for the degenerate age in which he lives. In his confession to the artist, its boots as well as its politics are equally damned: "'Master, when I was young there was gentlemen then. They wore fa-top-boots them days; to see a fa-top-boot was to see a gentleman. Nowadays since these storeboots come in, under the new constitution, there hain't no distinction; every thing is mixed up; every thing wars boots now, and sich boots! I'se afear'd to rub 'em hard, for fear to rub the sole off 'em. Them's gentlemen nowadays!'" In the manuscript version of *Virginia Illustrated,* there is another anecdote which was not published in *Harper's.* Doubtless the editors found it too harsh for their readers and therefore deleted it. It concerns Uncle Peter, an ancient Virginia Negro who has acquired a certain fame because in the old days he had been kicked by General George Washington. Mice somehow finds this character and brings Porte Crayon to hear the story, which Uncle Peter is delighted to tell again:

"I'se Uncle Peter, I'se de ole servant what Gen'l Washington kicked
. . . . Proper young man dat Mass' George was, eh gosh, he kick
like a blooded colt, four year old at dat," and Uncle Peter limped
about with such great vivacity as if he were still lame from the
effects of the kick . . . . "I was a boy den. General Washington
come down. Peter, says he, whars my boots? Den I was all over
a trimble, for believe me, Master, I hadn't clean 'em at all. So
when Mass' George seen dat, says he, you ordinary whelp, dat de
way you 'beys my orders, and he gin me a kick, Master, dat saunt
me across de yard; fust I thought my leg was broke and de fact is,
Master, I'se been sort of lame and unsarvicable ever sence." Uncle
Peter's reminiscence was duly rewarded and as they returned to the
hotel, Mice ventured to remark that when Uncle Peter told him
about it, he went lame in the other leg.

Placing the Father of His Country in the role of a Simon Le-
gree (for such would have probably been the reading in the
North) was too provocative for the 1850's, although a decade
earlier the anecdote would have been harmless enough. Strother
used the story elsewhere in his literary work, and it is quite
probable that he heard it from some old Negro.[29] In any event,
Uncle Peter is, like Billy Devilbug, a spokesman for the old regime and an enemy of the democratic leveling of the new.

Near the conclusion of the journey, the travelers visit the
University of Virginia to see a cousin, Ned Twiggs, who is one
of the five hundred students in attendance. Although Porte
is no advocate of classical education, he confesses that the University is a cut above most others. Ned humbles Porte in the
matter of Latin puns, but Crayon has his revenge in a comparison of beards. Dora avows that she likes scholars better than
scholarship. Minnie is more explicit; her conception of the literary man derives from the cavalier rather than from the metaphysical tradition. She speaks for the South when she says, "We
do not so much admire the laborious, pains-taking student, the
mere book-worm; but the brilliant, dashing genius, whose productions seem the results of intuition rather than of labor, whose
eloquence is unstudied, whose verses are impromptu." The
Philip Cooke, who could dash off a poem before breakfast, gal-

29. "The Young Virginians," *Riverside Magazine*, IV (August, 1870), 350.

lop a dozen miles, and hurl it into the window of his beloved—
this was the poet for the Southern woman.[30]

On their return home, Porte Crayon and his cousins meet
Squire Hardy, Strother's version of Frank Meriwether of
Swallow Barn. Squire Hardy is hospitable to a fault, somewhat
obtuse where politics is concerned, and good-humoredly provincial in his tastes and ideas. He haunts Boniface's Tavern on
the turnpike so that he can waylay travelers in order to invite
them to his house for an extensive visit. As the innkeeper says
to Porte, "This is a poor place, Sir, for my business, Sir. When
I do get a genteel customer, I can't keep him on account of
Squire Hardy and the like of him. He only lives two miles from
town, keeps a much better tavern than I do, and nothing to pay,
and good liquor in the bargain."[31] Porte and his group are
especially welcome, because the Squire is able to spell C-r-a-y-o-n
as C-r-a-n-e, the maiden name of his wife. Although Strother's
portrait of the Virginia squire has been criticized as one-dimen-
sional by no less an authority than Dr. George Bagby,[32] Hardy
is an improvement on Meriwether. Strother, who was in closer
touch with Virginia life than Kennedy, caught the defects—ar-
rogance, ignorance, narrowness—as well as the virtues of his
squire. Bagby was right in contending that the isolated rural
gentleman of Virginia could not accurately be portrayed as a
single type (his own characterizations and those of Arthur G.
Bradley are perhaps the best in literature), but Strother successfully avoids the pitfall of sentimentalism and achieves an impression which is within the tradition of the Theophrastians:

30. Alex Boteler recalled that in the early morning Cooke would ride to
"The Bower," home of his cousin Evelina Dandridge ("Florence Vane"), and
would deposit the bouquet and poem before the house was astir. See John
D. Allen, *Philip Pendleton Cooke* (Chapel Hill, N. C., 1942), p. 31.

31. There are many accounts of Virginia gentlemen virtually kidnapping
passers-by from the inns; see, for example, Matthew P. Andrews, *Virginia, the
Old Dominion* (New York, 1937), p. 263. Mention has been already made of
how Beverley Tucker tricked Strother into remaining overnight with him
in Williamsburg.

32. George W. Bagby, *The Old Virginia Gentleman and Other Sketches* (New
York, 1910), p. 28. Bagby groups together Strother's and Kennedy's squires as
"a Stout bluff, hearty, jovial old fellow, fond of juleps, horse races, and 'a little
game of draw.' "

The Squire, out of his own district we ignore . . . . At home he is invariably a great man . . . . Sour and cynical in speech, yet overflowing with human kindness; contemning luxury and expense in dress and equipage, but princely in his hospitality; praising the olden time to the disparagement of the present; the mortal foe of progressionists, and fast people in every department . . .; opinionated and arbitrary as the Czar, he was sauced by his negroes, respected and loved by his neighbors, led by the nose by his wife and daughters, and the abject slave of his grandchildren.

It would not be difficult to find a "source" for Strother's characterization—Addison and Steele, Goldsmith, Irving, and Kennedy had all portrayed similar individuals; but it is pedantic to assume that Strother relied upon literary models. Squire Hardy seems to resemble Colonel John Strother, Colonel David Hunter, and dozens of flesh-and-blood Virginians seen every day on the streets of Martinsburg or Berkeley Springs. For all their limitations, such men were both admirable and lovable, and Strother saw that as they became anachronisms in American life a certain nobility of character disappeared forever with them.

Virginia Illustrated ends where it began, at "Crayon Hall" in the village of Martinsburg. All have benefited by their excursion; Little Mice becomes, of course, the "African Lion" of the community, particularly when he finds his picture engraved upon the pages of *Harper's*. Though Strother completed his circuit of Valley and Piedmont shrines, the ending gave him a great deal of trouble, if erasures, inkings, and deletions in the manuscript version are an accurate indication. The stock ending for a story in the 1850's was a marriage, and Strother made use of this device. Fortunately, however, the marriage between Porte Crayon and Minnie May is suggested rather than described. The reader, therefore, is spared the inevitable ceremony with which thousands of stories have concluded. *Virginia Illustrated* is still an interesting and amusing piece of literature, valuable for its revelations of social history. It is a patchwork incorporating travel narrative, description, anecdote, satire, philosophy, and humor into a single work designed for the general public. Although uneven, the individual scenes have weathered the changes in literary climate from that day to this. Strother's book is perhaps the best written about Virginia during the 1850's. Certainly it was the most widely read.

Virginia Illustrated was reviewed widely and, for the most part, favorably, the reviewers usually accepting the author's discursive style for what it was. Some compared Strother with Irving (none suggested Kennedy). Most recognized the regionalistic nature of the work, with its portraits of Negroes and delineation of Southern landscape. Although reviews appeared in two English periodicals, none of the New England magazines descended from their transcendental ether to notice the work. *Harper's Weekly,* as one would suspect, praised it and quoted a blurb from a Mississippi newspaper which compared the work of Strother with that of Irving—the first published instance of the analogy that was made so often during Strother's lifetime.[33] The *Southern Literary Messenger,* ever on the lookout for promising Southern writers, called Strother the "American Doyle," and praised the pictures of Negro life in the book.[34] The most enthusiastic review appeared in *Graham's Magazine,* which called Porte Crayon a "man of genius." The *Graham's* reviewer said the book is "one of the most genial, whole-souled, amusing and descriptive works on local American scenery, manners and customs ever written, and will always be possessed as such of great value to the scholar and those who know a true, sound original work from an imitation or a piece of literary mannerism."[35]

When Strother received his first copies of *Virginia Illustrated,* he sent one to Henry Augustus Wise (not to be confused with Governor Henry Wise, his guardian), the author of several books of travel and adventure under the nom de plume "Harry Gringo." Wise saw at once the resemblance to Irving, but he did not feel that Strother was deliberately imitating him. Writing to Strother, Wise made some accurate and sensible remarks: "Your style approaches more nearly to the manner of Irving than any of his host of imitators; and this without striving or effort. My theory is, that you have never been what is called a 'practiced

33. *Harper's Weekly,* I (July 11, 1857), 438.
34. *Southern Literary Messenger,* XXV (August, 1857), 160.
35. *Graham's Magazine,* LI (September, 1857), 278.

writer,' and your success is the result of sound appreciative knowledge of the old English writers, acting upon a healthy imagination. No man or woman is born with this gift and it cannot be fished up like a fish from a stream."[36] In its digressive structure, its air of playful satire, and its strong flavor of sectionalism, *Virginia Illustrated* does have a distant kinship with *The Sketch Book*. However, it is most likely that the similarities are the result of both authors' dependence upon Scott's regionalism, romantic landscape, and retrospection. In 1871, the year when Harper's reprinted *Virginia Illustrated,* Strother read Irving for the first time since the war. His remarks in his journal are not those of an admirer: "Yesterday read in Irving's Sketch Book. They seemed like the work of a school girl or sophomore." These are not the words of a man who sought to imitate Irving. The only obvious borrowing was the name "Crayon," and it should be noted that as a name "Porte" is more humorous and less pretentious than "Geoffrey." If the literary sources for *Virginia Illustrated* are ever required, they will doubtless be found in books of Virginiana, and if Strother had any open books on his writing table while he was writing his own narrative, they were Samuel Kercheval's history of the Valley of Virginia, William Burke's account of the Virginia springs, and Andrew Burnaby's book of travel.

Because *Virginia Illustrated* was the first, the most popular, and the only separately printed Strother serial, more attention has been given to its content and its form than will be devoted to the rest of his work. Except for one or two articles during the eighteen-seventies, Strother's eclectic style and composite structure remained the same. However, his materials changed as he moved from one section to another, and these provided him with varied contrasts and impressions to be passed on to his readers. Making full use of the carte blanche given him by the Harper brothers, who were wise in permitting him to roam wherever he liked, Porte Crayon turned first south, then north, as he entered the larger frame of what might be called "The United States Illustrated."

36. Letter from Henry Augustus Wise to David Strother, August 16, 1857. In the possession of Boyd Stutler, Charleston, W. Va.

Chapter VI

Travels South and North, 1855-1859

AFTER his Valley of Virginia trip in the fall of 1853, Stroth-er's artistic excursions were restricted until the spring of 1856, when he set out with his sketch pad for North Carolina. He did, however, find time to assist John Esten Cooke with two projects. The Brothers Duyckinck were launching their antholo-gy of American literature and wished to include a portrait of Philip Cooke along with samples of his work. John Esten found to his surprise that there was no extant likeness of his brother, who had died from exposure after a duck hunt near his Shenan-doah retreat early in 1850, and he requested Strother to make a drawing. Strother obliged his cousin, although he found that Philip's appearance had slipped from his memory, so seldom had they met since their Martinsburg days. In the same letter John inquired whether Strother and Pent would "go in" the Duyckinck volume and added, "I'd give a dollar or more for the volume if your Bedouin phisnomy was in it."[1] Neither was represented in the Cyclopaedia, although George Duyckinck was a friend of Strother's. When John was preparing his novel *Ellie* for the press in the spring of 1855, Strother again obliged him by making two illustrations for the book. The novel, a chronicle of Richmond life, was a dismal failure, a result which Strother had doubtless foreseen, because he politely but firmly

1. Letter from John Esten Cooke to David Strother, December 5, 1854. Among the John Esten Cooke papers at the Library of Congress.

had written John, "You of course understand that my name
does not appear with the designs. As it is I have more engagements than I am willing to fulfill and if I were known I should
doubtless become so famous that I would be continually over-
taxed with work, a result which I very much dread."[2] Despite
these explicit instructions, the title page of *Ellie* included "with
illustrations after designs by Strother." The collaboration was
unfortunate for both writer and artist, the text and the drawings
being equally poor.

Although Strother was less guilty of rabid partisan politics
than most of his fellow Virginians, he found that as the 1850's
wore on it became more difficult to remain a moderate. The
election for the Thirty-fourth Congress in 1855 was the most
hotly contested in his district within memory, and it involved
Strother in one of the most notorious feuds in the history of the
region. Charles J. Faulkner, the Democratic candidate from
Martinsburg, and Alexander P. Boteler, the Whig from Shepherdstown, were both his lifelong friends. After his election,
Faulkner accused Boteler of having maligned him during the
campaign. Letters were exchanged, each growing more testy,
until Boteler challenged his opponent to a duel, Strother being
chosen as Boteler's second. On August 16, all parties went to
Washington for a meeting (as if there were not enough room for
a hundred duels in Berkeley), but they were promptly arrested
by the authorities. After their release, Strother made arrangements for a second meeting in Baltimore, but the misunderstanding gradually subsided. The whole fiasco was not without its
humorous side; during the heat of the preparations a friend of
Strother wrote him as follows: "I hear Faulkner has been most
industriously practicing pistol shooting, and has become a crack
shot at an *iron screw,* but I reckon if he had to look down the
muzzle of a pistol in a live man's hand he would think the hole
as big as the Mammoth Cave."[3] The episode showed that, if
Strother avoided political issues in his articles, this was no sign

2. Letter from David Strother to John Esten Cooke, May 23, 1855. Among
the John Esten Cooke papers at the library of Duke University.

3. Letter from A. V. Tidball to David Strother, September 4, 1855. Among
the Alexander Boteler Papers at the library of Duke University.

of his ignorance or lack of concern with them. Even in 1855, he saw in the Whig Party the moderate course which would prevent war and in the Democratic Party the frenzied excess which would encourage it. However, the greatest irony he could not foresee—the fact that both Boteler and Faulkner would support the Confederacy and under Jackson's command would oppose him and his political ideology during the approaching war.

In the winter of 1855, Strother lived with his family in New York. If he met any of the great literary personalities of the age at the salons of his friend, Anne Lynch Botta, he was not sufficiently impressed to record the fact. He lived at the Astor House, still the favored hotel for old-time visitors to New York, but avoided by the fashionable set. Across the street was Barnum's Museum and City Hall with its pleasant promenade for walks with Ann and Emily, slush permitting. Someone introduced him to Walt Whitman, whom he characterized thirty years later in his journal as "a coarse, healthy lout exhaling himself naked, sweating, and stinking before the public, without delicacy, depth, or dignity." This judgment, however, seems to have been directed toward Whitman the poet rather than Whitman the man. Certainly a more incongruous pair cannot be imagined: Strother reserved and aristocratic, Whitman forward and democratic—the symbols of two wholly different Americas meeting in a moment, yet centuries apart. Less strange perhaps is Whitman's affection for Strother, which will be mentioned later. New York was a pleasant interlude in the mid-fifties, but Strother appears not to have been reluctant to set out for North Carolina in the spring of 1856.

His new tour for *Harper's* was to do for the Carolinas what he had done for Virginia—to explore the less traveled byways in his search for local color. In both the North and the South, there was a demand for more and better pictures of Southern life. In Charleston, Simms wrote that before a national literature was possible, there must be adequate presentation of America in its regional phases. Writers had already explored New England and the Middle States, but except for a handful of informal humorists, the omnipresent European travelers (for the most part antagonistic), and a cluster of writers in one or two cities, the South was virtually untapped by the American writer. When Strother began his Carolina tour it was almost as if he were following Simm's recommendation: "to be *national* in literature, one must needs be *sectional*. No one mind can fully or fairly illustrate the characteristics of any great country; and he who shall depict *one section* faithfully, has made his proper and sufficient contribution to the great work of *national* illustration."[4] North Carolina, in particular, was an unknown region for most Americans. Certainly until *North Carolina Illustrated* appeared in *Harper's Monthly,* most of its subscribers knew more of life among the Patagonians than among the Tar Heels. Strother included the entire region from the Potomac to the Mississippi in his writing. Of all the writers of the Old South, Porte Crayon had the greatest geographical range.

His original plan was to travel through and to illustrate both North and South Carolina, but after two months on the road, Strother returned to Martinsburg without penetrating the latter. Since the days of William Byrd, Virginians had looked upon their neighboring North Carolinians with mixed feelings of pity and disgust. Strother's experiences were described in a similar vein, but with a great deal more bemused affection. His journal reveals his dissatisfaction more strongly than do his published accounts. The population was "lazy but civil" and the river towns were "stagnant as the Styx" or, less poetically, "dirty, forlorn, and ragged." Pipe-smoking females were common enough in the Virginia mountains, but in North Carolina he found a small variation. Jottings like the following did not make their way into *Harper's*: "J'ai dire que les femmes de N. Carolina fassait beaucoup l'usage de tabac. J'ai vu meme une fille avec une petit baton dan sa bouche." Some of the ratty little towns were perpetuated in his finished articles. Plymouth, for example, offered little to detain the traveler and less to amuse him except for "a dog-fight; a negro brat tumbling down the steps; and finally, about twelve o'clock, a drunken fellow who called for 'likker.' "[5]

4. Quoted in Jay Hubbell, *The South in American Literature* (Durham, N. C., 1954), p. 595.

5. "North Carolina Illustrated, The Piny Woods," *Harper's New Monthly Magazine,* XIV (May, 1857), 744.

Porte Crayon, however, had not come to North Carolina merely to scoff. At the Belvidere Fisheries he found a "frank hospitality which characterizes the region," discovered a peculiar bug-fish which he named for science *Harengus Porte Crayonensis,* and for a week lazed on the beach or on the Pamlico Sound. The pinewoods region around Washington was desolate and dismal, the forests seeming like a vast cemetery, but as he traveled west his spirits rose. From Raleigh he took the railroad to Greensboro, where he obtained a horse to ride out to Guilford Court House, five miles distant. Since boyhood he had been spellbound by stories and histories based upon the Revolutionary War; so minute was his knowledge of the battleground at Guilford that he recognized the place by intuition. Almost mystically he recorded his first impressions of the lonely and silent battlefield:

I reined up my horse in the midst of a group of ruined chimneys and decayed wooden houses, all, save one, silent and deserted. There was no human being in sight of whom to make inquiry, but I knew instinctively that I was upon the field of Guilford. The face of the country answered so well to the descriptions I had read, and there had been apparently so little change since the day of the battle, that there was no difficulty in recognizing the localities. Unmarred by monuments, uncontaminated by improvements, the view of the silent lonely fields and woods brought the old times back, so fresh, so real, so near.[6]

His sense of the past was completely integrated into his experience as he re-entered what for him was always the golden era of American history. Only five years separated him from his first sight of the bloody battlegrounds of the Civil War, yet he was more closely oriented to the historical patterns of eighty years before. He retraced the counterattack of the Virginia troops under Colonels Washington and Lee, and before leaving the field gave vent to his Virginianism by rising in his stirrups to release "a shout that made old Guilford's echoes ring again and alarmed a plowman on a hill half a mile off."

6. "North Carolina Illustrated, Guilford," *Harper's New Monthly Magazine,* XV (July, 1857), 163.

Strother's last article for *North Carolina Illustrated* described
a visit to Gold Hill in Cabarras County. At this boom town,
he met the Cornish and Welsh miners and descended with them
to watch them mine "earth's most operant poison." He observed
the contrast between the squalor above ground and the riches
below, and he did not fail to observe that although the resources
were Southern, the management was Northern. The grand
finale of his series treated a May Day picnic on the banks of the
Yadkin near Salisbury—a spree where "corks flew about like shot
in a sharp skirmish." Among the celebrants was Hamilton C.
Jones, author of "Cousin Sally Dillard," one of the most popular
stories in the pre-war South. Strother and Jones, who were
mutual admirers of each other's work, hit it off and exchanged
anecdotes, one of which found its way into Porte Crayon's next
Harper's series.[7] When the party ended in broken violin strings
and inebriate rhyme ("Verses Written by a Picnic Party on the
Head of a Broken Tambourine with a Corkscrew"), Strother
returned to Virginia.

North Carolina Illustrated is not Strother's best travelogue.
As social history, it will continue to draw readers (the work is
still well-known in parts of the Carolina Piedmont), and its details are accurate enough. It differs from his other serialized
travel narratives in abandoning the frame-story for literal re-
porting. There are no fellow sportsmen or cousins with Porte
Crayon to provide him with opportunities to digress, to satirize,
or to harangue. The four parts of *North Carolina Illustrated* are
unified only by his haphazard travels within the state.[8] While
his wit and style elevate the narrative above the prosaic level
of journalism, there is still a noticeable flatness. This was his
first literary venture beyond the Old Dominion. The new
materials were foreign, and he had not developed an ease with

7. Jones is the source for at least part of the anecdote about the debating
society, which appeared in "A Winter in the South, Fifth Paper," *Harper's
New Monthly Magazine,* XVI (May, 1858), 724-25.

8. While it does not treat North Carolina, his "The Dismal Swamp," *Harper's New Monthly Magazine,* XIII (September, 1856), 441-55, belongs to the
series, for it is based upon an excursion he made several weeks before he entered
North Carolina.

them. For the writer, North Carolina was to Virginia what Boeotia was to Attica. Only when he succeeded in accepting and exploiting regional peculiarities, as in his next two travelogues, would he find a suitable point of view. And to dramatize such peculiarities he needed one or two companions with him, a necessity which he never overlooked again.

In the late 1850's Strother wrote two other travel series, *A Winter in the South* and *A Summer in New England*. The first, which ran in *Harper's* from September, 1857, to December, 1858, consisted of seven articles based upon his tour with wife and daughter into the Deep South during the winter and spring of 1857;[9] the second, which ran from June, 1860, to July, 1861, consisted of five articles treating a tour with a male companion into New England during the summer of 1859. Both are fictionalized narratives, inasmuch as they contain characters—Virginians, of course—through whose eyes the respective areas are seen. Although the characters differ, the two chronicles are companion pieces in that they record the social history of two areas which were being fractured by the political crises of the age. Strother's narratives are non-partisan; as the nation split into two camps, the writer gave no sign of favoring either. He could not help satirizing the reforming zealots of New England, but, on the other hand, the cotton speculators of Alabama received their due. In a more placid time, his travelogues might have served to promote inter-sectional good will—certainly they did not hinder it—but the 1850's was not a period of good feelings.

A Winter in the South has a plot of sorts, the observations of a party of Virginians en route to New Orleans. Squire Broadacre, who travels for his dyspepsia, is a newer version of Squire Hardy, a rural gentleman "stranded high and dry on the rocks

9. In his journal, under "Points for Biography," Strother indicated that he made two trips into the South, one in 1857 and the other in 1858. As these "points" were based upon recollections made in 1886, it is probable that he was mistaken in thinking that he traveled to New Orleans in 1858. The dates upon some sketches—for example, "New Orleans, Feb., 1857" and "Vicksburg, Miss., Mar. 26, 1857—indicate that he went into the Deep South in that year. It seems incredible that he would have made such an arduous journey again in 1858.

of old fogyism."[10] He is accompanied by his wife and two daughters, Ann and Betty, and Leonore D'Orsay, his niece and ward. Robert Larkin, who replaces Porte Crayon, is a young and romantic dandy, and like Crayon has a talent for drawing and an urge to travel. A Negro driver, Jim Bug, completes the company, but he is far more sketchy than Little Mice. Although the characters and the places are different, the prevailing mood is the same as in *Virginia Illustrated*. Strother, however, was in a greater hurry to complete his series, and his haste is marked by the poorer quality of his illustrations. Many of them were prepared by an assistant, David English Henderson, an artist from Jefferson County, who relieved Strother of the tedious landscape and architectural sketches and gave him more time for caricature.[11] The series is misnamed, for six of the seven papers treat southwestern Virginia, western North Carolina, and eastern Tennessee, and only one paper the route from Chattanooga to New Orleans. It is probable that the series was unfinished, for the loose threads of the plot, particularly the attachment between Robert and Leonore, are never tied together. Such structural lapses seem not to have troubled the editors of *Harper's*; five of the articles were given the lead-off position in that magazine.

The party of literary tourists leaves Berkeley Springs, proceeds to Washington and Richmond, and then takes the canal-boat to Lynchburg. Squire Broadacre is little concerned about the careful planning of routes or time-saving travel, observing that "those who have nothing to do are most solicitous about saving time—to enable them to do it thoroughly, I suppose."[12] At secluded Saltville in the Holston Valley, the Squire indulges in castle-building as he dreams of "locating an El Dorado in that happy valley—a little world, where there should be wealth without envy, justice without lawyers, and freedom without

10. "A Winter in the South, First Paper," *Harper's New Monthly Magazine*, XV (September, 1857), 433.

11. The originals of Henderson's fine sketches are in the library at Princeton University. For a brief description of them, see the *Princeton University Library Chronicle*, XII (Summer, 1951), 222.

12. "A Winter in the South, First Paper," *Harper's*, XV, 442-43.

politicans,"[13] a sentiment that is clearly Strother's own. As Strother knew, the older Virginia idealism was breaking down, and political expedients having become hopeless, escape now remained the only answer to the impending chaos.

The travelers admire East Tennessee for its Spartan simplicity and the hardy independence of its inhabitants. This was an older region of "hard likker," horse thieves, and high mountains —a cultural salient bypassed by the civilized sameness of the East. They spend part of the winter in Jonesborough, a town built, as Strother says, by people who intended to live there for the rest of their lives. Nearby are the Smoky Mountains, which Larkin contrasts with the Alps and Apennines. "I never could appreciate," he says, "sights that have been so inked over with dottings and jottings, etchings and sketchings—besmoked, besmeared, bedaubed, bepainted—gaped at and slavered over, by every litterateur, artist, and snob in Europe and America."[14] The virgin forests and virtually untouched mountains lure the men to a climb, climaxing in the ascent of Mt. Mitchell in winter, an episode which is one of the most detailed in *A Winter in the South*. Strother was one of the first American writers to find a rich vein of materials in the Tennessee mountains, a vein not really exploited until the advent of Mary N. Murfree some twenty years later. His descriptions of dog-barking mountain settlements and apple-jack distillers resemble those in her book, *In the Tennessee Mountains*. Even the Virginia Canaan cannot compare with the Smoky Mountains, and Strother's enthusiasm is conveyed to the reader. The mountain isolation, remote in time and distance from the outside confusion, operated as a powerful stimulant upon Strother, and he viewed his subject without the trace of condescension which was evident in *Virginia Illustrated*. Supplementing the mountain excursions are some of his best anecdotes: a Kennedy-like recollection of an old-fashioned Christmas, old slave tales, and the description of the backwoods academy at Indian Creek.

When the travelers leave the Appalachian ridges behind and enter the Cotton Belt, they find a wholly different and uncon-

13. *Ibid.*, p. 450.

14. "A Winter in the South, Fourth Paper," *Harper's New Monthly Magazine*, XVI (January, 1858), 168.

genial world. As Virginians, they are struck by the unlicked and swashbuckling cosmos of the Southwest, where even the Negro waiters have caught the speculation-fever. "I tell you what," says one to his fellow, "I'll give you dis coat for a dollar and a half and take your paper at nine months, or ef you like better, one dollar cash on de button."[15] Aboard the river boat to Mobile, Strother introduces Jedebiah, the son of Simon Suggs, the notorious Southwestern sharper. Jedebiah flatters the Squire's vanity by calling him a "Virginian" and then vanishes with a fifty-dollar loan. Long before Melville and Twain, Strother caught the vivid contrast between palatial splendor and abject squalor in the characters on the "flush-times" steamboat. On one side were the cut velvet sofas and the French menus and on the other were the ten-bale cotton farmers "half afraid to sit on these fine seats, and not altogether sure of the propriety of spitting tobacco juice on these rich carpets."[16] The South-westerner is a man of deeds rather than of words; he asks but one question before going into battle: "How will it pay?"[17] In this traditionless society, Strother was as much the outlander as his fellow Virginian, Joseph Glover Baldwin, whose *Flush Times in Alabama and Mississippi,* published in 1853, epitomized the era. Bob Larkin makes his own summary: "Since the spirit of Democracy, not satisfied with political equality, is fast leveling all distinctions in morals and manners, it is hard to distinguish between a gentleman and a billiardmaker; to know the differ-ence between a rich banker and a swindler; or tell an M.C. from a black-leg."[18] Even Jim Bug seems imbued with some of the conservatism of his Virginia master, for at the railway depot in New Orleans he is indignant at hearing the Negro porters speaking French: "The idea of them black rascals undertakin' to talk larned, like ladies and gent'men."[19]

15. "A Winter in the South, Sixth Paper," *Harper's New Monthly Magazine,* XVII (August, 1858), 299.

16. "A Winter in the South, Seventh Paper," *Harper's New Monthly Maga-zine,* XVIII (December, 1858), 8.

17. *Ibid.,* p. 7.

18. *Ibid.,* p. 5.

19. *Ibid.,* p. 16. Jim Bug's astonishment at French-speaking Negroes re-sembles the reaction of another Jim in *The Adventures of Huckleberry Finn.*

Strother's travels into the Deep South were important in crystallizing certain conceptions he had partially formulated. He saw firsthand the enormous raw power of the Southern frontier, contrasting so markedly with the enervated Virginia Tidewater, but this power was, after all, only raw. It was nothing when compared with the immediate power of the North. He saw that there were really two Souths, the traditional, represented by Virginia, and the new, represented by the Southwest. The first had retained its social and moral superiority and lost its economic power, while the second had acquired this power without taking the responsibilities which should go along with it. In the melting pot of the Southwestern frontier, Strother envisaged a South which was greatly different from the one he had known in the Valley of Virginia, yet he also knew that a million bales of cotton were but a drop in the even larger economy of the North.

Having roamed through and described the South, Strother next turned for a subject to its antithesis, New England. The five numbers of *A Summer in New England* were written before the firing upon Fort Sumter, but before the last one could be published, the Civil War had made its halcyon scenes of New England life seem centuries old and irrelevant. The satirical treatment of the Yankee is so mild that it is difficult to conceive that a Southerner wrote it, and the content so removed from any suggestion of war that it seems impossible that its author would become a soldier in that war. *A Summer in New England* is more fortunate as to plot than most of Strother's narratives. The narrator is Bob Berkeley, who writes in first person. Accompanying him on his trip is Dick Dashaway, a brainless but generous young Southerner of many love affairs.[20] The guileless, amiable Dick serves the same function as the Chinaman in Goldsmith's *Citizen of the World*: he is almost painfully naive, but his comments upon the strange manners of the Yankee nation often cut to the heart of the matter. Dick's provincialism is balanced by Bob Berkeley's sophistication. We therefore obtain two interpretations of the events. Dick is an early example of the

20. The model for Dashaway was Berney Wolff, Strother's young brother-in-law. Two years later Berney entered the Southern army, rising to the rank of major.

Southerner described by Henry Adams: "Strictly, the Southerner had no mind; he had temperament. He was not a scholar; he had no intellectual training; he could not analyze an idea, and he could not even conceive of admitting two; but in life one could get along very well without ideas, if one had only the social instinct."[21]

Dashaway and Berkeley visit New Haven, New Bedford, Nantucket, Boston, and the White Mountains, all of which are described in detail. Dick learns early that Southern chivalry is misunderstood in the North. After offering a young lady assistance with her trunk, he is rebuffed by a threat to call the police, upon which he muses, "Up here ladies did not seem to be much accustomed to gentlemen's attention."[22] At New Haven he is horrified by the Yale students, who pass the Southerners loaded down with massive volumes under their arms; aptly he remarks, "I say, Bob, there goes a chap that has more learning under his arm than he'll ever have in his head."[23] Like most of his race, Dick prefers a sporting rather than an academic life, and he is gratified by their visit to Nantucket and Martha's Vineyard. Both are impressed by the whaling men, particularly by their self-reliance and efficiency. Yet even here, New England scenes provoke Virginian analogies: the sand dunes recall the Alleghenies, and the whaler's boat and harpoon are compared with the Southerner's pony and rifle. But there are differences, too. The natives seem to lack generosity and conviviality. Strother could not admire the New Englander who walked ten miles to obtain the dime owed for damage to his fence, although he admitted that a habit of exactness rather than miserliness prompted the act.

Thus far in their northern wanderings, neither Dick nor Bob have seen anything which resembles their preconceptions of the Yankee, but as their train nears Boston, they find what they have been waiting for:

21. Henry Adams, *The Education of Henry Adams,* ed. James Truslow Adams (New York, 1931), pp. 57-58.

22. "A Summer in New England, First Paper," *Harper's New Monthly Magazine,* XXI (June, 1860), 4.

23. *Ibid.*, p. 5.

We could recognize among the physiognomies around us characteristic marks of that great whittling, guessing, speculating, moralizing race whose destiny is—still a matter of guess-work.

This dapper gentleman, with a smirk on his face, which he thinks
is a smile, a shining, high-crowned hat, and a silk umbrella, I should
take to be the president of some railroad or manufacturing company,
a prince of button-makers, or principal stock-owner in a wooden
bucket-mill . . . .

This prim, tallow-faced individual, with a white cravat and
puckered month, is unmistakable—the traveling agent of some great
humanitarian society, whose plans, if universally adopted, promise
incalculable benefits to the human race. The specialty of this person
may be, perhaps, the propagation of vegetarian principles among
the Esquimaux . . . and the enforcement of monogamy among the
Roman clergy.[24]

Two Yankee stereotypes are included in Strother's satirical portrayal: the smug commercial man and the trouble-hunting reformer. Although Strother's description of the Yankee character
is mild when placed beside a Southwestern humorist's—particularly George Washington Harris's, whose Sut Lovingood hated
sheriffs and Yankees more than any other forms of animal life—
the attitude was Virginian enough. The basic difference between the Southerner and the Northerner was that the latter
wanted change, economic and social, while the former did not;
so far as this difference was concerned, Strother was wholly a
Southerner. "Why should a man carp at the world?" he wrote.
"Why undertake to tinker at Creation? Can he mend it? Some
people *think* they can; I do not."[25] This rhetorical question,
which Strother answered to his own satisfaction, was doubtless
provoked by the zealous visionaries of the North, particularly the
abolitionists, who, he thought, were allowing abstract principles
to lead a nation into a war that others would have to fight. As
we have seen, Strother had little faith in the theory that human
nature could be changed. He believed that living was a great
deal more important than theorizing. In Boston he noted that
Yankee humanitarianism was little practiced. An Italian beggar

24. "A Summer in New England, Third Paper," *Harper's New Monthly
Magazine*, XXI (November, 1860), 760-761.
25. "A Summer in New England, First Paper," *Harper's*, XXI, 2.

bitterly cried out, "What matters it to us poor people who
governs? All parties alike suck our blood and devour the bread
of our children."[26]   Bostonians found it easier to carry their
philanthropies to the rest of the globe than to apply them at
home.   Strother's antipathy toward abolitionism and other current "isms" was not the result of insensitivity to human suffering
but of a skeptical mind which doubted the sincerity and the
usefulness of high-sounding reforms.

The paper containing the analysis of the New England mind
is perhaps the best in the entire series.   Dick, of course, is more
impressed by the handsome dray horses than by the city's remarkable institutions.   At first he is infatuated by a Miss Teazle,
whom he had previously met at Berkeley Springs, but his interest wanes when he finds her at her home with "a book, a
bouquet, and a pair of specs—the usual complemental articles
of a Boston girl's costume."[27]   When he confesses to her that
he has not seen a man with a pleasant face since he arrived in
New England, she readily explains, "They have no time to look
pleasant . . . they are too busy for that."[28] Bob Berkeley, however,
explodes the myth of Yankee hostility.   He admires the order,
quiet, and application of the city.   Undoubtedly he is Strother's
spokesman when he says, "we found no exception to the rule
of obliging good-humour and fair dealing."[29]   Nor is he blind to
the superiority of the Massachusetts economy.   After a visit to
a great textile mill he notes that cotton from the Deep South
is shipped to Boston, where it is woven and then re-shipped to
the area from which it originally had come.   Perhaps he hoped
that his Southern readers would read in this wasteful inter-
change both a lesson and a warning.

There is no evidence that he made a pilgrimage to Concord—
certainly the last place in New England he would want to visit
—or that he met any of the notable literary figures of Boston
at the dinner held in his honor.   George William Curtis, the
editor of *Harper's Weekly,* could have supplied Strother with

26."A Summer in New England, Fourth Paper," *Harper's New Monthly
Magazine,* XXII (May, 1861), 723.
27.*Ibid.,* p. 724.
28.*Ibid.,* p. 727.
29.*Ibid.,* p. 722.

letters of introduction to most of the transcendentalists, but if he did, Strother apparently did not make use of them. While at the Parker House, he did have good news from Virginia. His friend Boteler had defeated Faulkner in the congressional election for the Eighth District, and in his victory Strother saw a hope for the resurgent Whigs and a favorable omen for the country. In no equivocal terms he wrote Boteler:

I hail the overthrow of a rule, the most despicable & degrading that ever cursed the soil of a free & civilized community, so dishonoring to my native soil that I loathed the land where I was born, and had not the bienniel hope of a change sustained me, I would most surely have sought a residence eleswhere. Now thank heaven, I can feel that the Eighth District is a fit residence for a gentleman . . .—that the jails and penitentiaries are no longer to be bilked of their just dues to furnish us leaders & public functionaries.[30]

Strother felt that the Democratic Party with its platform of states' rights threatened the Union, and that Boteler's victory marked the return of good sense and straight thinking. What he could not foresee was that the district was not indicative of Virginia at large, or that even Boteler would desert the Whigs at the first provocation.

Shortly after Dashaway and Berkeley leave Boston, they meet Squire Hardy and his daughter Ellen en route to the White Mountains. The competition for Ellen Hardy's attention is a series of scenes which feature Porte Crayon at his best. Dick manages to shove upon Bob a 240-pound New England bluestocking who is an ardent admirer of his literary work and is a poet herself: " 'I am altogether a creature of feeling—I feel entirely too much!' she exclaimed, pressing both hands upon her voluminous bust. 'It is a misfortune.' I agreed that it was."[31] Dick, meanwhile, escapes with Ellen Hardy.

In the White Mountains, Strother felt more at home than anywhere else east of New York. The grand and rushing mountain scenery evoked his highest praise, but this praise was

30. Letter from David Strother to Alexander Boteler, June 15, 1859, from Boston. Among the Alexander Boteler Papers at the library of Duke University.
31. "A Summer in New England, Fifth Paper," *Harper's New Monthly Magazine*, XXIII (July, 1861), 158.

not that of the tourist. Nature is the great restorative and pur-
gative which clears away congested sensations; she is the true
goddess who brings man to his real inheritance: "the instinctive
life-long yearnings of the soul are satisfied—you are free."[32]
Throughout most of Strother's literature, this idea, glorification
of nature, may be found. It is perhaps the only thought which
he shared with the Concord school; why else did he think that
Walden was the single New England book that made any sense?

Although *A Summer in New England* concludes on a familiar note, the suggestion of a marriage between Dick and Ellen,
the work as a whole presents as balanced a picture of New
England as could have been written by a Virginian in the 1850's.
The picture might have been useful, in less troubled times, in
dispelling by laughter some of the hard feelings, North and
South. Unfortunately the first shots at Harpers Ferry were only
months away, and within two years Strother's Martinsburg was
surrounded by hostile armies. At such times literature follows,
rather than changes, the course of history. Strother himself was
faced with the most important decision of his lifetime—to withdraw entirely or to fight, and if to fight, on which side? At
some time or another in the conflict, every Virginian had to
choose between his state and his country. The final paper of
A Summer in New England seems buried in the past. The
age wanted propaganda, not the reflections of a non-political
man. For the next five years the pen of Porte Crayon was dry.

32. *Ibid.,* p. 153.

Chapter VII

The Great Rebellion, 1859-1862

THE raid of John Brown upon the federal armory and arsenal at Harpers Ferry in 1859 proved to be the first military engagement of the Civil War, for it activated the dormant sectional antagonisms rooted in slavery and states' rights, antagonisms which had been festering for the past forty years. John Brown's fantastically ill-conceived and ill-managed invasion of Virginia soil was but a preview of the larger one by the Federal armies a year and a half later. By a stroke of good fortune or bad, David Strother was an eyewitness of both conflicts: At the first he was typical of most Virginians in abhorring the demonstration of belligerent abolitionism. At the second he was atypical in deploring the equally fanatical action of the Virginia militia, which demanded the surrender of the town. Better than most Southerners of his age, Strother knew that the South could not hope to win. Even a victory in arms over the North meant falling to the position of a third-rate power hopelessly dependent upon the economic patronage of a foreign nation. His hostility to Brown was no indication of a latent secessionism—far from it. He saw that the unprovoked attack upon Harpers Ferry was a reflection of that very sectional bitterness, that demarcation between North and South, that he so greatly feared. Nor was he wrong in his appraisal. The seeds planted by Brown were reaped, as Strother well knew they would be, in the whirlwind of civil war.

Prior to October 16, 1859, nothing much had ever happened at Harpers Ferry, a pleasant little town favored by excursionists out from Baltimore, and the location of a national arsenal since the presidency of Washington. When Brown and his marauders occupied the town on that evening in order to commence their freeing of the slaves, no one in northern Virginia had the slightest suspicion of the boldness of their plan. On the following morning while the first shots were being fired at Harpers Ferry, Strother was in his office at Martinsburg, about twenty miles away. According to his journal, when he first heard of the excitement, he supposed it to be merely another strike of disgruntled workmen at the government arsenal. With some scorn, he watched a band of citizen soldiery board a train for Harpers Ferry. These volunteers were armed with "squirrel rifles, fowling pieces, pistols, swords, and whatever was at hand." On the following morning, he heard that half a dozen of the Martinsburg volunteers had been hurt in a fight, and for the first time he realized that something was afoot down there. Largely out of curiosity, he boarded a train for the Ferry; unwittingly, he thereby stumbled upon the journalistic "scoop" of his career and the denouement of what was probably the most important event in American history during the nineteenth century. Writing his accounts in *Harper's Weekly,* he was the only newspaper correspondent to be on the scene at Harpers Ferry.[1]

Although his *Weekly* correspondence treats the details of the raid and the trial, an unpublished manuscript provides one of the best eye-witness accounts in existence. He arrived too late to take in the storming of the engine house by the marines, but he did catch the bedlam which immediately followed it. He overheard a Maryland congressman talk about the whole affair in terms of an additional three hundred votes in the next election. He watched the half-drunken and brawling militia milling about the dead bodies, some of which were being rooted over by stray hogs. He saw the macabre comedy of the mountain beau who

1. Two articles were published: "The Late Invasion at Harper's Ferry," *Harper's Weekly,* III (November 5, 1859), 712-14, and "The Trial of the Conspirators," *Harper's Weekly,* III (November 12, 1859), 729-30. A third article, apparently written for the *Weekly,* described the hanging, but public feeling veered so strongly in Brown's favor that the editors declined to print it.

was outraged when the crowd shouldered him and his two girl friends away from the bloodstained bodies ("Gentlemen, just give room here. Can't you stand back and let the ladies see the corpses?") and he listened as Lieutenant Jeb Stuart cried out to a wounded conspirator in words which have not found their way into Southern history books ("You son of a bitch. You had better keep silent. Your treatment is to be that of midnight thieves and murderers, not of men taken in honourable warfare.") Because he was a well-known figure to the authorities, Strother was permitted to enter the room where Brown lay upon his pallet and was soon engaged in sketching the old man. He discovered that there was nothing of the heroic about Brown, for he "denoted the most ungovernable fear" when he heard a movement outside which he interpreted as the first sounds of a lynching. Having completed his sketch, Strother was introduced to Colonel Robert E. Lee and Lieutenant Stuart, and not until this time did he become convinced that the raiders were not just a band of robbers who had come to divest the paymaster of his bankroll and who had raised an alarm of Negro insurrection in order to cover their retreat into Maryland. With increased interest, he returned with Stuart to draw Brown more carefully, and in the process he witnessed the interview conducted by Governor Wise, lately arrived with further regiments of Virginia militia.[2] Strother thought the interrogation, which took several hours, was tedious and poorly conducted, but as Brown's quixotic plan unfolded, Strother shared with the others the astonishment attending such a wild confession.

The presence of the Governor flattered his vanity (which was excessive) . . . . He candidly stated that the subject of his inroad into Virginia was to free the slaves and by their asisstance with the aid or connivance of the non-slaveholding whites to overthrow the social and political institutions in the Southern States and to erect in their stead a government and laws already organized by himself and followers. This plan of government recognized complete equality between whites and blacks and all existing rights of property except the property in slaves and all property owned by slaveholders. All such

2. Among others privileged to attend the interrogation were Senator J. M. Mason, Colonel Lewis Washington, and Andrew Hunter.

property was to be forfeited to the state and given over to the eman-
cipated negroes and the needy leaders in the war of freedom.

The prospect of a slave insurrection was not a new one for
Virginians; since the Nat Turner incident nearly thirty years before, the state had been on the alert for emergencies of that kind.
But the earlier outbreak had been forgotten because of its aimless
spontaneity, while the John Brown plan was characterized by the
plotting of a madman who had retained only one faculty—an
obsessive sense of abstract justice. The raid itself was so poorly
managed that its destructive effect was nearly negligible, but
for the South it sounded like the crack of doom. The Southerner
had to consider the question: how much does John Brown rep-
resent Northern sentiment? The animosity which had been
lurking in the background for a generation had at last come
to the surface. At no time did Strother sympathize with Brown
on the matter of slavery. Even during and after the Civil War,
he retained his Southern viewpoint that "Ossawatomie" Brown
was a blackguard rather than a saint. On the other hand, he did
not sympathize with Southerners like Edmund Ruffin, who saw
in the Harpers Ferry affair a torch by which to light the dry tin-
der of secession. Strother did not confuse John Brown with politics. He was simply a "greasy old thief" who had come in the
night and was bent on vicious destruction.

Brown and the remnant of his band who had not been killed
were placed in the Jefferson County jail at Charles Town and
were tried immediately. Northern Virginia lay virtually under
martial law. Outsiders, including newspaper reporters, were
scrutinized carefully or were denied access to both Brown and
the region. Plots to rescue the prisoner were uncovered, most
of which made the Harpers Ferry raid seem less fantastic by comparison. Strother's cousin, Smith Crane, brought a well-substan-
tiated report that a band of Kansas desperadoes were planning
a forcible rescue.[3] The result of these alarms was that armed
patrols of Virginians scoured the highways day and night, looking for suspicious characters. In Martinsburg, Strother assisted
in organizing one of these border guards, but he was nevertheless

3. Oswald Villard, *John Brown: A Biography Fifty Years After* (New York,
1943), p. 523.

on hand from time to time to watch the proceedings of the trial. His personal friend, Judge Richard Parker, presided at the trial, and his uncle Andrew Kennedy was the prosecuting attorney. Consequently, Strother was enabled to cover the courtroom scenes for *Harper's Weekly* almost without competition from other newsmen. He watched Brown with interest, and admitted that the prisoner was cool and unapologetic—qualities which Strother admired—but saw nothing supernatural about the old man who picked his teeth with a pin as he listened to his death sentence. Strother expected that the country at large would agree with him that Brown deserved the death sentence as an insurrectionist and murderer. He could not have believed at that time that many Americans saw anything heroic or martyr-like in Brown. His correspondence published in *Harper's Weekly* is explicitly Southern in its tone: "We owe him one good turn: with desperate hand he has blown up the whole magazine of abolition pyrotechnics—pray God there may not be a cracker or a squib remaining unburned! Brethren of the North, when hereafter any man shall attempt to profane your rostrums or your pulpits with incendiary abuse and revilings against any section of our common country, I charge you smite him on the mouth— with the word Harper's Ferry."[4] Little did Strother know that the abolition fireworks were just beginning. Three cartoons in the *Weekly* about this time were probably drawn by Strother, who amusingly caught the total unconcern of the Jefferson County slaves for their deliverer. One depicts a robust Negro workman armed with a ferocious-looking pike and a wicker basket who says to a fellow Negro, "Much obliged to dat ar possum wattomie for dese pikes he gin us—dey's turrible handy to dig taters wid."[5]

By early December, however, the editorial policy of the *Weekly*, ever alert to public opinion, underwent a transformation in its attitude toward the John Brown affair. Northern radicals were making a tremendous racket and Brown was finding so many followers that the *Weekly* dared not publish Strother's

4. "Trial of the Conspirators," Harper's Weekly, III, 730. John Brown's first biographer called Porte Crayon a "fiendish historian of the holy invasion." James Redpath, *The Public Life of Captain John Brown* (Boston, 1860), p. 264.

5. *Harpers Weekly*, III (November 19, 1859), front page.

third report, an account of the hanging. Not until 1955 was this manuscript published.[6] Several hours before the execution, Strother found a suitable spot near the gallows from which to observe. Ascending the empty platform, he could see white farmhouses and corn shocks in the fields adjoining them, symbols of peace and prosperity. Looking toward Harpers Ferry eight miles away, he realized that Brown's last sight would be "the spot where his enormous crime first took the form of action."[7] At eleven o'clock the prisoner arrived and ascended the scaffold without trepidation. Strother from his position next to the steps saw no sign of fear during the five-minute delay before the sheriff released the trap door. The conclusion of Strother's narrative indicates neither hostility nor admiration: "At the end of half an hour the body was taken down & placed in the coffin—the people went home, the troops wheeled into columns & marched to their quarters, and the day concluded with the calm & quiet of a New England sabbath. No man capable of reflection could have witnessed that scene without being deeply impressed with the truth that then and there was exhibited, not the vengeance of an outraged people, but the awful majesty of the law."[8] His acount does not mention the grisly aftermath. According to Andrew Hunter, Strother received permission to ascend the scaffold, to lift the hood, and to sketch the visage of the hanged man. "He said that the celebrated Lydia Maria Child had published that she wanted to have a portrait or likeness of Brown in every condition of life to hang in her room, and that he had taken this sketch to send her that 'she might have him too when he was finished.' If he sent it she has the best portrait of Brown ever taken."[9] Strother's grim joke was at least consistent with his theory that the two sections, North and South, would be recon-

---

6. "John Brown's Death and Last Words," in Boyd Stutler, "An Eyewitness Describes the Hanging of John Brown," *American Heritage*, VI (February, 1955), 4-9.
    7. *Ibid.*, p. 8.
    8. *Ibid.*, p. 9.
    9. Andrew Hunter, "John Brown's Raid," *Publications of the Southern History Association*, I (July, 1897), 175. Members of the Strother family say this sketch survives; however, the author has not seen it.

ciled when radicals on both sides desisted from their rabble-rousing. John Brown was dead: that was certainly a condition not admitting change. Like Hawthorne, Strother felt that "nobody was more justly hanged."[10] What he could not comprehend was the ultimate triumph of the cult fostered by men like Emerson, who saw John Brown as "the new saint . . . who will make the gallows glorious like the cross."[11]

For many Southern leaders, the John Brown episode was an opportunity to make converts to the principle of secession. During the trial, Governor Wise, Senator Mason, and Edmund Ruffin, among others, met at Andrew Kennedy's house on the outskirts of Charles Town to discuss the possibility of forming a confederacy of Southern states which would ally with France and then seize Cuba, Mexico, and Central America as part of an empire which would be developed by slave labor. Arming and equipping the South for war could be conveniently masked by the popular fear of further slave uprisings. Strother frequented his uncle's house many times during the trial and because of his obvious aversion to Brown's ideas, he was invited by the others to join their conferences. Perhaps, too, the conspirators thought that his reputation as a writer, particularly his association with a powerful organ like *Harper's,* would be of great value to them. When he refused to have anything to do with their plan, he was dropped by them and thereafter heard little more of the discussions.[12] Although he had no sympathy with the abolitionists, he had less with the secessionists. Governor Wise did not forget Strother's Unionism, for when Dave tried to recruit a militia company at Martinsburg on the eve of the Civil War, a request to have his company supplied with arms was rejected by the

10. Nathaniel Hawthorne, "Chiefly About War Matters," *Atlantic Monthly,* X (July, 1862), 56.

11. Quoted in Villard, *John Brown,* p. 563.

12. Strother outlined the plans of the conspiracy in his journal (February 28, 1865). Fire-eater Edmund Ruffin was quite impressed by Porte Crayon: "I also met and made the personal acquaintance of Strother, (Porte Crayon) whose delineations with both pencil and pen I have seen with much pleasure, & whom I have long desired to know personally." Boyd Stutler (ed.), "The Diary of Edmund Ruffin, Ardent States-Righter, 1859," *The Jefferson Republican* (Ranson, W. Va.), September 20, 1951.

state authorities. The rejection was a tribute to Strother's well-known loyalty to the Union.

The fifth decade of the nineteenth century closed for Strother in clouds of political chaos and domestic grief. In the middle of the John Brown fracas, he lost his wife, Ann Wolff Strother, who died on November 6, 1859.[13] During the following year, he applied himself to his literary activities, the completion of his series about New England, and "endeavored to ignore the Revolutionary excitement which disturbed society around him." He became as despondent as he had been during his Baltimore period. While his contemporaries were filled with speculations upon war, he retreated more deeply into himself. Human efforts seemed futile and vain; progress was only temporary. Without success, he fought against his principal enemy, procrastination. There were countless opportunities for his pen and pencil. *Harper's* would use all the literature he could produce, but writing became more and more distasteful. In 1860, politics penetrated into every conversation, and his journal for this year shows that his private grief was exchanged for public regret. The Whig Party seemed dead, and the Democrats were determined to have their war: "From a rationally conservative republic we have in thirty years degraded into a howling democracy, as a gentlemanly drinker degrades into a bestial sot. Each symptom of deterioration was met with a fresh and increasing dose of democracy, as the drunkard cures headaches and fits with more strychnine and whiskey until delirium tremens carried off the man and civil war the nation." He felt that ultimately the United States would accept one of two kinds of despotism: either anarchy or dictatorship. There was a remedy consisting of a return to strong centralism in government and a frank acceptance of inequality in human society and national government. "Inequality is the law of nature," he wrote in his journal.

13. The cause of her death is not known. Four years earlier, her health had been poor, for Strother wrote: "She has been suffering a great deal lately & is indisposed to go out at all." Letter from David Strother to Alexander Boteler, October 28, 1855. Among the Alexander Boteler Papers at the library of Duke University. No portrait of Ann Wolff Strother has survived, nor did her husband mention her death in his autobiographical sketch. She is buried on his right side in the Green Hill cemetery at Martinsburg. His second wife is buried on his left.

"Equality is a dream of the poets." Such speculations anticipated the reaction against the liberal tradition in the twentieth
century, and the rejection of the common man ideology. Ever
able to see the sham underlying verbal adornment and emotional
appeals, Strother avoided the pat generalizations of both Northern and Southern demagogues and planned, if the worst came, to
isolate himself from the confusion of the age in the sleepy village
of Berkeley Springs.

In December, 1860, he became engaged to marry his cousin,
Mary Eliot Hunter of Charles Town, the niece of Andrew
Hunter. On one of his courtship rides to Charles Town, he
turned aside to visit "Park Forest," where his grandfather Strother had labored and his father had been born. South Carolina
had seceded from the Union and a convention had been called
at Richmond to determine the status of Virginia. Standing in
the oak grove, full of trees that had matured half a century before, Strother looked across the fields and prophesied what would
happen in the event of war:

These fair and fertile fields will be laid waste. Bleak chimneys
rising from an ash heap will mark the site of these pleasant homes.
Kindred will be divided by the sword. Ancient friendships changed
to bloody feuds; peace, security, and plenty give place to war, watch-
fulness, and famine. And yet no upright and sound thinking man
can give a human reason why this war should be . . . . There is not
a moral or political principle insisted on by either side which can
not be more advantageously settled by reason and forbearance.[14]

Strother was not carried away by romantic illusions about war, as
were so many of his contemporaries. All of his predictions were
fulfilled, and, ironically, much of the blame for destruction of
the north Valley was placed upon David Strother, one of the
few who believed in peace at any cost.

His views upon Virginia's course paralleled those of John
Pendleton Kennedy, who warned that the border states had less
at stake in the arguments of the Deep South and more to lose
if they did not reject them.[15] Both men sensed that the Con-

14. "Personal Recollections of the War, First Paper," *Harper's New Monthly
Magazine*, XXXIII (June, 1866), 7.

15. John Pendleton Kennedy, *The Border States: Their Power and Duty*
(Philadelphia, 1861).

federacy was helpless without Virginia, Maryland, Kentucky, and Tennessee, which with their diversified commerce and industry did not need the Deep South at all. Both were aware that the Republican Party would not much concern itself with the slavery issue, but would insist upon preserving the Union at all costs. This was not the time, however, for moderation and compromise, and the arguments of Kennedy were drowned out by the trumpetry which called men to war. "Secession," wrote Strother, "is like fire, easily extinguished at the commencement, but the longer it burns, the more fiercely it blazes."[16] With disgust he watched the quasi-legal action of the governor's calling out state troops *before* the Ordinance of Secession had been ratified by the people. This to him was proof that a few demagogues were plunging Virginia into a conflict with which the people had little to do.

When in April, 1861, reports reached the Union Association at Martinsburg that an armed band was preparing to seize the Harpers Ferry arsenal in the name of Virginia, the Association requested him to take command of five hundred local volunteers to prevent it.[17] He refused on the ground that if the rumor were true, the Army of the United States did not lack the power to cope with such an attack. However, on April 18, while he was en route to Baltimore to make final arrangements for his approaching marriage, his train stopped at Harpers Ferry. With great surprise, he noted that the armory shops were closed and was told by Turner Ashby that the town would soon be seized by the militia. Ashby, an old friend of Strother's, assumed that Dave would be on the side of Virginia and showed great surprise when Strother told him that "neither Governor nor Convention had a right to give the order."[18] From a legal point of view, he was right, for the Ordinance of Secession was not voted upon by the people until over a month later. Governor Wise, who had abhorred John Brown's treasonous breach of due process at Harpers Ferry a year and a half before, now seemed to be taking a lesson from him. Strother followed the secession-

16. "Personal Recollections, First Paper," *Harper's*, XXXIII, 4.
17. *Ibid.*, p. 8.
18. The quote is from Strother's journals (April 18, 1861).

ists to Charles Town, where the militia was assembling, most of the members of which he had known all his life. He told the officers that it was the duty of the state troops to march on the Ferry, not in order to attack but to offer their commands to the United States government. So persuasive were his arguments that the commander, Colonel Allen, refused to move his regiment until he received an official order in writing from the adjutant general of the state. The order was duly received and the militia began their march upon the federal arsenal, but to Strother belongs the credit of having delayed Virginia's first action in the Civil War for eight hours. At the request of some of the officers, Strother accompanied the militia in order to dissuade the troops at the first opportunity from going through with the attack, but the opportunity never came. Harpers Ferry fell during the evening and was wantonly burned. For the second time the little river town became a point of violent eruption, and by a curious directive of fate, Strother was again on hand to sketch the burning town. The fact that he followed the militia led many Virginians to believe that he was one of them, a theory completely false. On the following morning he saw the stars and stripes being lowered to be replaced with the flag of Virginia. Of this he wrote dramatically:

Once in my early youth I visited the crater of Vesuvius, and, venturing down the interior I stood for a time looking down upon the sea of smoke that concealed everything around and beneath, when a sudden breeze rubbed the clouds away and for a moment my eyes beheld the hideous gulf that yawned below. So it seemed that the sudden gust of emotion excited by the lowering of our starry flag had swept away the mists of speculation and revealed in its depths and breadth the abyss of degradation opened by secession.[19]

Despite the rumblings of war about them, David Strother and Mary Eliot Hunter were married on May 6 and prepared to follow his plan of complete withdrawal from the chaos of the time by retiring to his cottage at Berkeley Springs.[20] It was

19. "Personal Recollections, First Paper," *Harper's,* XXXIII, 14.
20. Miss Hunter's family, which was well-to-do, considered Strother a poor marital risk. All her property was held in trust and was to be "free from all . . . debts, contracts and engagements of the said David Hunter

a cheerless honeymoon. A drizzling rain followed them from Charles Town, one of the wedding party was Judge Richard Parker, the man who sentenced John Brown—a grim reminder of the outside world—and Berkeley Springs was bleak and dismal. Nor was there a festive tone about their dinner that evening: talk settled on the imminent war. In the weeks that followed, the couple realized that their plan to ignore the war was impossible. It was possible to hide a copy of *Battles of the French Revolution* from sight, but even walks in the forest brought encounters with backwoodsmen, who invariably asked, "What news from the war?" The honeymoon cottage provided all the articles for seclusion—parlor organ, paintings, violin, guitar, and books—but there was also a room the door of which was kept locked: the armory. Although his wife had died six months before, Colonel John Strother was as full-blooded as ever. After Lincoln's inauguration, he had hastened to Washington in order to offer his services to the country. While Lincoln did not accept the offer of the old veteran of the War of 1812, the mission proved that some of the fire that had taken him to the Canadian frontier half a century previously had not burned out. The example was not lost upon his son. A fortnight after their marriage, the couple packed their bags for Charles Town, ostensibly for a visit with his wife's mother, but actually in response to a compulsion to return once more to the outside world.

During the next six weeks, Strother watched the two armies encamped along the Potomac without committing himself to either. There were minor skirmishes across the river. He noted wryly that no one was ever hurt on the Virginia side "but if reports could be believed the slaughter on the Maryland bank must have been prodigious." On May 23, polls in Virginia opened to record the vote on the Ordinance of Secession, a mockery considering the fact that Virginia was already at war. Even so, and despite the Southern troops which hung about the precincts, the counties containing Martinsburg and Berkeley Springs returned a Union vote, the latter by a six-to-one count.

Strother." Jefferson County Court Records, Deed Book 39, p. 510. Most of her inheritance did not fall to her until after Strother's death in 1888.

The Berkeley County company, drafted unwillingly into the Confederate Army, had a mutiny which resulted in half the men deserting, although most were dragged back into ranks. But as the Northern armies continued to squat in Maryland, confidence in the Secession cause mounted. It seemed that fire-eating Southerners had proved their boast that the North was too cowardly to fight. Strother noted that even the poor-white population began to parrot phrases like "our slave property" and "no right to coerce a state," none the less zealously for not having any idea what they meant. Freedom of speech and liberty of movement seemed to have been abolished. On one occasion, Strother was arrested at Harpers Ferry for a short time, the charge being that his pencil and sketch pad were obviously the equipment of a Yankee spy. On another, he turned away a Confederate recruiting party at his door with a loaded pistol—and after that was left unmolested. In the midst of such frenzied emotionalism, he wrote in his journal that he "felt like a sane man in a mad house."

Neutrality was obviously becoming impossible. Civil had given way to martial law. Strother saw the choice to be between government and anarchy; for him the side of the true Virginian was with the forces of the national government. "Virginia," he wrote, "now lay subjugated by armed strangers, groveling at the feet of the Cotton Confederacy."[21] On July 9, he delayed no longer. Confiding his plans to Colonel John Strother alone, he saddled his horse and rode to Martinsburg, then occupied by the Federal armies, where he offered his services to General Patterson. He was aware that his extensive knowledge of northern Virginia would be valuable for any commander leading an army south from the Potomac. The war, for Porte Crayon, had at last begun.

Strange to say, the topographical corps of the United States Army had no accurate maps of Virginia. For years before the war, no government dredge or engineer's tripod had been permitted to cross the state line. It took three years before the North fully realized the strategic importance and military value of the Shenandoah Valley, which the Confederates always

21. "Personal Recollections, First Paper," *Harper's*, XXXIII, 22.

managed to occupy—and not by chance—during harvest time. Strother's familiarity with this terrain was apparent to all the federal commanders who campaigned in the Valley. Less apparent to them was his insistence upon the military weakness and confusion of the Southern armies during the first months of the war. Without exception, the general officers under whom he served overestimated the numbers of their enemy, and throughout the war Strother stood beside them like an oracle urging attack. Not until 1864 did the Federal armies find commanders who would mercilessly and relentlessly hammer the South into defeat. History proves that Strother's military ideas —when finally applied by Grant, Sheridan, and Sherman—were the proper ones for winning the war. The soundness of his views was illustrated by his advice to General Patterson immediately after joining the Union Army. Having received reliable information from a Unionist that General Joseph Johnston's army, which opposed Patterson, contained only thirteen thousand men, Strother urged an immediate advance. The general staff listened attentively to Strother's synopsis, then concluded that Patterson was faced by an enemy whose numbers were three times as great. Had Strother's advice been followd, one of the most fatal blunders of the Civil War would have been avoided—permitting Johnston to retire, remove his whole army to Manassas, and turn the tide of Bull Run into an overwhelming Southern victory. Patterson's delay cost him his generalship and the nation an untold amount of time, money, and men.

One of the unwritten chapters of the war, according to Henry Tuckerman, is the "record of moral sufferings of those who had to endure the alienation of life-long friends and the perverse violence of kindred."[22] The suffering, alienation, and violence were particularly strong in the case of David Strother, who even today is abhorred by distant cousins with long memories. Of his nearest relatives, the Strothers, Pendletons, and Kennedys adopted the Union cause, while the Hunters, Cookes, and Dandridges were strongly Confederate. Strother's own brother-in-law by his first wife became a Confederate officer, as did John Esten Cooke, who never again appeared at Berkeley Springs as a

22. *The Life of John Pendleton Kennedy* (New York, 1871), p. 275.

guest at the hotel or discussed Virginia and literature with Porte Crayon. In this wide family relationship, there is no case of brother fighting brother and dying in each other's arms (a familiar subplot of later novelists), but the bitterness of cousin against cousin makes up for the lack of dime-novel melodrama. Something of the developing family hatred is seen in a letter from Philip Cooke's daughter to John Esten early in the war. She wrote:

I am so mad whenever I think of Phil Kennedy's being on the other side, it is disgraceful the way in which the Kennedys and Pendletons have turned out. I hate to be any kin to them! And I used to be so proud of the Pendletons . . . If they ain't on our side I rather they should be against us, than take no part in the conflict. Oh if I could only change with some of the hateful "stay at home" men, and go off to the wars I would be perfectly happy! I so long to kill some of the northern wretches.[23]

Nor was the bitterness sweetened by time; as the war wore on, the damnation of opposing relatives became stronger. The case against David Strother was even stronger than some, largely because he was not commissioned as an officer in the Union army until 1862, a condition which was interpreted by many as expedient fence-straddling. Yet Strother's political opinions were obvious from the beginning. Only faulty logic could have put him into the Secessionist camp. He entered the war with only his self-respect and his father's blessing—these seemed to him enough. He came out with a conviction that he had done his duty—that was all he expected. He was always something of an alien in the Union army, separated by the Potomac from friends and kinsmen. "That fair valley was now the land of mine and my country's enemies," he wrote. "On this side I was alone."[24]

The fall and winter of 1861-62 were the quietest of the war as both armies marshaled their strength for the spring campaigns. The protection of Washington (against an enemy that

23. Letter from Nannie Cooke to John Esten Cooke, June 8 [1861]. Among the John Esten Cooke Papers at the library of Duke University.

24. "Personal Recollections of the War, Third Paper," *Harper's New Monthly Magazine,* XXXIII (September, 1866), 411.

had no intention of moving anywhere except south) became the urgent policy of the Federal forces, and Strother accompanied the concentration toward the capital, wintering in the vicinity of Rockville, Maryland. The army had grown so demoralized that "the sight of a negro in a canoe will stampede a whole regiment."[25] He was now assigned as a civilian assistant to General N. P. Banks, whom he found unsure and vacillating. Despite his anomalous position, Strother was a gentleman and was treated accordingly. There was not time for literature, but there was for dinners with the generals, who came to respect the views of their Virginian associate. Ward Lamon, a boyhood friend who had become Lincoln's law partner and the chief marshal for the District of Columbia, arranged a meeting with the President, who spoke of the visit Dave's father had made to offer his services to the country. Colonel John, said Lincoln, had given him much encouragement at a time when there seemed to be no solid political opinion upon which to base a hope.[26] The younger Strother left the interview with a feeling that the President was a typical representative of the American people, "neither great nor small."

Weighty subjects, however, did not destroy his sense of humor. Porte Crayon went to war along with David Strother. In his journal he recorded amusing side lights of the day, such as the account of a horrified Southern lady awaiting the first appearance of the dreaded Yankee army: "Good Heaven, quoth she, we will all be ruined, our houses burned, and our throats cut. On being assured that there was no reason to apprehend such treatment, she replied, Ah, don't tell me, look what they have done in Baltimore. Well, what have they done in Baltimore? Why, said she, holding up her hands in horror, I hear they play Yankee Doodle up and down the streets on Sunday!" He also recorded the short-lived history of the Home Guard, a Berkeley Springs organization that was formed to protect the village from marauders and to supplement the Union army in that area. They sat up nights in their headquarters in the courthouse and arrested everybody and each other until it was

25. *Ibid.*, p. 415.
26. *Ibid.*, pp. 416-17.

"shrewdly suggested that the peace of the lonely village might have been better preserved if everybody went quietly to bed and minded their own business."[27]   The town bully arrested a stranger one night, and conducted him toward the court house until the stranger balked, pulled a pistol, and killed his jailor. Abruptly the activities of the Home Guard terminated. Strother's sympathies were with the stranger.

When it became evident that the rebellion would not be a matter of months but of years, Strother made efforts to obtain a commission in the United States Army. The prospect of serving without pay or rank, of supporting a wife and daughter within the Rebel lines, and of being shot as a spy in the event of capture was not attractive. Francis Pierpont, who had been elected governor of loyal Virginia with its capital at Alexandria, saw in Strother a man of his own convictions and promised to obtain a line commission for the spring campaign. Strother's feeling against the Confederacy became bitterly personal in October when he heard that Colonel John Strother had been captured and maltreated by the Secessionists. Troops from Winchester had ridden over to Berkeley Springs and arrested him in August along with Edmund Pendleton, another staunch Unionist of Morgan County. Although Pendleton was at once released, Colonel John had been imprisoned in a tent for five days by order of the Confederate provost and a one-time friend, Colonel Angus McDonald. The charge was treason against the State of Virginia, which, so far as his public declarations in favor of the Union were concerned, was accurate enough. There is little doubt that Colonel Strother was a difficult prisoner. At the public hearing, with flame in his eye, he burst out, "My opinion is that you are the traitor and instead of sitting in judgment should be hung yourself." When McDonald's Scottish temper died, the prisoner was released. Even such an arch-Confederate as Trip O'Ferrall, who had been county clerk at Berkeley Springs before the war and became governor of Virginia after it, thought the episode of sufficient importance to include in his memoirs forty years later: "I have always regarded the arrest, confinement, and treatment of this hoary-headed, decrepit, yet superb grand

27. *Ibid.*, p. 410.

man as an outrage upon the instincts of humanity and a shame and disgrace to the Confederate officer who was responsible for it."[28] Stubbornness on the part of both men prolonged an uncomfortable situation which would have been smoothed over quickly had either been less hidebound—the Confederacy, after all, could not hope to bring to trial every Union man in the South. Colonel John Strother, a specter from another era, returned to Berkeley Springs, where he died of pneumonia on January 16, 1862.[29] It is impossible to say whether his incarceration by McDonald hastened his death, but his son always thought so. The result was a deep bitterness toward the Confederacy which had not been evident before. Along with the news of his father's death came the report that Stonewall Jackson had invaded Berkeley Springs, plundered the hotel, destroyed Dave's collection of private papers and drawings, and stabled horses in his cottage. With his father's last words, "Forward, McClellan," ringing in his ears, Dave prepared in the same spirit for the spring campaign of 1862.

Early in March, 1862, he was commissioned as assistant adjutant-general of volunteers, with the rank of captain, and again joined General Banks, who was preparing to move up the Shenandoah Valley as a complemental move to McClellan's peninsular campaign. Strother obtained the information that Winchester would be abandoned by Jackson at the first sight of the Federal army, information which proved true but which Banks ignored. Quickly Banks proved that, however well he presided over the House of Representatives, he was little fitted for a

---

28. Charles T. O'Ferrall, *Forty Years of Active Service* (New York, 1904), p. 25. O'Ferrall, who became a colonel in the Confederate Army, is said to have commanded the last Virginia troops to surrender. His regard for Colonel Strother is all the more remarkable because his mother had operated the principal rival hotel in Berkeley Springs, and feelings between the two families had often been strained.

29. Among the final words of Colonel John to his son were, "I can not go to war; but I feel that it is my mission to face these people—to show them on all occasions that there is one Virginian, at least, who abhors their treason and despises their usurped authority." "Personal Recollections of the War, Fourth Paper," *Harper's New Monthly Magazine,* XXXIII (October, 1866), 554. To General Banks, Strother quoted his father in a slightly different form. See letter from David Strother to Major General N. P. Banks, January 23, 1862. Among the N. P. Banks Papers at the Essex Institute, Salem, Mass.

command against Stonewall Jackson. Days lengthened into weeks as the Army of the Shenandoah crept up the Valley turnpike. Week after week Strother urged a strong advance, to be overruled each time by the rest of the General's staff. "Such a staff, some said, would have wrecked the great Napoleon,"[30] wrote Banks' biographer. Near Harrisonburg, Jackson vanished and in desperation Banks retreated back toward the Potomac, to be hit in the flank at Middletown by the Confederate army and nearly cut in two. What followed was called by Strother "a miniature Bull Run stampede"[31] and was certainly one of the worst routs of the war. So many Federal supplies fell into Rebel hands that Banks was henceforth called "Jackson's commissary general."[32] Strother himself narrowly escaped capture in Winchester as he galloped out of the town with the Rebel cavalry just behind him. Ironically, much of the blame for the debacle must be placed upon Captain Strother himself, who had scoffed at the idea that Jackson might attempt to circle Massanutten Mountain and attack the Union flank; on the single occasion when the Captain was wrong in the campaign, Banks accepted his judgment. Notwithstanding the defeat of the army, Strother had proved himself an able tactician, for had his advice been followed from the beginning, Jackson would not have been able to disappear from Banks' front. As the army regrouped on the northern side of the Potomac, Strother had severe misgivings about political generals. The trouble with the Northern army seemed to be Washington.

On June 16, 1862, he was commissioned lieutenant colonel of the Third Mounted Regiment of Virginia Volunteers by order of Governor Pierpont. As his companies were scattered among

30. Fred H. Harrington, *Fighting Politician: Major-General N. P. Banks* (Philadelphia, 1948), p. 63.

31. Quoted, *Ibid.*, p. 73.

32. Banks remained the laughingstock of Virginians for many years. After the war, when he was readmitted to Congress, a country editor wrote waggishly: "We are at a loss to know how Genl. Banks could take the Congressional Test Oath which among other things, requires a man to swear that he has never given 'aid or support' to the late so-called Confederate Army. It is well known that this redoubtable hero was for a long time Stonewall Jackson's Commissary General in the Valley . . . yet we find him sworn in as a member of the House from Massachusetts." *Spirit of Jefferson* (Charles Town, W. Va.), December 19, 1865.

different military departments or existed on paper only, his commission was essentially that of a staff rather than a field officer. Technically, he was under the command of the loyal Virginia government rather than the United States Army, and was therefore enabled to serve under whatever commander requested him. He was not long in waiting. General John Pope, fresh from minor victories in the West, was put in command of the Union armies in northern Virginia at the end of June. The day before he received a telegram from Pope summoning him to Washington, Strother had written, "I know nothing of the merits of this new commander, but thank God that the military anarchy heretofore existing is about to end."[33] He found the new commander at Willard's Hotel interrogating Virginia loyalists on the conditions of roads around Gordonsville. Pope was a man of impatient energy who looked every inch a soldier. Strother accepted the invitation to join his staff and for the next three weeks assembled topographical information for the Federal advance, which was effected during the first week in August.

As a general, Pope proved to be no worse than Banks but scarcely better. Brusque to the point of rudeness, confident to the bounds of conceit, he looked with scorn upon his staff and his soldiers. His address, "Headquarters—in the saddle," is perhaps the classic bit of pomposity to come out of the Civil War. But he was eager and willing to fight; his difficulty was that he never seemed to be able to find just where his enemy was. Jackson's habit of making himself felt before seen was perhaps not how they fought battles in the West. Of all the battles in which Strother served, Cedar Mountain and Second Manassas were the most confusing and uncoordinated. No one, including the staff and the commanding general, seemed to know what was happening. As a courier, Strother found that it was sometimes impossible to deliver messages to generals only a few miles away. Several commands did not trouble to fight at all, largely through distrust of Pope. At the most crucial moment in the campaign, Strother personally delivered Pope's message to Fitz-John Porter, which if acted upon, might have crushed Jackson before the

33. "Personal Recollections of the War, Seventh Paper," *Harper's New Monthly Magazine*, XXXIV (May, 1867), 733.

arrival of Longstreet. Porter, addicted to the McClellan worship so characteristic of the army, did not attack and was later dismissed from the service.[34] The Northern forces were driven back toward Fairfax, Pope's campaign having ended in an utter failure. Yet Strother did not blame Pope for his failure. Personal jealousy and political party-spirit had undermined the general strategy. After the war, the damnation of General Pope became a frequent pastime, but Strother generously wrote in *Harper's,* "I am but little disposed to indulge in unkind or unecessary criticism of an officer who . . . has exhibited in so high a degree the intelligence, energy, and fighting animus which characterizes a first-class soldier."[35] After the exhausted and bedraggled army had straggled back to the fortifications at Centerville, a well-heeled politician confided in Strother that politically speaking, "the success of such a man as John Pope would be a misfortune to the country."[36] This remark speaks volumes for the Washington brand of patriotism.

When the army of Lee invaded Maryland in September, 1862, McClellan claimed Strother for his staff of the Army of the Potomac. Warned by Strother that Harpers Ferry could not be defended, McClellan hurried to Washington to advise either the relief of the garrison or its abandonment, but the War Department did not act upon the recommendation and Harpers Ferry fell with its 11,000 men to the Confederate army. In the Battle of Antietam that shortly followed, Strother for the first time in the war felt proud of the Union army, which had now erased its ignominious defeats by nearly crushing the Southern army. While he recognized that in strategy, secret maneuvering, and audacity the Rebels were superior, he pinpointed qualities of

34. Strother's military recollections placed much of Pope's failure upon the shoulders of Porter. In 1878 Porter was officially cleared of the charges against him by a court of inquiry. Strother was summoned to this trial, but at the last minute illness prevented him from going. He did, however, write Porter a letter which retracted his accusations, and this was published in *Harper's.* Perhaps more than any other public document it exonerated Porter in the public eye. See "Editor's Easy Chair," *Harper's New Monthly Magazine,* LVIII (January, 1879), 306-7.

35. "Personal Recollections of the War, Ninth Paper," *Harper's New Monthly Magazine,* XXXV (November, 1867), 728.

36. *Ibid.*

the Federalists which ultimately won the war for them: "There is in our favour the usual advantage that the army of a civilized power has over that of a semi-barbarous people, better organization, provision, and equipment but less of energy, astuteness, and fortitude." The North was waging the kind of war which would be fought in the twentieth century, logistical rather than heroic. The South was fighting like Horatius at the bridge, emphasizing individual rather than collective superiority.

On a reconnaissance party to Charles Town after Antietam, Strother experienced the first of a series of unpleasant scenes enacted over and over in future years. General Hancock and several other Union officers were quartered at Andrew Hunter's house on the edge of town. Dismounting in the rain, Strother entered the familiar house to find Hancock. In the library he found several officers sitting around with Mrs. Andrew Hunter and her daughter Florence. He entered the room and greeted them, and Mrs. Hunter sprang to her feet with an exclamation, "Good Lord—in my house!" and calling her daughter to her, fled the room. The officers were astonished and Strother mortified by his aunt's demonstration of horror. He thereafter found that many other doors in Virginia were closed to him.

Early in November, McClellan crossed the Potomac to search for Lee, and Strother was sent to Washington to secure all available maps of the territory in front. At Willard's, he was shocked by the news that McClellan had been replaced by Burnside as head of the Army of the Potomac. Once again Strother was without a commander. At dinner he ran into General Banks who called him over and invited him to accompany an expedition getting under way, presumably for Texas. Strother accepted the proposal and accompanied Banks to New York, by a coincidence taking the same train occupied by McClellan, who was being carried northward into oblivion amid the sounds of "cheering and music which greeted the deposed commander at every stopping place." When these had died away so ended the military glory of the army's most popular general. In his journal Strother summarized his impressions of that officer:

My opinion in regard to McClellan is that he is the most capable man we have in military affairs. His head is clear and his knowledge complete. He wants force of character and is swayed by those around him . . . . The people around McClellan without taking into consideration their social and characteristic merits, were the most ungallant good for nothing set of martinets that I have ever met with. I do not mean that they were inefficient in their special duties, but not a man among them was worth a damn as a military adviser—or had any show of fire or boldness in a military campaign.

McClellan campaigned in the European manner with a brilliant staff in handsome uniforms, but long before armchair strategists reached similar conclusions, Strother discovered his major limitation—a lack of self-assertion. Yet if he was looking for bold plans and dashing tactics, Strother should have known from experience that Banks would provide neither of them.

His visit to New York was a re-entry into the world he had known before the war. He called upon the House of Harper and was told by Dr. A. H. Guernsey, editor of the *Monthly,* that his articles were sorely missed and the vacuum created in the magazine by his military service had never been filled. Strother noted also that "the old fogies [the Harpers] were equally complimentary." New York was untouched by the war, and his visit with the Kembles and Pauldings recalled the gracious leisure of an era receding far away. Gouverneur Kemble was on hand at Cold Spring to do the honors. There was a strange contrast in the quiet Hudson village between the Parrott-gun foundry near the river and the artistic villas on the bluff, one of which was occupied by his friend of Italy, Thomas Rossiter. It seemed difficult to believe that "a few days more and I must again enter on my career of hardship, danger, and death." Before he left New York, William Kemble took him to call upon General Winfield Scott, who like Strother had given up Virginia for the nation. Strother regarded with great interest the old soldier who had been a comrade-in-arms of his father and whose biography he had illustrated while Scott was winning his victories in Mexico. His description, with its emphasis upon eccentricity and incongruity, is in the Porte Crayon vein:

The veteran of three wars sat enveloped in shawls under the chandelier and near a table in the middle of the room, his countenance full of dignity and benignity. At the table three of his grandchildren were eating grapes under the direction of the General. He received us with great courtesy and recognized me when my name was spoken and made kind enquiries of my father. He spoke of his daughter Camelia and his grandson Winfield who spoke French more fluently than he does his native tongue. Why does the General consider it important that his grandson should speak French better than English? He spoke of a dinner at Mr. Blodgett's as a very superb affair, said he corrected the hostess's pronunciation of *girl* and his comment brought on a conversation on philology in which the lady showed much knowledge. This is one of the General's weaknesses.

Scott, who had once rebuked a member of his staff for confusing Dryden with Shakespeare,[37] represented the urbane and elegant general of the old school who combined the social and intellectual graces with the business of war. That same night Strother walked down to the East River and boarded the steamer *North Star,* bound for some indeterminate port of the Deep South. His idyllic interlude in New York was over. "I got a bunk and covering myself with a dirty matress I slept tolerably, dreaming of being hunted by Confederates and making desperate defence from houses and log cabins."

37. Charles W. Elliot, *Winfield Scott, The Soldier and the Man* (New York, 1937), p. 391.

Chapter VIII

The Great Rebellion, 1862-1864

NOT until the *North Star* was off the Florida Keys did Banks reveal to Strother the objective of their movement—to replace General Ben Butler at New Orleans, to re-Unionize Louisiana, and to cooperate with Grant in investing Port Hudson and Vicksburg.[1] The prevailing tone was to be firm but conciliatory, but Strother, who knew the temperament of the Louisianans, doubted from the first that such a program could succeed, and subsequent events proved him right. New Orleans, by far the largest city in the Confederacy, had fallen a year earlier and under the regime of General "Beast" Butler had become the setting for scandals and corruption without parallel in American history.[2] Banks hoped to win the people's affection as rapidly as Butler had lost it, but his staff, consisting for the most part of zealous abolitionists, too often expended its energy in reclaiming the Negro rather than in winning Louisiana.

On December 15, the detachment landed at New Orleans, and the following day Butler read his farewell orders to his staff officers amid weeping. Things began well. The city was elated at Butler's removal, and the newspapers had praise for Banks

1. The extreme secrecy of the expedition was ridiculed by Banks's soldiers: "Possibly they were afraid that some indiscreet soldier might put the secret in his letter, which he intended to send home after arriving at their destination." Frank Flinn, *Campaigning with Banks in Louisiana* (Lynn, Mass., 1887), p.8.

2. John Fiske, *The Mississippi Valley in the Civil War* (Boston, 1900), p. 130.

and kind words for Porte Crayon. Much to his grief, Strother was placed on the sequestration committee, where he was an intermediary between the civilian population and the military government. Had he been a dishonest man, he could quickly have made his fortune, as his predecessor had done. To John Pendleton Kennedy he wrote: "I have been approached twenty times by men of substance with offers of from one to twenty thousand dollars, if I would procure a permit to trade with the enemy in provisions, medicines, etc. The applicants seemed innocently to be following their accustomed business and quite taken aback when they found it could not be done. They say they have always transacted business in that way heretofore and could buy a permit to anything whatsoever."[3] A captured Rebel officer told him that while New Orleans had been in Union hands it had furnished the Confederacy much more assistance than before, because supplies which had formerly been unavailable at any cost could now be bought without great inconvenience. This was, indeed, a curious manner of waging war. Banks was successful in cleaning up the graft in the city, and Strother was instrumental in the restoration of many estates to citizens from whom they had been seized unlawfully.

The problem of what to do with the Negroes gave Banks the greatest amount of trouble. Legally they were free—at least to starve. A plan to force them to work for a quota of the harvested crop was scrapped because of Banks's fear that this might arouse political animosity in Massachusetts. When the plan was changed to put work on a voluntary basis, few Negroes returned to work. As a result, the planters, the Negroes, and the Federal government were denied the profits of their labor. Strother urged compulsion, but quoted Banks's reply "that public opinion is to be considered, and that it is more important that public opinion should be satisfied than that the planters here shall be saved from ruin." This did little to forward the principal objective, re-Unionizing Louisiana. Many of the former slaves were recruited into the army, but the white officers commanding such regiments threatened to resign. Efforts to enforce equality be-

3. Letter from David Strother to John Pendleton Kennedy, March 7, 1863. Among the John Pendleton Kennedy Papers at the Peabody Library, Baltimore.

tween white and Negro troops ended in race riots, principally incited by the Massachusetts contingents. The Negro found life among his liberators little better, and probably worse, than among his former owners. Strother observed the transformation of the New England soldiers, who had originally been so solicitous about the Negroes' welfare: "The white soldiers won't do anything now except make the negroes work for them. They are more exacting and brutal than the masters were originally. A vulgar fellow unaccustomed to be waited on is always so with servants." It seemed to be easier to talk about abolition than to practice it. On one occasion he saw an orderly order a Negro captain out of a hall "with the same contempt he would have shown to a mangy dog." The captain tipped his hat and left without a word. The confusion was such that within a few months many Louisianans, white and black, were looking back fondly upon the days of Ben Butler.

The assault by Farragut and Banks upon the stronghold at Port Hudson in March did not accomplish much in a military sense, but it provided a great deal of humor for Strother's journal. At the review of the army at Baton Rouge, naval officers assisting, the ground was muddy and the parade ground cut with ditches, which the officers were forced to jump. It was expected that Farragut's staff, mounted on motley horses, would be thrown, but the only casualty was one of Banks's staff, who slipped into a ditch "leaving only the horses heels sticking out." A horse was not the only thing that Farragut could manage. While Banks vacillated at Port Hudson, the Admiral plowed through the Confederate batteries with the tenacity of one of his rams, then, nautical-fashion, sent a message to Banks by floating it down the Mississippi in a bottle. The testy confidence of Farragut was one of the most impressive things Strother found in Louisiana. There was a salty pungency in the Admiral's prophecy about the outcome of the war that admitted no argument: "General Banks, we must beat these people in the end. We have twice as many men and ten times as much money."[4]

4. Quoted in Strother's article, "Campaign on the Teche," *Weekly Times* (Philadelphia), March 29, 1879.

Strother never found out why the army did not attack Port
Hudson, but the soldiers did keep up "a skirmishing fire all
around on pigs, poultry, and cattle [until] the whole land was
covered with blood, guts, horns, hair, and feathers." To Strother, Banks plumed himself on their fortunate "escape" from
Port Hudson, although the land forces were never completely
engaged.

The army returned to New Orleans and prepared for a campaign against the scattered Confederate forces to the southwest
of the city, most of which were around Opelousas, the state capital, in the Teche country. Before operations began, Strother
submitted his resignation to Banks, to be effective at the term-
ination of the campaign. Affairs in the Department of the Gulf
were becoming worse rather than better. Discipline seemed
entirely gone. Even a council of war could be interrupted by a
private soldier seeking to find the location of his regiment, all
of which Banks accepted without rebuke. After the usual delays, the Teche campaign opened in the early part of April, and
for the first time in his military career General Banks found
himself in hot pursuit of a Confederate army, in this instance
the outnumbered force of General Sibley. Strother, who had been
with his general in less triumphal situations, watched Banks's
jubilation as he "cavorted like a young colt." Strother himself
was caught up in the enthusiasm of the engagements as he
wrote in his journal: "Man the peace lover is simply a poltroon
and a coward. Roll your drums, flaunt your banners and advance to the battlefield. War is a joy and glory of our race."
For all the glory, there was still excessive plundering, often under the very nose of the commander, who seemed powerless to
prevent it. Perhaps the stolen prize of greatest significance was
the pilfering of the General's own boots by some brave soldier.
The campaign ended at Opelousas, which was surrendered without a struggle. The Union success was doubtless of greater importance for psychological reasons than for tactical ones. The
United States was running low on victories, and to the readers of
Eastern newspapers the Teche might well have appeared as important as Waterloo. But southwestern Louisiana had been

Self-portrait of David Hunter Strother in hunter's garb. "There stands before you a slight, elastic, and somewhat gaunt gentleman, with dark, concentrated e . . . *Head-Devil* in all matters of feud, foray, or whatever enterprises that ight be classed under the designation of marauding—all dare-devil achieve ents. . . ." (From the original in the possession of Porter Strother.)

Left, Mary Eliot Hunter Strother, the second wife of "Porte Crayon." From a photograph made about the time of her marriage in 1861. *Right,* Mary Eliot Hunter Strother—"Mrs. 'Porte Crayon' "—in later years. (Photographs courtesy of Louise Strother Shepard.)

"Porte Crayon" standing in front of his home in Berkeley Springs, "where the newspaper enters but once a week, the telegraph is unknown, and honor is spelled with a *u.*" Probable date, the 1880's. (Photograph courtesy of Fritz Newbraugh.)

cleared of Rebels for the time and five thousand bales of cotton and three thousand mules and horses had been seized.[5]

At the end of April, the army again returned to New Orleans, where Strother's resignation was accepted with flattering praise by Banks, who said, "The Colonel has always voted for pitching in. At all times and under all circumstances." The pity was that the General so seldom followed his subordinate's advice. In later years Strother contended that family distresses drew him from the Department of the Gulf, but his journals imply that the pandemonium there was the most important reason he left. Not without symbolic import did he jot on the flyleaf of his journal at this time—"The tower of Babel for vignette of this American Revolution." On April 30 he boarded the commercial vessel which was to carry him to New York, walked the deck in the moonlight until a late hour, and then wrote, "I think that I have fought my last battle." He had not, but in a military capacity he had seen the last of General Banks.

His steamer stopped over at Havana for three days, and Strother was impressed with the crowded harbor, churches, castles, and forts, all of which recalled Europe. Yet the strangest scenes of all were the Confederate blockade runners and their captains, tall gallant fellows with cravats blazoned with the stars and bars of Secessia. On May 9, the ship docked at New York, and the first news was ominous—Joe Hooker had been thrashed by Lee along the Rappahannock. "All this I had been apprehending," he wrote, "and consequently was not so furiously anxious to get to land as some of our passengers were." In Washington he found his wife waiting for him and obtained a two-month leave. Before leaving for western Virginia, they drove to the Capitol, then nearing completion. On the ground

5. Flinn, *Campaigning in Louisiana*, p. 71. During the advance upon Opelousas, Strother impressed a clergyman-soldier by his Homeric observations on death: "He surprised me by telling me of the perfect indifference on such matters that characterizes the soldier. He said, that, after the battle of Antietam, the over-wearied boys lay down on the field, by the side of the killed, to sleep, and sometimes even used their dead comrades for pillows. One man he told me of, who brought his fiddle, which he had carried through the campaign, and, sitting down on the nearest dead body, began to play and sing." George Hepworth, *The Whip, Hoe, and Sword; or, the Gulf Department in '63* (Boston, 1864), p. 277.

was the Liberty statue which had not yet been lifted to the cupola. Thinking of the crucial condition of the nation, Strother remarked, "The Goddess of Liberty in bronze has a flamboyant air and the colours of a coppersnake. I don't think she will ever mount that dome." Nor was the prospect at Berkeley Springs much brighter. Although officially the village was within Federal lines, a guard of twelve infantrymen was necessary to protect the Strothers from a sudden raid of Rebel guerillas, who were in and out of the town almost at will. War had emptied the place, the great hotel was silent and vacant, and Colonel John's portrait stared vacantly at him in the back parlor.

It was unsafe to remain in Berkeley Springs, so the Strothers returned to Washington for the remainder of his leave. In two years of war, patriotism seemed to have disappeared, and the subjugation of the South seemed even further away. Strother found the cause of the national chaos and moral deterioration in Carlyle: "Carlyle says a country falls into wars and disorders when its *able* men are cast aside and foolish men are in the land. Never was a stronger illustration of this idea than the condition of the country at present. 'When the wicked rule, the people mourn.'" The wicked to his mind were the politicians, who too often insisted upon party favorites for commanding generals.

Toward the end of June, the Civil War reached its climax. The army of Lee vanished from Hooker's front and the capital city was in a state of panic until Lee reappeared in Pennsylvania and thereby indicated that Washington was not his objective. The Gettysburg campaign had begun. Strother, without a command or a commander, volunteered immediately, but his orders were not served in time. Instead, he fought his own battle of nerves in the tense capital, haunting Willard's and the telegraph offices. Conflicting reports came in, the armies were engaged, but the outcome was unknown. The fourth day of July was a day of leaden gloom. Strother's journal records something of what proved to be perhaps the most important single day in American history:

The events of today will be decisive of the war if favourable to us . . . . Walked into the grounds back of the President's house where I found a great crowd of people in holiday attire. They were collected to hear the Declaration of Independence read and an oration by an Honble. Mr. Wallbridge. There was a canopy of board where the orators and the marine band sat. One was reading the Declaration of Independence and then read the names of the signers by states. At each state there was a faint round of applause. The band then played the star spangled banner. As the Southern seceded states were read out, Virginia, North Carolina, South Carolina, Georgia, there was dead silence. I had been trained from youth to a great veneration for our national history and all these national Dei Majorum Gentium. What a mockery seemed their celebration, how painful the recapitulation of these honoured names and themes. The star spangled banner seemed a funeral dirge, the national flag a pall, each venerated name a burning curse on the page of history. I left the ground . . . . As I approached the street I met Hall, our fellow boarder, who told me that news had arrived of the defeat of Lee. We had captured Longstreet and six thousand prisoners, the enemy in full retreat. This he said was official. I hastened to the office of the Herald agent where I found the statement recapitulated. I hurried to the house and seeing Mrs. Randolph in great tribulation I told her the news. She was in such excitement that she wept. Mrs. Wade came in and joined the chorus. I ran upstairs and told my wife who looked as if she would presently cry. I went down and got an extra Star which modified somewhat the news, yet left us substantially victorious. All Lee's attacks were repulsed with great slaughter and failure to beat us must destroy him. Now let us throw every man, horse, and gun upon them and the war is ended with a blow.

Contrary to Dave's hopes, Lee managed to escape back to Virginia, but Strother was correct in his surmise that the events of that day were decisive. The end of the war now seemed but a matter of time, and he was anxious to begin campaigning again. Although he was commissioned colonel of the Third West Virginia Cavalry on July 18, 1863, he remained until the end of the war an officer with neither men nor horses. His command was split up into fragments assimilated into detachments from the Rappahannock to the Ohio; they were never mustered together and his colonelcy existed on paper only. At an interview with the Secretary of War, Stanton offered him assignment to any staff he named.[6] He chose the Department of West Virginia, which was commanded by General Benjamin F. Kelley, an able but underpraised soldier.[7] His choice revealed an interest in the new state of West Virginia, which had been admitted to the Union only a month before. He had long realized that Virginia's western counties, including Berkeley and Morgan, had little relation to the rest of the Old Dominion; most of them had remained loyal to the Federal government and welcomed the opportunity to break away from the mother state. West Virginia became a buffer state between the North and South, and General Kelley had the difficult and important job of guarding several hundred miles of mountainous frontier and of mediating between the divergent interests of a heterogeneous population. Martial law provided the only stability and discipline in the region, so that, virtually if not officially, Kelley was the first governor of the state. This was the area of partisan rather than systematic warfare, an area where marauding bands were guided on weekdays by Baptist ministers and friend was often pitted against friend. It was also the familiar stamping ground of Porte Crayon—his choice then was a wise one.

Other than natural scenery, the new state contained little to attract the eye or to stimulate the mind. West Virginia, born of revolution, had had little time to adopt the social graces of the more settled seaboard. Its scenery was alpine and its people, in the main, unlicked. The roads were poor, the railroads were few, and the communities, particularly in the central part of the state, were isolated. In all of Strother's ramblings through America, he found nothing quite like West Virginia. At the state capital, Wheeling, illiterate politicians gorged themselves on French dishes misspelled on the menu. Clarksburg was a fair specimen of a West Virginia town at this period:

6. Edwin Stanton was an admirer of Porte Crayon's writings. After the interview, Strother wrote in his journal, "He spoke to me kindly of the pleasure my writings had given him, taking me familiarly by the arm and asking me questions about the personages of my work."

7. Even Colonel Fremantle, who found little to praise about any Union soldier, admitted with surprise that Kelley was a "gentleman" who gave him every attention. Walter Lord (ed.), *The Fremantle Diary* (Boston, 1954), p. 235.

The most wretched hole I have yet seen is Clarksburg on first acquaintance. I called at the best tavern I could find and asked for a room and breakfast. A potbellied, red-faced, grey-headed landlord received me and a dirty clay-coloured negro showed me to the dirtiest room it has yet been my fortune to occupy. Three beds that were positively and undisguisably filthy. They looked as if they stunk. A wash bowl with a gap in it, an empty pitcher with the mouth broken off and a glass tumbler with one side broken off and half full of dead flies . . . . The whole face of the country here looks dingy and neither the grass nor the foliage looks as fresh as that east of the mountains. The dwellings and settlements look mean and the people rough and uncouth.

It was little wonder that Kelley had his headquarters at Cumberland, Maryland. Strother served first as his acting ordnance officer and later as chief of cavalry. Plain in his background, simple in his habits, Kelley was full of good sense and a spirit of liberality. Despite continual political pressure from the state legislature to adopt harsher measures toward the Confederate sympathizers, Kelley stood firmly upon his convictions, even though he knew that ultimately he would be relieved for them. So rarely had Strother encountered such qualities in a commander that he rapidly became a warm friend and defender of General Kelley.

In February, 1864, Strother missed a superb opportunity for communicating his name to posterity as a literary figure. John P. Kennedy was assisting the sanitary fair commission at Baltimore in getting up a lithograph album of contributions from America's foremost writers. He was especially eager for Strother to give him a sketch and an article for inclusion in the volume: "I think considering your fame as an artist as well as a writer, some neat little sketch in outline of a descriptive character by way of illustration of the text, would be very unique and striking in the collection . . . . Two or three little interpolations of this kind in the text would give it a distinctive character as your work."[8] Duties in the Department prevented Strother from obliging Kennedy "within a fortnight," as had

8. Letter from John Pendleton Kennedy to David Strother, February 22, 1864. In the possession of Boyd B. Stutler, Charleston, W. Va.

been directed. Although he did prepare the article and sketch, they arrived too late to be included in the first edition of *Autograph Leaves of Our Country's Authors,* and the promised second edition was never brought out.[9] Had it arrived in time, it would have appeared in the notable company of Longfellow, Bryant, Lincoln, Holmes, Hawthorne, Emerson, and many others. After receiving the belated contribution, Kennedy wrote Strother:

Your excellent paper with the beautiful Vignette arrived here on Thursday. On going to our workmen I found them finishing the last form of the Volume, and as our time was narrowed to less than three weeks for completing the work—in binding &c—for the Fair, we found we could not venture to attempt to insert it in this edition . . . . It so happens that we have two or three other most valuable communications in the same predicament—one from Motley, one from Agassiz and one or two others. These give us an additional inducement to press for a second edition.[10]

Such an opportunity never came again. In the later anthologies of American authors, except for those more restricted in scope, the work of Strother was not included.

Military activities in the Valley of Virginia during the spring and summer of 1864 fell under three heads: the advance of Sigel's army and its defeat at New Market; the subsequent advance of Hunter with a path of destruction carried as far south as Lynchburg; and the counter-offensive of Early, who took the Southern army to the outskirts of Washington. Colonel Strother was engaged in the first two campaigns, and at their conclusion he retired from the army. It was his service with Hunter as chief of staff which, more than any other, caused some Virginians to hate Strother. They blamed him for the particularly severe depredations which accompanied Hunter's advance

9. The original manuscripts for the volume remained in the family of Colonel Alexander Bliss until sold at private auction by the Parke-Bernet Galleries of New York on April 27, 1949. The various pieces have been separated, but the Strother manuscript, describing the Rebel destruction of the railway yards in Martinsburg, is now owned by T. H. Hanley of Bradford, Pennsylvania.

10. Letter from John Pendleton Kennedy to David Strother, April 2, 1864. In the possession of Boyd B. Stutler, Charleston, W. Va.

up the Valley. However, Strother had nothing to do with the burning of private houses and the destruction of personal property. His tour of duty in the Department of West Virginia was marked by strenuous efforts to save, not to destroy. As we have seen, one of his reasons for electing to serve there was to assist the people of his native region. To Kennedy he wrote:

Civil law is entirely subverted in West Virginia and all along the border. Men bring their cases to the Military Provost Marshal's and consult soldiers in regard to their disputes instead of lawyers. Besides being the center of military command, Headquarters is the grand court of Equity where anybody has to apply for justice and protection. I am continually besieged with clients by letter and in person—and my acquaintance with the country and people enables me to have some influence in modifying the hard condition of this region. Not much, however, but I can at least protect my own family and property and sometimes oblige my personal friends and prevent outrages that are continually occurring through want of justice in the troops and ignorance or rascality in the officers.[11]

Three times he saved Charles Town from the torch. Once he intervened with General Kelley to save the life of a Confederate cousin who was charged with murder (and from whom in later years he received no thanks). His journals are filled with instances in which he begged off other property and lives from destruction. Yet this was the man whose name was anathema to a generation of Virginians.

When General Franz Sigel relieved Kelley from command of the Department in March, he retained Strother for his staff and requested that the Colonel prepare a confidential notebook for the War Department and the General. Strother was never close to Sigel, nor was anyone else, unless it was the "penitentiary birds" he adopted. Of all the Federal generals whom Strother had met, Sigel was the least fit to command an army in the field. When excited, he could not speak English. He informed a member of his staff that he had once earned his living by playing the piano in a London beer saloon. It was generally assumed that he had been appointed as a political gesture to flatter the

11. Letter from David Strother to John Pendleton Kennedy, April 14, 1864. Among the John Pendleton Kennedy Papers at the Peabody Institute, Baltimore.

German constituency of the country. Always a shrewd judge of character, Strother was not fooled by Sigel's cocksure manner. When the army was transferred to Martinsburg preparatory to its march up the Shenandoah Valley, Strother intuitively sensed disaster and left his private notebooks at home so that they would not fall into the hands of the enemy. Throughout the campaign Sigel seemed to have little idea of what tactics he was expected to employ or what force he was expected to defeat.[12] His general objective was to "threaten" Staunton, but preparations for this were hopelessly tangled. As the army left Martinsburg, Sigel appropriated Strother's horse for one of his civilian scouts. A probable battle lay ahead, but Strother and another aide-de-camp were without the means of accompanying the army. "Bier was furious," Strother wrote, "and declared he would resign. I told him there was a campaign and probably a battle ahead and we must go if we went afoot." Both officers managed to hitch a ride in a passing carriage. On the morning of the fatal Battle of New Market, the staff was astonished to see the General at full run toward the camp of Negro servants, his boots down-gyved, exclaiming, "By Got, I vill catch dot dam tief." They learned that his brandy flask had been lost. When he failed to discover it among the servants, he accused his hostess, a Virginia lady whose house he had appropriated. She was outraged and cried out bitterly, "May the vengeance of the Almighty follow that man. He has wounded my feelings too deeply for healing or apology." Her curse was fulfilled on the same day at the Battle of New Market.

Most of Sigel's army, scattered along the turnpike for five or ten miles, never arrived on the field in time for the battle. At midday on May 15 fierce cannonading on the northern end of New Market forced the Federal line to retreat to its second position. As the action waxed hotter, Sigel's command of the English language waned. "Sigel seemed to be in a state of excitement and rode here and there jabbering German. In the excitement he seemed to forget his English and the purely American portion of his staff were totally useless to him." When

12. George E. Pond, *The Shenandoah Valley in 1864* (New York, 1883), p. 21.

the Federal lines broke under the Confederate charge, Strother and others of the staff drew swords and attempted to rally the stragglers, but all organization and coordination had dissappeared. Strother's suggestion for placing batteries on a nearby hill to cover the retreat doubtless saved the Federal army from a worse defeat, although New Market became one of the most ignominious turnbacks of the Civil War. In his thirty engagements of the war, Strother was struck by the enemy's lead only at New Market—a spent musket ball struck him in the chest, bounced off, and while giving him something to think about did not injure him. The Confederates failed to push their advantage, and the army was successful in withdrawing from the field during the later hours of the day and the rest of the night. Sigel had failed disastrously in his march to Staunton, for he was defeated by a force of inferior size, much of which was composed of the young cadets of the Virginia Military Institute under their first fire. Strother summarized the feelings of the army when he wrote, "We can afford to lose such a battle as New Market to get rid of such a mistake as Major-General Sigel." More memorable was Porte Crayon's barbed witticism, which swept like wildfire through the army: "We are doing business in this Department. Averell is tearing up the Virginia and Tennessee Railroad while Sigel is tearing down the Valley turnpike."[13] That Sigel was defeated is less surprising than the fact that he was given the command in the first place. Even the supreme commanders had no illusions about his ability; General Halleck wrote to Grant, "He is already in full retreat on Strasburg. If you expect anything else from him you will be mistaken. He will do nothing but run. He never did anything else."[14]

13. Miles O'Reilley [C. G. Halpine], *Baked Meats of the Funeral* (New York, 1866), pp. 300-301. Halpine also records Sigel's reaction when he heard what Strother had said: " 'By Gar,' he exclaimed, 'I vill not haaf beople's saying dem kind o'tings! By Gar, I polief dere are beoples on mein staff who are not griefed to zee me dearin' down de 'pike! By Gar, Colonel Stroda re must not zay dem kind o' tings, or he veel be court-martial!' " Halpine further quotes Strother as saying, "There was no trace of cowardice in General Sigel, as there certainly was none of generalship."

14. *The War of the Rebellion: A Compilation of the Official Records of the Union and Confederate Armies, Series I*, XXXVI, Part II, 840.

If Sigel was despised by Virginians, his successor, General David Hunter, was feared and hated. Even before taking command on May 19, Hunter was running a close second to Ben Butler as the most hated Union general in the South. The Confederate government had officially declared him a felon for his use of Negro troops and his enfranchisement of the Negro in North Carolina, and Confederate newspapers vied with one another to find a suitable epithet to fit their indignation. Two printable and representative samples were "ferocious barbarian," and "brutal bandit chief."[15] Even members of his command in later years found little to say in his favor. Colonel H. A. DuPont wrote caustically: "His mentality was largely dominated by prejudices and antipathies so intense and so violent as to render him at times quite incapable of taking a fair and unbiased view of many military and political situations."[16]   Hunter unquestionably had a deep hatred for the South, and his wholesale depredations by torch and his occasional use of the hangman's noose were reflections of this antipathy. Yet one must admire, at times, the courage of a man who knew what would happen if he were captured and who still persisted in waging a deadly, quarterless war well beyond his lines of supply deep in Virginia. That he ordered the wanton burning of private homes is undeniable, but it should not be overlooked that it was ferocious bushwhacking by armed civilians that gave rise to the "retaliation orders" of General Hunter. He was no student of chivalry, no McClellan carefully protecting fence rails and chicken coops from Yankee soldiers. But unlike Banks, Hunter did not permit his troops to plunder because he was too weak to stop them. There was a kind of method in his madness, and there was certainly power in his army, which struck up the Valley as far as the outskirts of Lynchburg, farther than any previous Union general had penetrated. Although new at the time, his conception of war as involving not just the defeat of armies but the destruction of morale and supplies has been accepted as an axiom in warfare of the twentieth century. When his army got

15. These appeared in the *Register* (Shepherdstown, W. Va.), May 5, 1866, and the *Whig* (Richmond), June 28, 1864, respectively.

16. H. A. DuPont, *The Campaign of 1864 in the Valley of Virginia* (New York, 1925), p. 44.

under way on May 26, the smoke from a burning house, the
rendezvous of Confederate bushwackers, rose in the morning air
as a grim portent of the coming campaign.

Strother's service as chief of staff under General Hunter requires extended discussion. It was by far his most influential
position during the Civil War, and it climaxed his career as a
soldier, for at the conclusion of the campaign he resigned his
commission and returned to civil life. The appointment was
regrettable for one reason: Strother was accused of having mas-
ter-minded the destructive maliciousness that was actually ordered, as we shall see, by General Hunter. Even the similarity
of their names, David Hunter and David Hunter Strother,
seemed to indicate to a later generation a fiendish union of
blood. Hunter and Strother were distant cousins, but kinship
ended there. Actually Strother regarded his General with mixed
emotions. Personal acts of kindness sometimes made Hunter
the most generous and thoughtful of men. At other times he
seemed to be unbalanced with his own perverse brand of malice.
Strother was too much a man of honor and too much a soldier
to tolerate a single word of abuse aimed at his commander by
his fellow soldiers. This same stoical loyalty restrained him
from answering public attacks and accusations after the war;
a word in his own defense would, in effect, have served to implicate Hunter more deeply, and Strother therefore suffered in
silence. He did what he could to countermand the harsher orders of the general, but he obviously could not override his commander. Nor is there any reason why he should have been a
a Southern watchdog devoting his waking hours to performing
missionary work among the Southron. However mixed his
feelings toward Hunter were, Strother was convinced that he
was a competent and a fearless soldier.

With his army, Hunter began his march up the Valley of
Virginia to threaten Staunton. At Woodstock, Strother began,
as his private journal shows, the first of many services to the
civilian population. The following is a fair sample: "Passing
through the town of Woodstock the General halted and had the
jail searched but found no one in it. He was evidently seeking
an apology to burn something and proposed to set fire to Hol-

lingsworth Hotel, but I told him that our wounded had lain there and had been well cared for while the place was occupied by the enemy." Popular legend has it that Southern womanhood was abused shamelessly by the Yankee cohorts under Hunter. It is not difficult to see how the following incident could be used to great patriotic advantage by an imaginative Southern editor:

Another woman was then brought in having been arrested trying to pass the pickets outward. When she found she would be detained for a day or two, she broke into loud lamentations, wringing her hands and tearing her hair. She had left a baby at home six weeks old and it would certainly perish with hunger as there was no one on the place. [Colonel] Starr felt her breasts which were entirely flat and showed no signs of milking. He told her that from all appearances she would be of little use to the baby and so she must be content to stay. She abused Starr and then laughed and when I saw her she was sitting quietly under a tree smoking a short clay pipe and chatting in a friendly manner with the guard . . . .

As Strother ironically said, "Rough are the wages of war."

At Harrisonburg, Strother's minute knowledge of the Valley as a *Harper's* correspondent paid an ample dividend. The Confederate army lay in wait along the turnpike beyond North River, and he recommended a march to the left along the Port Republic road to flank the enemy. Despite the slowness of the movement, the Union army easily crossed the river without opposition, forced the Confederates to regroup hurriedly at New Hope, and almost totally annihilated them at the Battle of Piedmont on June 5. In the heat of the battle, the derisive cry, "New Market— New Market," could be heard drifting from the Southern lines. However, it soon subsided when the Federals made a crushing attack, which proved that, whatever his faults, David Hunter was no Franz Sigel. This victory, the first total one ever obtained by a Northern army in the Valley of Virginia, owes its general strategy to David Strother. On June 6, Hunter's army entered Staunton, the objective of the Federal armies for the past three years. Only eleven years before, "Little Mice" had drawn attention to Porte Crayon and his "Cousins" during their visit to the town by strolling about with copies of *Harper's* under his arm and a June-bug stick pin in his cravat. Strother's entry into the town now attracted attention: "I got two bands with a large American flag to accompany the staff as we entered the town. We made a tour of the principal streets playing Hail Columbia and Yankee Doodle and other such airs as we thought might be useful and pleasing to the inhabitants." The humor soon disappeared from the scene, giving way to pandemonium. The jails were thrown open, and the riffraff of the town descended like locusts, looting the Confederate military stores at the depot. The provost guard knocked off the heads of barrels of applejack, and the liquor ran down the curbs in cascades, carrying along sticks, paper, horse dung, and dead rats. Suggesting a scene in *A Tale of Two Cities,* the soldiers and vagabonds on hands and knees drank the mixture without a qualm, while "the more nice were setting their canteens to catch it as it flowed over the curbs." Despite the confusion, Strother was able to pledge his word that the insane asylum and the female seminaries in the town would not be harmed. The Confederate government, however, lost an estimated $400,000 in military supplies at Staunton.[17]

Hunter did not rest on his laurels. Reinforced by nearly ten thousand troops from the commands of Averell and Crook, who arrived from the west, he called a staff meeting to determine his next move. The commanding general favored a move on Charlottesville to connect with Sheridan, who was moving in that direction from the eastern theatre, but it was Colonel Strother's plan which was adopted—to proceed upon Lexington and Buchanan, then cross the mountains and fall upon Lynchburg, the grand depot and principal railroad junction of the Confederacy connecting with the West. No one supposed that Lee would allow Lynchburg to fall without a fight. The whole plan was dependent upon the utmost speed. The Confederates, used to vacillation and hesitancy among the Union commanders in the Valley, might not suspect that so daring a raid would even be conceived, much less executed. The movement was particularly hazardous because it necessitated severing most of the communication and supply lines from the north, forcing the

17. Pond, *Shenandoah Valley,* p. 34.

Union troops to live largely upon the land and the limited provisions which the army could carry with it (this was the same logistical problem which Sherman faced during his march from Atlanta to the sea some months later). The plan would have succeeded had not a lack of ammunition held the army in Staunton until June 10.

On June 11, after a rear-guard action by Confederate General McCausland, the Army of West Virginia entered Lexington, the "West Point of the South." By the time Strother arrived in the town, the looting of the Virginia Military Institute was well under way. The plunderers came out loaded with a ridiculous collection of beds, carpets, cut-velvet chairs, stuffed birds, charts, books, and cadet uniforms. The burning of the Institute gave rise to a flurry of indignation among short-memoried Southerners who seemed to have forgotten that the cadets had fought in the field against the Union soldiers at New Market. General Hunter on June 12 asked his chief of staff whether the school should be burned, and Strother replied without equivocation:

I told him I looked upon it as a most dangerous establishment where treason was systematically taught, that I believed the States Right conspirators had with subtlety and forethought established and encouraged that school for the express purpose of educating the youth of the country into such opinions as would render them ready and efficient tools wherewith to overthrow the government when the hour and the opportunity arrived. Throughout the pamphlet literature of the school, addresses, speeches, and circulars, we saw one prominent and leading idea—that the Cadet in receiving his education from the sovereign state owed his allegiance and military service to the state alone . . . . This was the paramount reason for its destruction by fire.

The people of Lexington were little surprised by the destruction of the school—most expected it. Margaret Junkin Preston, whose husband was a member of the faculty, wrote in her diary four days before the town was occupied, "As the Institute is Government property, they will most likely burn it; that, at all events, is what we apprehend."[18] No malice prompted Stroth-

18. Elizabeth Junkin Preston, *The Life and Letters of Margaret Junkin Preston* (Boston, 1903), p. 184.

er's recommendation, nor did guilt compel him to assist in re-building the Institute a year later while he was adjutant general of Virginia. Both acts were in line with his sense of duty. As Strother watched the volumes of black smoke rolling upward from the flaming building, a clerk handed him his only trophies —a new gilded button marked "V.M.I" and a pair of gilded cadet epaulettes. The burning of ex-Governor Letcher's house which followed was an unwarranted piece of destruction, the blame for which Hunter must carry alone.

There seemed to be great concern among the citizenry that Washington College (now Washington and Lee University) would also be put to the torch. However, such fears were groundless. Even Hunter knew that the college had no connection at all with the Confederacy. The theory was given credibility in later years by a Colonel Schoonmaker, a Union officer, who wrote the following:

After burning the Virginia Military Institute buildings, he [Hunter] announced his intention to burn the Washington College buildings also, and, knowing the sentiment among the rank and file of the army was averse to the burning of the Virginia Military Institute . . . and that no such reason could be given for burning the Washington College, I went with two other officers to see Colonel D. H. Strother, Hunter's Chief of Staff, a noted author and warm personal friend of his, and urged him not to permit Hunter to make another mistake in this direction as it was certain to lose to him the moral support of his army, which was opposed to the unnecessary destruction of property. Strother succeeded in doing this and to him, rather than to myself, belongs the credit for saving the Washington College buildings from destruction.[19]

19. Letter from a Colonel Schoonmaker, July 27, 1922, as quoted in William Couper, *One Hundred Years at V.M.I.* (Richmond, 1939), III, 32-33.

The Lexington *Gazette* for August 2, 1864, has this to say of Strother at Lexington: "We understand that he made three sketches of the Institute, and Governor Letcher's house—one before the buildings were fired—one while they were burning—and another of the ruins—all for Harper's *Weekly*. This man has long been employed in this business, and figured very conspicuously at the time of the trial and execution of old John Brown. He was thoroughly Southern in his feelings then." Also quoted in Couper, p. 42. The drawings in question have not been found.

Schoonmaker's story, while flattering to Strother, was written
nearly sixty years after the events and his memory was muddled.
His recollection is a bit hard on Hunter. Strother's journals
are full and detailed on the whole affair. The truth is far less
dramatic. There was an unauthorized demonstration by Federal
soldiers around the Washington College building. An alarmed
trustee called frantically for a guard. Strother ordered it immediately, and explained to the gentleman that "we were disposed to treat his college in a different manner from the Institute." This explanation was cut off rudely by the trustee's "I
do not wish to discuss the matter, Sir," to which Strother pointed
to the blackened ruins of the Institute and wryly said, "You
perceive that we do not intend to discuss it either." Riding to
the College to assist in the matter personally, Strother found
that the disturbance was caused by soldiers who were pelting
the statue of Washington on the cupola, thinking it was Jeff
Davis! The truth, while less melodramatic, is somehow more
revealing. As for the bronze statue of Washington in front of
V.M.I., that was another matter. It was a spoil of war, and as
he looked at the symbol of American unity, Strother "felt indignant that this effigy should be left to adorn a country whose
inhabitants were striving to destroy a government which he
founded and by their daily acts insulting his memory." He
arranged that the statue be crated and shipped by train to
Wheeling, West Virginia, as a symbol of Federal victory in
Virginia. This transfer set off another flurry of indignation
after the war, as we shall see.

On June 14, the army left for Lynchburg, and the following
morning General Hunter entered Strother's room with a start-
ling announcement—Angus McDonald, the man responsible
for his father's imprisonment nearly three years ago, had been
captured and was now sitting on the front porch of headquarters.
Although stunned by the news, Strother showed no sign of vindictiveness. Hunter offered to turn the prisoner over to him to do
as he liked with the old man. Strother replied that he "did not
care to use [his] position in the United States service to avenge
a private quarrel or injury." If Strother had his revenge upon

Left, Major General David Hunter, United States Army, under whom "Porte Crayon" served as chief-of-staff in the Valley of Virginia and Lynchburg campaigns of 1864. Hunter, who ordered the destruction of the Virginia Military Institute, was a distant cousin of David Hunter Strother. *Right,* John Strother, only son of "Porte Crayon" to reach manhood, wearing the uniform of the Peekskill Military Academy. (Photographs courtesy of Emily Strother Kreuttner.)

A previously unpublished photograph of the Virginia Military Institute after its destruction by fire on June 11, 1864. Strother wrote, "If in war I was instrumental in destroying the Institute, in peace I should like to be instrumental in restoring it to greater prosperity than it ever had before." (Courtesy of Colonel William Couper.)

THE STORMING OF THE ENGINE-HOUSE BY THE UNITED STATES MARINES.—[Sketched by Porte Crayon.]

Sketch by "Porte Crayon" of the storming of the engine-house at Harpers Ferry by the United States Marines. Strother arrived on the scene several hours after the actual assault, but has re-created it in considerable detail. (*Harper's Weekly,* November 5, 1859.)

Strother's portrait of John Brown, the first made after the attack upon the Harpers Ferry armory. In an improvised bed made from an upturned chair, Brown awaits his interrogation by Governor Wise. (*Harper's Weekly,* November 5, 1859.)

Angus McDonald it consisted only of descending the stairs, coming face to face with him, and exchanging the following words:

He seemed as if about to accost me again when I said, "Do you know me, Sir?" He replied, "Yes, I know you and you know me very well. And yet, Sir, you do not know me. You do not know me." This was said apologetically as if to open an opportunity to explain his treatment of my father. I could not listen to more, but said quietly but emphatically. "I think I do know you, Sir," and then turned on my heel and went away. My blood boiled but I could not insult a prisoner, especially one with gray hair . . . . That single look was vengeance enough for me. I could see remorse in his countenance when he recognized me and his aged appearance filled me with pity. If I had followed my impulses at the moment I should have liberated him.

McDonald was turned over to the provost marshal to be treated neither better nor worse than the other Confederate prisoners, and Strother never saw him again. The prisoner was taken to Wheeling, where he died early in 1865. Charles Halpine, the New York writer better known as "Miles O'Reilley," was a staff officer with Strother at this time and substantiates the latter's account:

"I can only regret my civilization," said the Colonel [Strother], when the capture of this miscreant was announced. "Just for this one morning, Miles, I should like to be a Comanche or Sioux Indian, and have their privilege of vengeance." Not being a Comanche but a gentleman, however, he took no other notice of the prisoner, than to see that he was not better and no worse treated than his fellow-captives of higher and lower rank.[20]

The episode did not die with Halpine's objective appraisal, written in 1866. In a recollection of McDonald written in 1867, an ex-Confederate wrote, with greater imagination than truth, that the old man had died of "the shock which his system had received from the torture inflicted by Genl. Hunter and David Strother, those *inhuman monsters*."[21] Unless torture be defined rather loosely as treatment identical to that of fellow imprisoned

20. O'Reilley [Halpine], *Baked Meats,* p. 323.
21. James Avirett, *The Memoirs of General Turner Ashby and His Compeers* (Baltimore, 1867), pp. 356-57.

officers, the charge must be regarded as inaccurate. Nor did the
matter die here; the sore was reopened as late as 1934, when one
of Colonel McDonald's descendants elaborated upon the incident by reprinting the version left behind by Angus' wife. As
an example of the kind of emotional frenzy with which Strother was viewed by many Virginians, it is an interesting artifact:

He [Angus McDonald] had learned that he was indebted for all his
cruel treatment to a creature named David Strother, alias "Porte
Crayon," a cowardly renegade, who after having offered his services
to the Governor of Virginia to help her in her need, became alarmed
over the prospect of losing his gains as a writer and caricaturist in
the Northern journals, as well as that of the hard fighting and pri-
vation he would have to undergo if he cast his lot with his own
people, [and] fled . . . beyond the Confederate States . . . . It was
said that he went to the enemy because they offered him better
pay and higher rank.[22]

The editor of Mrs. McDonald's diary expends an additional
twenty-two pages to show exactly why and how David Strother
was a lying, hypocritical, brutal, cowardly renegade. It is difficult
to believe that such gibberish has been taken seriously and
without question for the past ninety years, and the whole affair
might be somewhat amusing but for the malicious spirit which
inspired it. The McDonald clan systematically set about to
blacken the Strother name, and whatever may be said against
them, they met with remarkable success. Although without
foundation in fact or probability, the accusations were accepted as definitive by many Virginians, who seemed not to
have thought that there was another side to the matter. The
following letter, indicative of the length to which the McDonalds
were prepared to go, was sent to Strother's wife:

My father, Col. Angus McDonald of Winchester, Virginia, was
recently arrested by the forces of Genl. Hunter as a prisoner of war;
and taking into consideration his feeble health, should have been
at once parolled, but for the influence of your husband, David Strother . . . . I have taken this means to give Col. Strother notice that

22. Cornelia McDonald, *A Diary of Reminiscences of the War and Refugee
Life in the Shenandoah Valley, 1860-1865,* ed. Hunter McDonald (Nashville,
Tenn., 1934), p. 227.

the measure of pain, which, to gratify his private malice, shall be visited on my father, shall be meted out to him even unto death, if death be the result of my father's confinement and this determination will survive, no matter when the war ends, and where he may be found. To this purpose I pledge the lives of nine sons.[23]

With respect to this letter, it is difficult to see how the attempt to frighten Mary Strother could gratify a masculine revenge. It might, also, be noted that the 1st New York Cavalry captured "feeble" Angus with a wagon train filled with arms—muskets, carbines, pistols, and double-barreled shotguns—all of which he used against his pursuers with as much rapidity and energy as they could be loaded. As an epilogue to the pledge of "nine sons," it should be remarked that Strother died quietly in his own bed twenty-three years after the Civil War.

When the Army of West Virginia crossed the Blue Ridge and descended into the Piedmont near Lynchburg, Strother became aware that its situation was perilous. It had, like the force of Xenophon, cut itself from all communication, except for a trickle of supplies sent by Sigel at Harpers Ferry, and was in the middle of the enemy's territory. Strother's apprehensions were borne out by the subsequent events. Lee had dispatched General Early from the Richmond sector with a force larger than Hunter's in order to prevent the fall of Lynchburg. Ironically, but perhaps characteristically, Hunter burned the home of the informant who told him of the Confederate reinforcements. As Strother had predicted, Union delays had been costly and the opportunity to capture Lynchburg had flown. On June 18, skirmish fire on the outskirts of the city became increasingly heavy by the hour. Only with difficulty was Hunter's army able to disperse the Confederate counterattacks of that day. The question was no longer how to advance, but how to save the army from total destruction. At the final staff meeting, Strother revealed his practical good sense: "Averell was excited and angry. He said to me, I would give my head this night if we could have taken Lynchburg. I replied that the desire was past. We had but to make good our retreat. He said he was not afraid of them. I said neither was I and be damned to

23. Quoted, *ibid.,* p. 231.

them, nevertheless we should have to retreat. Genl. Hunter immediately ordered the trains to move on the back track."

The retreat began, with the light of a full moon falling upon the congestion of marching men, and piles of burning equipment flickering in the faces of the soldiers passing by. The staff, Hunter assisting personally, cut telegraph wires in abandoned railway shacks. After two days of continual fighting and harassment, the army was demoralized, but by June 22 it reached the comparative safety of New Castle at the foothills of the Alleghenies. The army rested while the staff decided what to do. Strother's proposal, to provide each man with three days' rations and to fall upon Charlottesville, where communications could be opened with Grant, was overruled. Instead, the plan of General Crook was followed—to withdraw to the Kanawha Valley where the unprovisioned army could find ample rations at the supply depot. Jubal Early was already moving away from them on his celebrated march to the outskirts of Washington, and had Strother's plan been adopted, the Confederates would have had an army in their front and one in their rear. Who can say what might have happened?

The march to Charleston, West Virginia, was one of the most grueling of the war. The terrain was the same that had been traversed by Porte Crayon and his "Cousins" a dozen years before, but the tour this time was in sad contrast to the earlier one. At White Sulphur Springs, the magnificent hotel lay abandoned and desolate. Soldiers rooted about the empty rooms and corridors, which had been stripped of everything portable long before. "Miles O'Reilley" wrote: "The scene appeared to the writer all the sadder for the reason that it was witnessed in company with 'Porte Crayon,' who never wearied of relating droll and varied anecdotes of its former greatness and splendor before the 'chivalry' had determined that Southern rights must be achieved by war."[24]

On June 30, the army arrived in Charleston and the Hunter raid came to its close. The troops were put aboard steamers and then on railroad cars to rush to the defence of Washington, but Early had withdrawn before they arrived. During the recent

24. O'Reilley [Halpine], *Baked Meats*, pp. 370-71.

operations, Strother had played an important role with greater responsibilities than ever before in his military career. In the Congressional report which he wrote for his commander, Strother called the Hunter Raid "one of the boldest and best-conducted campaigns of the war."[25] This is an exaggeration but it is not too serious a one. For the first time, a Federal army had successfully engaged the enemy in the Valley of Virginia, too long known as the "Valley of Humiliation" for the Union forces which met the Rebels there. Although Hunter allowed Early to get between him and Washington, the threat to the capital city was overrated by the public, as Early himself knew. The tide of war in the Valley of Virginia had turned, as Sheridan proved during the next few months.

With the conclusion of the campaign, Strother's active part in the Civil War also came to an end. Officially he served as Hunter's chief of staff until the general was relieved by Sheridan in August, but after the army moved from Charleston to Harpers Ferry he had no important duties to perform. On July 17, he noted in his journal that Hunter had received an order from Halleck to devastate the Valley of Virginia south of the Baltimore and Ohio Railroad "so that crows flying over would have to carry knapsacks." The metaphor was an effective one, but it was unfortunately ambiguous. Halleck doubtless intended to suggest that the summer harvest of Valley crops should be destroyed so that the Confederacy could not reap them. Hunter, interpreting the order as a vindictive one and perhaps embarrassed by the raid upon Washington, gave orders on the same day that the houses of Andrew Hunter, Edmund Jennings Lee, and Alexander Boteler, all of whom were among Strother's oldest friends, be burned to the ground. Because he was chief of staff, Strother was accused of having ordered their destruction.[26] Nothing could have been further from the truth, because

25. Thirty-ninth U. S. Congress, First Session, *House Executive Document No. I,* p. 1261.

26. In a letter which Henrietta Lee, wife of E. J. Lee, wrote to General Hunter several days after the destruction of her house, she implies that Strother was partially to blame: "I, therefore, a helpless woman whom you have cruelly wronged, address you, a Major-General of the United States Army, and demand why this was done? What was my offense? My husband was absent

he did not even hear of the burnings until after they had occurred. However, it is gratifying to find that both Andrew
Hunter (who, by the way, was a cousin of General Hunter)
and Alex Boteler were steadfast in their conviction that Strother
had no hand in the unreasonable destruction. Strother, in fact,
did what he could to ease the situation but was forced to write
sadly in his journal: "A war of mutual devastation will de-
populate the Border counties which contain all my kindred on
both sides of the question. I would fain save some of them but
fear that all will go under alike in the end."

At this time "Porte Crayon" became in the public mind a
mythic villain, a Yankee Mosby who galloped by night in raids
through northern Virginia, plundering from rich and poor. The
real raiding parties did not discourage the misconception. Tales
like the following came back to Strother: "A sergeant of cavalry
spoke to me this morning, asking if I was not Col. Strother. On
being answered, he said . . . sometime ago when scouting up the
Valley near Millwood he talked with a young lady who was
curious to know his name and after pressing, she at length hit
upon 'Porte Crayon.' Upon this, he laughed knowingly and left
her fully under the impression that she was right. This shows
how stories of my scouting through Virginia have obtained
credence." Even his first wife's mother, who should have known
better, confronted him with the question of how much he was
responsible for the Hunter burnings. Charges against him appeared in Richmond and Wheeling newspapers, yet he refused to answer them and thereby implicate his general. It is
little wonder that in his journal he wrote in desperation, "They
talk as if I was commander-in-chief of the national armies." As
Virginia, exhausted after three bitter years, was pushed deeper
into the quagmire of defeat, Strother was seized upon as a
scapegoat who could be blamed for many personal sufferings.
Circumstantial and often contradictory evidence, as we have
seen, was used by many Virginians to weave a fantastic tapestry

—an exile. He has never been a politician or in any way engaged in the
struggle going on, his age preventing. This fact your chief-of-staff, David
Strother, could have told you." Quoted in Millard K. Bushong, *A History of
Jefferson County, West Virginia* (Charles Town, W. Va., 1941), p. 175.

of villainy and to emblazon before the world the names of an ignoble triumvirate: Ben Butler, David Hunter, and David Hunter Strother.[27]

By mid-summer, 1864, the war seemed to be no closer to a successful conclusion than it had been three years before, when the Federal army first started up the Valley of Virginia. In July, sunstroke mowed down the army more effectively than Confederate lead, yet there seemed to be a never-ending supply of green boys ready to take the places of the disabled soldiers. Strother had grown miserably tired of war, and the thought of returning once more to art and literature became increasingly attractive. Although his old world existed no more and his region was a wasteland gutted by war, it seemed somehow better to pick up what charred remnants he could find than to remain in the army. When Sheridan replaced Hunter as commander of the Department on August 7, Strother received a leave of absence with his official resignation from the army to take effect at the end of it. On October 3, 1864, he received a discharge and terminated his military career.

27. Popular opinion assumed that Strother was engaged in these Jefferson County burnings, and it was strong enough to be carried into a later generation. John Peale Bishop, a native of Charles Town, used Strother as a villain in his novelette, *Many Thousands Gone.*

Chapter IX

General Strother and Virginia, 1864-1871

ALTHOUGH Strother's campaigning had ended, the war had not. Because of the raiding parties of Confederate guerrillas like Mosby and McNeil, he was unable to return to Berkeley Springs with his family.[1] Until the surrender of Lee, they lived in Baltimore, where Strother was a frequent guest of John P. Kennedy, who loved the war chatter with which Strother was filled.[2] At Kennedy's, Strother was amused by an account of a Rebel officer's dream: he had been asleep twenty years and on waking saw General Lee with a long white beard, sword in hand, and followed by six men and a wheelbarrow starting on the twenty-fourth invasion of Maryland. Strother was finding his old vein of humor again, and he was even prepared to learn a few new things, among them an appreciation of the intellectual potentiality of the Negro. After hearing a lecture by the famous Negro speaker, Fred Douglass, he wrote, "I was astonished and humiliated that I, an educated Anglo-Saxon, a traveller, a philosopher, and scholar, should have lived for forty-eight years to receive instruction and feel my prejudices rebuked by a negro and a freeman . . . . I shook hands with the orator and thanked

1. Even as late as 1865, a part of McNeil's rangers rode into the city of Cumberland, Maryland, and kidnapped Strother's old comrades-in-arms, Generals Crook and Kelley. Berkeley Springs was raided incessantly during the war.

2. Henry Tuckerman, *The Life of John Pendleton Kennedy* (New York, 1871), p. 333.

him for the instruction I had received." Douglass was the only sincere abolitionist Strother had ever known.

The long-sought return to literature and art was not accomplished as easily as Strother had hoped, even when hostilities finally came to an end. For one who had fought in thirty engagements of one of the greatest wars in history, literature appeared tamer and less impressive than before the war. Strother found that even his oldest and best-loved author, Walter Scott, seemed flat and affected: "Upon what small capital has Scott founded some of his novels. Rob Roy was a small cattle thief compared with McNeil or Gilmor, two of the poorest of our Border ruffians. What a poor figure the Border Raider cut in his day, beside the raids of this war! What tremendous chapters of history are we enacting and how tame is romance compared to our daily life! It is no wonder after what I have seen that I cannot read and that all romance seems trivial and contemptible to me." Not only had his appreciation of literature been dampened by his participation in the war, but so had his enthusiasm for writing it. Although he abhorred "tame romance," his confession nevertheless foreshadows his next literary endeavor, the recording of this contemporary drama in his series, "Personal Recollections of the War." Strother knew that his copious journals contained a wealth of material of interest to readers of *Harper's,* and he wrote to Editor Guernsey to arrange for a new series based upon the war. The proposition was at once accepted, but with an ominous reservation: Guernsey protectively but firmly warned that there were many disadvantages in relying upon literature for a living in those troubled times. Strother was touched to the quick by the implication, but he knew that the amiable editor meant no personal offense. Early in December, Strother went to New York to make arrangements for the serial and to work out the financial details. His hopes of earning his prewar price of five hundred dollars per article were shattered. Because the *Monthly* had been damaged by the war, particularly in the loss of its many Southern subscribers, payment would be at twenty dollars a page or what would amount to about four hundred dollars per article. Although Strother signed the contract, Fletcher Harper gave him the option of canceling it within a month if he decided that the price was insufficient. Perhaps the Harpers felt that Strother's views upon the war would be the last thing Southerners wanted to read after the cessation of the conflict. While in New York, Strother stopped to see his friends the Kembles, learning from them that his old tutor, John G. Chapman, was living in destitution in Rome. Like Morse's warning thirty years before, the news of Chapman's poverty struck him forcibly: "What an idea! A man of near 60 who has pursued a profession with apparent success to be in want in his old age, and with a wife and daughter dependent upon him. What a warning! 'Put money in thy purse.'" The analogy between Chapman's condition and his own was too close for comfort, and Strother decided to find a position which would permit his literature and art to be avocational.

An opportunity soon arose. At the end of the month he encountered Francis H. Pierpont, governor of "restored" or loyal Virginia. They were kindred spirits in many respects. Both were Virginians who had remained loyal to the Union during the war and who had suffered great criticism. During the war, Pierpont had assisted Strother in obtaining his commissions. Renewing their friendship now, the two men shared a hope that Virginia could be drawn painlessly back into the Union after the war ended. The governor, at his own suggestion, promised to make every effort to obtain for Strother either a consular post at Buenos Aires or the ministry to Sardinia, but before either offer was acted upon, Richmond fell and Pierpont was called upon to re-establish the government of Virginia. As he prepared to transfer his government from Alexandria to Richmond, Pierpont invited Strother to join his staff. The invitation was accepted.

The "restored" Virginia government was a curious mongrel in American politics. During the remainder of the war its legislature met with only thirteen members seated in both its houses, and its constitution had been carried by an election which numbered only five hundred voters.[3] This government could hardly

3. Matthew P. Andrews, *Virginia, the Old Dominion* (New York, 1937), p. 492.

have been expected to meet with the enthusiastic support of Virginia at large, but doubtless it was better than no government at all. Pierpont was a highminded and liberal statesman who desired to re-establish local government throughout the state as quickly as possible, but he found himself in an untenable position. Richmond Democrats regarded him as a vacillating carpetbagger, while the Washington Republicans of the radical camp thought him dangerously conciliatory. Pierpont, forced to mediate between two irreconcilable factions, found himself alienated from both. By the end of 1865, the Radicals had undermined his policy of enfranchising ex-Confederates and had compelled him to adopt harsher methods. A native of western Virignia, Pierpont was little better than an alien in Richmond society, which looked in scorn upon the governor's cow grazing on the capitol lawn.[4]

Before he left for Richmond to join Pierpont, Strother revisited Martinsburg, which was now filling up with troops returning from both the blue and the gray armies. Everything seemed changed. Old landmarks had disappeared in four years of fighting during which the town had changed hands too many times to be counted. Across the streets there were barriers, and the few familiar faces seemed to be withered and old. At the house of one of his aunts, he met quite unexpectedly his cousin Bob Hunter, one of Lee's soldiers at Appomattox. Both were embarrassed, and the tension was not relieved until the old Negro servant of the house took both men by the hands and united them with a word. This touching demonstration was in striking contrast to others in which Strother and a former friend would become accustomed to passing each other on the street without exchanging an overt look, word, or gesture. Martinsburg was a chapter from the book of the past, and without regret Strother hastened to Richmond to commence a new page in his career.

His official position in the Pierpont government was adjutant general of Virginia, which made him responsible for the militia of the state. The post was, in effect, a sinecure, because Federal troops occupied the state and it seemed unlikely that Virginia

4. Charles H. Ambler, *Francis H. Pierpont* (Chapel Hill, N. C., 1937), p. 307.

troops would be raised at any future time. It was ironical that
he succeeded General William H. Richardson, the officer who
four years before had ordered the militia to march upon Harpers
Ferry and had precipitated the entrance of Virginia into the
war.[5] Strother, however, was not a grasping carpetbagger prey-
ing upon the state treasury. His salary was only fifteen hundred
dollars a year, which barely paid for the expenses incurred by his
family in Richmond's inflated economy. Pierpont leaned upon
him heavily for advice and suggestions, and for a time Strother
lived with the governor in the executive mansion. Many people resented his appointment, assuming as they did that he had
been responsible for Hunter's campaign. While former Rebel
officers, men like Generals "Billy" Mahone and George W. C.
Lee, bore no grudge, politicians and other non-combatants complained vociferously to the governor, who, greatly to his credit,
stood firmly behind his adjutant general. The following missive,
written by an Ohioan, is representative of many which Pierpont
received:

. . . I heard from persons entitled to credit, in the Valley, after I left
Richmond, the reasons of the hostility to Mr. Strother. And whilst
I claim some credit as a Union man, and differing even as I did
with them in regard to secession, and the war, I do not know that
I blame them in this regard. Mr. Strother was a Virginian "to the
manor born" as were his forefathers. He was for years the pride
of the Valley especially. He was raised there. His father and
family lived there and were honorably and well known. He was
intimately acquainted with the topography of the country, from
having traveled much and written sketches of its unrivalled scenery.
He was "Porte Crayon." Well, Sir, an order was issued which will
in all time be execrated by every man of honor and generous impulses, to burn all the mills and grain in the Valley, which was most
thoroughly executed, and more also. For a marauding band of cavalry prowled through the desolate country, robbing and plundering,
wherever they went, and Mr. Strother was their pilot. I say, therefore, who wonders that the people of Virginia, Union, as well as
Rebel, for there was not distinction when playing that game, I say

5. Richardson had held this office since 1841. One Virginia historian has
implied that Strother was an interloper, but it is difficult to credit this view.
See William Couper, *History of the Shenandoah Valley* (New York, 1952), II,
964.

who wonders that they loathe and execrate a man, raised amongst them who would engage in such an unnatural and barbarous system of marauding warfare.[6]

This serves to summarize one view of David Strother during Reconstruction. One wonders why similar charges were not brought against General Winfield Scott or General George Thomas, both Virginians, who directly and indirectly caused greater damage to the South than did Strother. The charges presuppose that a single colonel in the United States volunteers was almost an epical embodiment of all the villains in history and one who not only carried out the orders from Washington but apparently had a hand in writing them. The greatest wonder is how otherwise rational people could credit such an outlandish myth.

Had men of Strother's caliber been in complete control of national policy during the Reconstruction, that period would not have been one of the blackest in American history. He felt that the perpetrators of secession were not the men who had fought the battles but the demagogues who had led reluctant or indifferent Southerners into the holocaust. As he saw it, the task of Reconstruction was to subjugate a partisan minority, rather than to crush the personal and property rights of the people. Both he and Pierpont made assiduous efforts to assist ex-Rebels in obtaining pardons in Washington. He did not, like many victorious Republicans, lose his sanity and his sense of justice through an overly zealous dedication to party spirit. He was and remained a Virginian who hoped to see his state changed for the better, not crushed and humiliated. As he rode to Washington by train on one of his many trips for the governor, Strother was depressed by the desolate wasteland he saw on every side. In his journal he penned a literary vignette contrasting the Northern and the Southern people he saw: "On the cars a Chicago family with rings and bracelets galore. Figetty fat husband buying chicken at every station. Old Virginian, seedy, sad, and silent. Old man with a white hat and crape on it. Men and children sitting heavy on their hands by a chim-

6. Letter from B. H. Bunley (?) to F. H. Pierpont, August 10, 1865. Among the Pierpont Papers at the library of West Virginia University.

ney of burnt house." It is not difficult to see where Strother's sympathies lay.

On August 23, 1865, David Strother was commissioned as brevet brigadier general "for faithful and meritorious service during the war."[7]   Although one of 1163 brevet brigadiers in the United States, he was one of the few literary figures to hold this comparatively high rank. Almost at once he turned to the task of rebuilding the Virginia Military Institute. By virtue of his position as adjutant general, Strother was *ex officio* a member of the board of visitors of the institution which he had helped destroy. At first there was hesitation by other members of the board to proceed with their plans for reopening the school, for all of them knew Strother's previous role at Lexington.[8] However, at a meeting in September all misgivings were dispelled. Strother favored the proposal to install a former Confederate general—George W. C. Lee—as professor of military and civil engineering, although he successfully opposed a suggestion that the United States be sued for the destruction of the place. Such a suit Strother knew would be "futile and injudicious." Soon thereafter, he was engaged in an attempt to obtain for V.M.I. a part of the ninety thousand acres of land due Virginia by the Land Grant Act of 1862, but because Virginia was regarded as a seceded state, the recommendation was not acted upon.[9]   He also favored the uncarried proposal of removing the school to Richmond and of converting it from a military to a polytechnic institution.   Although it was many years before V.M.I. regained its prewar prosperity, Strother had amply shown by his energy and cooperation that he wished the school well. In his journal is found the striking line, "If in war I was instrumental in destroying the Institute, in peace I should like to

7. Strother's photograph and the date of his commission appear in F. T. Miller (ed.), *The Photographic History of the Civil War* (New York, 1911), pp. 311, 314.

8. The historian of V.M.I. has written: "By a strange twist of fortune the new adjutant general was none other than "Porte Crayon," General Hunter's chief of staff, and this caused the unreconstructed Richardson to 'doubt the propriety of putting the Institute in operation until we have a legitimate State Gov't . . . .'" William Couper, *One Hundred Years at V.M.I.* (Richmond, 1939), III, 105.

9. Couper, *One Hundred Years*, pp. 114-15.

be instrumental in restoring it to greater prosperity than it ever had before."

Despite this, Strother had no intention of appeasing the South. His spirit of justice and frankness was not a reflection of obsequious pacification. The North, not the South, must determine what is owed and who should pay. As we have seen, when Hunter destroyed V.M.I., a statue of Washington had been seized as a prize of war. Along with it went two bronze cannon. While Strother was adjutant general, authorities of the school requested the return of these trophies. He at once complied with part of the request and the statue was returned. However, he did not press for the return of the cannon. These, he knew, were military emblems wholly out of character with the peaceful reconstruction of Virginia. With characteristic tact and openness he wrote to Governor A. J. Boreman of West Virginia in October:

The war is ended. The great Cause has triumphed gloriously. Peace covers the land with her healing wings. The military institute phoenix like is rising from its ashes. Its mission hereafter will be more peaceful and more in accordance with the spirit of the age . . . . With such views and aims for the future, the statue of George Washington can with great propriety resume its position as patron of the Institute and under these circumstances we wish to replace it.[10]

The statue was returned to Lexington by September of the following year. It is regrettable that Strother's part in capturing it rather than in returning it has most often been alluded to by Virginians.

In the late months of 1865, it became increasingly evident that the Pierpont government was being choked by the growing Radical element in Washington. Strother saw that his presence in Richmond was of little assistance to the governor in mediating between his snarling adversaries. Indeed, Strother often found that his presence caused no little embarrassment. One night a prominent Richmonder, James Lyons, gave a dinner for the governor and his staff. When they arrived, a reception line had formed in the dimly lighted corridor of the house, and

10. Letter from David Strother to A. J. Boreman, October 14, 1865. In the West Virginia Archives.

Strother followed the governor, shaking hands with the other guests. Suddenly Lyons introduced him to a man he could not at first see. "General Strother—Governor Wise." He felt the grasp relax, giving way to a cold formal bow. At dinner the company noticed that Wise was absent. Some said he was sick; others remarked that he would return. Wise, however, did not come back.

Not only was Strother an alien in Richmond, a situation he could have tolerated, but also he developed misgivings about Pierpont's accomplishments. It seemed that the restored Virginia government was becoming merely a tool in national politics. As far back as July, Andrew Johnson had told Strother that the governor should "be firm with these people as well as merciful and not trust them too soon or let them off too easily." This was not the admonition of a man who hoped to accomplish the difficult task of peaceably restoring a Southern state to the Union. In December, it took no great perception to see who truly governed in Virginia. Strother's request for five thousand arms to resist the threat of Negro uprisings was referred to the commander of the United States troops in Richmond. Soon afterward, despite Pierpont's entreaties, Strother submitted his resignation and magnanimously recommended his predecessor, General Richardson, to succeed him.[11] Not without relief, Strother retired to the tranquillity of Berkeley Springs, "where the newspaper enters but once a week, the telegraph is unknown, and honor is spelled with a *u*."[12] In this placid environment, he hoped to re-enter the lists as a writer for *Harper's*.

In preparing his recollections of the war, Strother hoped to find the link to the old way of life he had enjoyed before the war. Although the exigencies of a troubled era had drawn him into military and political affairs, deep down he was not cut out for these weighty but fruitless responsibilities. First and foremost he was an artist and writer; he now wished to create his masterpiece. In his journal he wrote: "I cannot take interest

11. Strother's resignation was effective on December 31, 1865. Couper, *One Hundred Years*, p. 129.
12. "Home," *Harper's New Monthly Magazine*, LVIII (January, 1879), 237-38.

in the ordinary avocations of men. They are horribly stupid and uninteresting. Therefore I have never made money, nor have I a desire to succeed in a career that cuts me off from the worship of the beautiful. 'A thing of beauty is a joy forever.' This has been the ruling idea of my life. Without this all else has been dullness and inanity .... I must write and sketch pictures." Despite his disaffection with practical affairs, it must be admitted that he had done extremely well in them—better by far than most artists of his day. His next *Harper's* series, "Personal Recollections of the War," owed more to his experience in the world than to his aesthetic sensibilities. It was unquestionably his least "literary" endeavor.

Since the cottage at Berkeley Springs where Strother and his wife had spent their honeymoon in 1861 had been sold, for a time they boarded with his sister, Emily Randolph, at Norborne Hall in Martinsburg. Here, in late January of 1866, his "faculties began to flow" as he reviewed his journals and sketches of the war period. By the end of February, he mailed to Guernsey the initial paper of his series, which became one of the first Civil War narratives to appear in a major American periodical. An agreement was struck for eleven articles chronicling Porte Crayon's part in the war from Fort Sumter to Antietam, although Strother originally had hoped to carry his narrative through to his retirement from the service. In any case, the project occupied his spare moments for the next two years. The reappearance of Porte Crayon in the pages of the *Monthly* after a five year absence was hailed with enthusiasm by the editor in his department, the "Editor's Drawer."

Porte Crayon—now a General, a real General, a General in the Union Army—once on a time wrote a series of articles in this Magazine. Who that read them has forgotten them? . . . So entertaining were they that there was hardly any need of a Drawer, or funny department, when Porte Crayon was along. Well, he is back again, and with this the first number of a new volume he begins his "Personal Recollections of the War." The Drawer gives him a welcome, and so will all the Drawer's readers.[13]

13. "Editor's Drawer," *Harper's New Monthly Magazine,* XXXIII (June, 1866), 129.

The editors completely misunderstood Strother's purpose. For him, the Civil War was a deadly, shocking catastrophe, not the subject for satiric chuckling. Porte Crayon was no "Orpheus C. Kerr." While the editors expected a series of light and humorous pieces, Strother wished to show the war as it had been and to clarify its issues for himself as well as for the reader. But the public was sick of war and wished to be entertained. Strother's narrative was too careful, too detailed, and too accurate. Its merits were appreciated more by military historians than by the general public.

Nearly all possible reactions to war are treated in his narrative—triumph, despair, confusion, loneliness, boredom, cynicism, amusement, courage and tragedy. Strother had a dual method of picturing the conflict; he outlined the general progress of the rebellion, and he elaborated upon the particular events which he actually observed, presenting, as he said, "Scenes where the greatness of little things, and the littleness of great things, will sometimes be strikingly illustrated by juxtaposition, where tragedy and comedy . . . , frenzy and farce walk arm and arm together."[14] Yet this is perhaps the greatest weakness of the work. The universals and the particulars do not always coalesce into a unified and relevant whole. Grand strategy and broken wagon tongues defy Strother's ability to link them together, and at times the author's meticulous care leads him into a narration of picayune details, such as the search for a lost block of ultramarine in an abandoned camp site. Because the work has a chronological structure, long drab days in bivouac sometimes figure as prominently as the climactic hours of heated battle. Often Strother was simply too careless and hurried. For example, in one paragraph we are told of a Colonel A—and in another of Colonel Averell. *The Personal Recollections of the War* is neither pure history nor pure literature, but a conglomeration of both with strong admixtures of tedium. Ennui, his old *bête noire,* caught up with him in the middle of the narrative; in the later papers, in particular, he relied too heavily upon the dry leaves of his journals without firing them with his

14. "Personal Recollections of the War, First Paper," *Harper's New Monthly Magazine,* XXXIII (June, 1866), 2.

imagination. As we have seen, unity had always been his literary pitfall, and his failure in this rhetorical principle here undoubtedly weakened a promising work. As a series of vignettes, anecdotes, and introspections, his narrative will always retain some value and interest, but the reader must be prepared to sift through a great deal of chaff to find the rewarding grains. Had he developed more fully the deeper emotions felt in battle, he would have given us better literature. Had he subordinated irrelevant details to important ones, he would have given us better history.

There are, however, positive things to be remarked about *Personal Recollections of the War*. Today it is all too easy to forget the tremendous popularity of Strother with his public. As an intimate friend known to all classes of society in the 1860's and as a writer who entered the homes of countless numbers of Americans, his smallest actions were of consuming interest. Because of this popularity, Strother wielded an influence upon public thought which few American writers could match, and yet he always used his power with justice and discretion. His former commanders—Banks, McClellan, Pope, and Porter particularly— were virtually at his mercy. He could have ridiculed them or made them laughingstocks had he so chosen. Strother, of course, did nothing of the sort. When he did make a mistake which seriously endangered the reputation of an unfortunate general, he was sufficiently magnanimous to make a public retraction.[15] His recollections reveal no rancor nor prejudice, despite the fact that he was writing about one of the bitterest periods of American history. They present the war in terms which transcend the partisan reportage of the newspapers and which bring a semblance of order into many facets of widely dissimilar campaigns. Strother was probably the first literary figure to make use of the cleavage wrought by war upon a single family whose members fought one another with a bitterness belying their kinship— John Esten Cooke developed a similar theme, but Strother anticipated him. The massive leather volumes of *Harper's* were a staple of many private libraries for over half a century, and many boys first learned about the Civil War by reading Strother's

15. The Fitz-John Porter case has already been mentioned.

articles. One of these was the late Elmer Davis, whose impressions are probably representative.

My favorite author in the *Harper's* of that time was David H. Strother, who wrote as did many of his contemporaries under an alias; his was "Porte Crayon." . . . It is a long time since I have read those reminiscences, but I have an idea that they might prove a useful commentary on the recent neo-Confederate renaissance; at at least you could see how the performances of tidewater Virginia look to an up-state Virginian, of a nationalistic and military family, who saw the forest when some of his contemporaries saw only the trees. General Strother's type of hand-illustrated travelogue eventually went out of fashion, and he ended his days in relative obscurity; but to judge from the evidence that unintentionally presents itself in his writings he seems to have been quite a man, in his time, and at least one of his readers gratefully remembers him.[16]

Until the end of his life Strother speculated upon the causes and the ultimate results of the Civil War, but his germinal idea was that it had been a conflict between feudalism and republicanism, or between "the barons and the burghers." The South had become an anomaly in the modern world, "a stumbling-block in the path of the nineteenth century."[17] The North had nearly failed for a single reason: strong leadership had been emasculated by a generation of rule by popular opinion. He confessed that the South had produced greater individuals than the North, but saw that in a technological war, collective rather than individual action was of the greatest importance. Courage and heroism had less to do with winning a war than sheer material strength, something Strother had known in 1861 but which many Southerners did not find out until Appomattox. War was not romance. John Esten Cooke, whose post-war novels embody the romantic tradition of war, confessed to a friend, "In modern war, where men are organized in masses and converted into insensate machines, there is really nothing heroic or romantic or in anyway calculated to appeal to the imagination."[18] The

16. Elmer Davis, "Constant Reader," *Harper's Magazine,* CCI (October, 1950), 164.

17. "Personal Recollections of the War, Third Paper," *Harper's New Monthly Magazine,* XXXIII (September, 1866), 149.

18. John O. Beaty, *John Esten Cooke, Virginian* (New York, 1922), p. 109.

charge of a light brigade amounted to little within the range of a Parrott gun.

The greatest wonder was how, coming from nearly identical environments, members of one family broke into separate factions, some joining the North and some the South. For Strother, there seemed to be some strange fatality at work, completely inscrutable. It was as if a drop of water falling upon a peak of the Alleghenies was split by a blade of grass, part making its way to the Atlantic and part to the Gulf of Mexico. The individual will seemed to be of little importance. "We are nurtured at the same breast; drink from the same cup, and read in the same book; we . . . divide on a blade of grass; we drift apart; each thinks the other deviating, perverse, absurd. Then comes the sweep and power of passion, and in the end we are as far apart as the frigid and torrid zones."[19] Unlike a native of states farther north or south, whose course in the war was usually determined by the nearest mustering trumpet, Strother, like many northern Virginians, had been forced to choose between conflicting loyalties. His journal is different from most Civil War diaries, for page after page is occupied by explanations of his choice of the Union position. Although he never gave a sign that he could have taken any other course, the great concern he displays for vindicating his part in the war seems to point to the fact that he was emotionally—if not rationally—still very much a Southerner.

Because Strother was a trained writer before he was a soldier, *The Personal Recollections of the War* rises above the average eyewitness account of the war. Yet defeat rather than victory seems more congenial to such narratives—the Confederate ones are vastly superior to the Federal ones—and in this sense, Strother was on the wrong side. Jackson, Ashby, Lee, and Early readily became epical characters, as Banks, Pope, and Sigel did not. Strother's work does not have the dramatic highlights of Henry Kyd Douglas' *I Rode with Stonewall* or Richard Taylor's *Destruction and Reconstruction,* to mention only two of many. Even in the early days of the war, the South was synonymous

19. "Personal Recollections of the War, Fifth Paper," *Harper's New Monthly Magazine,* XXXIV (January, 1867), 175.

with the gentleman soldier, chivalry, and most significant of all, the "underdog." For example, while the armies were quietly bivouacked along the Potomac River in the winter of 1861, Strother noted that the Maryland girls, without casting an eye upon the Northern soldiers, would stroll throught their camps to the river bank for a distant and exciting view of the "chivalrous" Southerners. And certainly there was nothing very heroic about an army which spent more of its time concentrating its forces than fighting. Strother's recollections, then, are neither more nor less than the sum of his experiences. They are valuable for revealing the man and for portraying the age, but seldom in them does one find the dramatic material which transmutes the military reminiscence into the nobler substance of literature.

Other pressing problems required his attention after his retirement from public life. As a coexecutor of Colonel John Strother's estate, he found to his surprise that the hotel was debt-ridden, some of the notes going back as far as 1832, with interest amounting to three times the principal. Despite his appearance of affluence, the Colonel had left behind him an indebtedness which his son and daughter were forced to bear. Rising costs following the war did not make the burden easier (wages at the hotel increased three hundred percent) and for the first time in his life Strother had to struggle for financial solvency. Early in 1866, he moved from Martinsburg to Berkeley Springs, where he purchased the Duckwall property on South Washington Street, which became his home for the remainder of his life.[20] Private servants—for he was a gentleman—alone cost him five hundred dollars a year, and Strother had good reason to look forward to the reopening of the hotel in the coming summer.

The season at Berkeley Springs in 1866 was a nightmare. It began with the hottest season on record, but ended with rain and cold, which drove away all the guests. His sister's son, Edmund Randolph, the favorite grandson of Colonel John, died unexpectedly, crying out in his last moments for Abe Lincoln and the Union. For Strother, as for the stricken family, the

20. This house is treated in Charles Carpenter, "The Berkeley Springs Home of 'Porte Crayon,'" *West Virginia Review,* XIV (February, 1937), 184-85.

child's death and the financial failure were portents. Even his journals—faithfully kept for years—faltered, whole weeks passing without a single entry. When the last visitor had left the hotel, the weather turned mild. The rains passed but the guests were gone. Net profits amounted to less than five hundred dollars, half of which was Strother's share. The heyday of Berkeley Springs had passed forever. Many Southerners boycotted Porte Crayon's spa, particularly those from Baltimore, Mobile, and New Orleans. Despite Dr. Guernsey's admonition that total dependence upon writing was folly, Strother knew that he must write or starve. On his fiftieth birthday in September, 1866, he took stock of his limitations in an effort to overcome them:

In love, fine arts, literature, and war I have played my part, not undistinguished. I have even meddled in affairs of state, but soon wearied. With more persistency and more industry I might have gone farther in all these careers, but it invariably happened that when I had learned an art I wearied of it, dropped it and sought the incentive to action in exploring a new road. In all these varied pursuits there is one most important point I have neglected. I have never paid the slightest regard to my money interests. This neglect now begins to pinch and stare me in the face . . . . A little more industry and a little more method are all that is wanting.

The hotel, put up for sale at $75,000, attracted no buyers. Each year the owners decreased the price, but capitalists of the postwar decade preferred more promising investments than the patrician enterprise of hotelkeeping. Berkeley Springs continued to draw a small, select group of bathers, but its decline was steady until the great hotel finally burned down in the 1890's.

In October, 1866 Strother received a letter from Horace E. Scudder, who was planning to launch a juvenile publication called *Riverside Magazine*. A contribution was requested from the Virginian. He would receive from $100 to $150 for each article running from five to seven pages, each being accompanied by three illustrations. The magazine, an excellent one, lasted only four years (1866-1870), but its contributors were a distinguished group, including Winslow Homer, Thomas Nast, John

La Farge, and F. O. C. Darley.[21] Largely to add to his income, Strother wrote and illustrated a twelve-part serial entitled "The Young Virginians." Imagination and recollection were fused together in the narrative of Beverly Moreland of Norborne Hall in the Valley of Virginia. Beverly is a composite re-creation of the boyhoods of both Strother and his father. Beverly's lively adventures at possum hunting, jousting, and hiking are treated realistically without the syrupy moralizing that too often accompanies children's stories. As usual in a Strother serial, there is a gap between intention and accomplishment. Three years of intermittent writing is a long time to sustain a narrative with strict attention to unity, and Strother, like Dickens and other serial writers, often brought into his story such a wide variety of characters that he was faced with the disturbing problem of what to do with them at the conclusion. Generally, he depended upon the reader's forgetting them and dropped them accordingly. The value of *The Young Virginians* lies in its graphic power within its episodes, many of which are rich in local color, rather than in its total effect.

There are some splendid scenes and anecdotes scattered about in *The Young Virginians*. Squire Stockfield is a more convincing representation of the Virginia farmer than the stereotypes of Thomas Nelson Page and John Esten Cooke. Lazy, lovable, and unpretentious, the Squire detests both ice and warm water. He therefore stations four Negro urchins at relay points between the spring house and his chair so that cool pitchers can be rushed to him on hot days. When firewood is short, he has a servant tear down a fence rail rather than fell a tree, because "it isn't healthy to wait so long for one's meals."[22] One of the best episodes is the militia muster and the adventures of Tom Mullinix, a befuddled mountaineer, and his son Toby. Toby is "skeered" by the unfamiliar world of three-story houses, glass show-windows, and gilded signboards. When Tom becomes lost in the crowd of drunken revelers, Toby is terrified

21. *Riverside Magazine* was important enough in the history of American wood engraving to be cited in W. J. Linton, *The History of Wood-Engraving in America* (London, 1882), p. 31.

22. "The Young Virginians, Chapter Five," *Riverside Magazine*, II (August, 1868), 375.

and runs from place to place trying to find him. A town boy asks him if his daddy wears "long leggings" and has a "chaw of tobaccer" in his hand. Toby replies affirmatively and is led to a wooden Indian in front of a tobacco shop. "There is your daddy, with his leggings and a big chaw of tobaccer in his hand," says the town boy. "He's been waiting for ye this hour or more." Fear gives way to rage as Toby works his tormentor over with a handy pile of rocks. Yet the mountaineer is characterized with respect. If Tom Mullinix is rather loutish in town, Beverly finds after a visit during the following summer that in the mountains he has "an air of native dignity, that would have done credit to a feudal baron in his castle hall."[23] Strother shows an understanding and appreciation of the mountaineer which is particularly striking during an age when the infrequent appearances of this regional type in literature are marked by either condescension or idealization.[24]

The birth of his sons, David Hunter on December 24, 1866, and John on March 13, 1868, were additional reminders that he must acquire financial security. For a time, Strother thought of publishing a drawing book—"Porte Crayon's Drawing Book for Children, for the million"—but nothing came of the idea. Something was urgently necessary, for his income from writing dropped off sharply after reaching a peak post-war year in 1867. In a miscellaneous notebook, he listed his earnings from literature: 1866—$1750; 1867—$2401; 1868—$1150; and 1869—$987. A windfall was needed, something less arduous than writing but more interesting than business. He determined to try lecturing.

The decade following the Civil War was the Lecture Age. As American prosperity hurtled to unparalleled heights, so the demand grew for better (defined as "more famous") lecturers, and humor was most popular of all. For Artemus Ward, Mark Twain, Petroleum V. Nasby, and many others, the platform had

23. "The Young Virginians, Chapter Ten," *Riverside Magazine,* IV (June, 1870), 257.
24. Mountaineers also figure in *Virginia Illustrated* and *A Winter in the South.* In his literary portrayal of this regional type, Strother anticipated Mary N. Murfree by nearly twenty years. George Washington Harris described Tennessee mountain men a few years before Strother, but Harris was almost solely concerned with the humor rather than the local color.

been the way to fame and fortune. Porte Crayon had been in Richmond during the winter when Dr. George William Bagby took the city by storm with his humorous lectures. Therefore when George Alfred Townsend ("Gath"), the war correspondent, appeared at Berkeley Springs during the summer of 1867 with assurances that the fame of Porte Crayon was sufficient to fill a house, Strother was excited by the prospect: "He [Townsend] says I should make my lecture personal and need have but one for a season, speaking but once in a place. $100 a night and expenses. Thinks on account of my literary notoriety I would take. A lecturer is most kindly received with far more indulgence than an author. The very sight of his face engages friendship and good feeling and seems to increase interest in his work." A number of possible topics came to mind—the Valley of Virginia, the Art of Sketching, John Brown— all of which he weighed during the ever-widening gaps between the appearance of his articles in periodicals. A Cleveland agent invited him to speak on John Brown, booking him for a December evening in 1868. The remuneration would be one hundred dollars, no expenses paid—a generous price for an untried speaker. Somewhat grandiloquently Strother summarized his feelings about his entry into a new career: "It is like the sound of a trumpet to an old war horse. Arise my soul. Put off the furred and silken garment of sloth and on the burnished armour of action to strive in a field beset with untried difficulties and dangers. To arms! To arms! Forward!"

He was right about the difficulties and dangers. The rate of mortality among lecturers was notoriously high, a fact which Mark Twain knew but Porte Crayon did not. Most speakers trained for months in back-country hamlets before venturing before a critical urban audience. With one swoop Strother descended upon a city which had heard the best as well as the worst lecturers of the nation. The result was a dismal failure. A stormy night in Cleveland prevented a full turnout at Case Hall, and Strother prickled with indignation when the manager checked his notes to be certain that he would not offend the ghost of old John Brown. He had no gimmick like Nasby's *"We are all descended from grandfathers"* with which to capture his audience, and humor, one of the best ingredients of his essays, was conspicuously inappropriate in a speech on John Brown. Strother's voice was not distinguished and his stature was small. His mind took in far too many points of view, particularly about a subject as complex as the one he had chosen. Although his audience expressed moderate interest in both Porte Crayon and his speech, he knew that he had failed to reach them. The Cleveland experience proved that if he expected to exchange pen and pencil for something else, it would not be for the platform. By the time he had returned to Berkeley Springs, the golden opportunity had turned into a leaden disappointment.

Temporary relief came in 1869, when the hotel was sold to a stock company in which Strother retained some of the shares. The price has not been determined, but it was probably no more than $45,000, of which he apparently received little or nothing, so large were the debts. Shortly after the sale he wrote in his journal, "L'honneur sans argent, n'est pas que une maladie," which implied that his money worries had by no means ended. Even his writing for *Harper's* took a commercial turn. In May, 1870, he traveled to Watkin's Glen, New York, to write about the scenic wonders of that place, but he was not proceeding there in the easygoing manner of his prewar excursions. A publicity organization had commissioned him to write the article. This was the first time Porte Crayon had resorted to hack work for which he was paid in advance and largely for his name. While he was at the Glen, the question arose whether or not to include a private sanitarium in the article. In the end it was included—but a special fee procured its inclusion, something new in Strother's experiences as a travel writer. The article, "An Excursion to Watkin's Glen,"[25] was one of his poorest, as might be expected. It was at first rejected by the editors, but the energetic efforts of the commercial interest were able to persuade the Harpers to bring it out in June of 1871. Even so, for the first time an article by Porte Crayon had been turned down by the *Monthly* staff, and it was humiliating to Strother to find that his manuscript had been marked "not of sufficient general interest."

25. "An Excursion to Watkin's Glen," *Harper's New Monthly Magazine,* XLIII (June, 1871), 32-49.

The bond which had joined *Harper's Monthly* and Porte Crayon for nearly two decades was now weakened, although the final break did not come for several years. The joy of traveling and writing was gone. Henceforth, Strother would write only about subjects and places he had known before the war in western Virginia. Something of the old intellectual curiosity had departed.

Chapter X

The West Virginia Phase, 1871-1879

IF to many Virginians Strother was a renegade, apostate, and traitor, to West Virginians he was, by virtue of his status as a writer and his service in the war, one of the first citizens of their state. Within a short time he became associated with West Virginia in many ways, and is now regarded as its earliest and foremost man of letters. Late in 1869, he was signally honored by his election as vice-president of the newly organized West Virginia Historical Society, the purpose of which was to preserve and publish all important documents and papers pertaining to state.[1] All present at the charter meeting were agreed that West Virginia was backward in matters of education and general culture, and the Society hoped to remedy these deficiencies by encouraging an indigenous art, literature, music, history, and education. Strother admired the unaffected zeal of the members and wrote in his journal: "Want of money is going to be the weakness of the new society. . . . On the subject the Legislature won't vote any funds. Yet if I was independent in that particular I would like to devote my remaining years to that purpose." Strother was far from financial independence, yet he did what he could. In June of 1870, he delivered a lecture on the fine arts as part of the graduation exercises at West Virginia University.

1. Strother was a charter member of the Society, which held its first meeting in Grafton on December 30, 1869. For particulars, see Charles H. Ambler, *Francis H. Pierpont*, (Chapel Hill, N. C., 1937) pp. 343-44.

This, his second major public lecture, was scarcely better than the first. He broiled under the hot kerosene lamps, which gave off so little light that he could not see his notes. But he was pleased and flattered with the reception he received in Morgantown and was pleasantly surprised to see that the region had improved so greatly since his first introduction to it during the war period on Kelley's staff.

When in December he was invited by a group of Charleston businessmen to visit the state capital with a view toward writing something about the booming Kanawha Valley, he accepted at once. Here was an opportunity to do something about his constructive interest in the new state. It was a coincidence that on the day of his departure from Berkeley Springs he received from Scudder the last issue of *Riverside Magazine* ever published, and within its pages was his last installment of *The Young Virginians*. With the demise of *Riverside* and the snub from *Harper's*, Strother's literary obligations were behind him. If the 1870's required commercial brochures, he would write them. He knew that Charleston was no tramontane Athens, but he was not so cynical as to believe that its case was hopeless. For a decade he had remarked that Virginia was bogged in the past; certainly there was no such ground upon which to criticize West Virginia, for that seven-year-old state had little past to speak of and a future that was at best a guess. Although it was not forced to undergo Reconstruction along with the South, its heterogeneity in population, its inadequate communications and transportation, and its lack of political or social roots produced enough problems to occupy its leaders for half a century.

In 1870 Charleston was an unfinished monument to great expectations. Frontier sports like eye-gouging and ear-biting, which had shocked early travelers, had given way to a more dangerous pastime—speculation. It seemed to Strother that everyone was a Colonel Sellers with a private scheme for realizing a fortune in a single night. The tempo was fast; impulse governed decision. Two days after he had arrived in the city, he was offered the editorship of the Charleston *Herald,* a weekly newspaper published by John Brisben Walker.[2] Walker, who had

2. John Brisben Walker (1847-1931) had a varied career as promoter, edi-

all of the drive and ambition of a Horatio Alger hero, was enthusiastic about the Kanawha "boom" which he thought his paper could touch off (a few years later he was bankrupt). Such excitement was contagious, and Strother wrote in his journal, "It is difficult to resist the current of an earnest and excited opinion, and even I am decidedly Kanawha bitten." He realized that speculation was the stuff of dreams, but the prospect of piloting the *Herald* appealed to him. Therefore he accepted Walker's proposition but committed himself only for the first three months of 1871. Walker was delighted and shrewdly suggested a share-the-profits partnership (the *Herald* was not making much money). With a newspaper, Strother could assist in bringing three sorely needed things into the state—railroads, education, and outside capital. Material progress, he knew well, was the immediate need for West Virginia—the finer things of life would follow these or not arrive at all. In mid-December he returned to Berkeley Springs to await the *annus mirabilis*.

Strother never found his duties as an editor wholly congenial. Filling the maw of the press with copy was quite different from penning leisurely essays in his study at Berkeley Springs. Walker did leave his editor alone and welcomed his increased spare time for further speculative plans and for the courtship of Strother's twenty-year-old daughter, Emily, who had followed her father to the Kanawha country. Mrs. Strother, a skeptic, remained at home. Only two copies of the *Herald* are extant from the period of his editorship; neither reveals anything extraordinary in either content or style.[3] As he had promised, Strother took a strong stand upon internal improve-

---

tor, and manufacturer. When only twenty-one, he served as military adviser to the American minister to China. He settled in Kanawha about 1870 and engaged in the manufacture of iron. His fortune of half a million was wiped out by the financial panic of 1873, at which time he tried journalism with little success. He moved to Denver in 1879, and in ten years was wealthy enough to buy *Cosmopolitan Magazine*. He later was a manufacturer of automobiles. His first wife was Emily Strother, daughter of David Strother. They were later divorced. Walker published a posthumous Strother story, "A Schatterndorff Episode," *Cosmopolitan*, IX (May, 1890), 94-112.

3. The extant copies are for January 21 and February 11, 1871. Strother's name appeared on the masthead of the *Herald* as late as May of that year, but he had nothing to do with the newspaper after March. Copies of the *Herald* are in the West Virginia Archives.

ments. In particular, he recognized the necessity for better communications between all sections of the mountain-ribbed state. There was no state, he wrote, where the inhabitants of the different areas knew less about each other, and this ignorance had "engendered many prejudices and misunderstandings, adverse to the common welfare."[4] Material progress was the remedy for curing the singularly clannish political complex of West Virginia, but at the same time Strother knew that West Virginia would not be transformed into a homogeneous entity in a decade or even in a generation.

As a man who, even in the intimacy of his own private journal, referred to his "matutinal or post-prandial coffee," Strother must have been an anachronism in a city like Charleston, but the *Herald* office soon became a headquarters for mountaineer raconteurs who wished to trade stories with Porte Crayon. The Kanawha, like the Washoe, had a humor all its own, exemplified even in the name of its ferry, the *Shoo Fly*. One garrulous Webster Countian, John Cole, gave the writer so many mountain anecdotes and tall tales that he unwittingly became Strother's Holinshed.[5] This "mountain genius," as Strother called him, would talk for hours during lulls in the *Herald* office. His favorite story concerned the Negro minister who quoted from the Apostle Clover. When told there was no such apostle and that he must mean Timothy, the clergyman replied, "Ah, well, I knowed it was one of the small grasses." The humor often ran in channels less pure, and here, too, Strother proved his mettle. When a poem written by a famous actress and circuit rider who was said to have been the mistress of Dickens and Dumas, was discussed, Strother drily remarked that doubtless "she took her *inspiration* by *injection*." Porte Crayon was as adept in barroom humor as in salon wit. Moreover, he observed at first hand the incongruities of politics in an unpolished state. Even the inauguration of a new governor provided him with vivid entries

4. *Herald,* (Charleston) January 21, 1871.

5. Rowzey's story of the drunken bears in "The Mountains, Ninth Paper," *Harper's New Monthly Magazine,* XLIX (July, 1874), 159-65, was originally told to Strother by Cole. On June 25, 1874, Strother wrote to Cole expressing his indebtedness. For a biographical note on Cole, see George W. Atkinson, *Prominent Men of West Virginia* (Wheeling, W. Va., 1890), p. 537.

for his journal. Pomp gave way to brawling among the legis-
lators after the drinks were passed around. "Young Kenna,"
Strother wrote, "struck a man over the head with a bottle,
cutting him badly. A piece of shell struck Old Sam Early on
the head and he went around with a pistol enquiring, 'Who
flung that last brick?'" The American frontier, having passed
West Virginia in its westward march, was now curving back to
pick up the new state. Strother had arrived in Charleston at the
right time to observe some memorable absurdities before they
disappeared forever.

Although he continued to admire the rough tone of Charleston, the very lack of tradition which brought forth his praise
became one of the most persuasive causes of his departure. "The
inhabitants," he wrote, "have no idea of fixedness and consequently do not collect about them books, pictures, and the lux-
urious appliances of a permanent civilization." Worse than
this was the mad scramble for easy wealth. The sight of otherwise sane men who sold their very souls to the crazy devil of
speculation was appalling: "Charleston is full of land speculators, schemers, stock jobbers, and people so occupied with their
own affairs that they are obvious and dreary, incapable of con-
tinuous conversation on other subjects, mouthing money by
thousands and handling it by fractional currency. One indeed
has to use a strong magnifier to see the cash used, after having
his imagination stimulated by the talk." Retaining his conviction
that the public welfare was of greater importance than private
fortune, Strother could not admire the indecent devotion to the
pursuit of personal wealth unaccompanied by anything else.
In a letter to Mrs. F. H. Pierpont, he emphasized that his own
role was to assist in establishing general education, industrial
acts, manufactures, schools, and railroads.[6] His vision did not
include making the private fortunes of particular individuals.
In addition to his editorial work, Strother also wrote a thirty-
two page commercial brochure, *The Capital of West Virginia
and the Great Kanawha Valley: Advantages, Resources, and*

6. Letter from David H. Strother to Mrs. F. H. Pierpont, February 4,
1871. Among the Pierpont Papers at the library of West Virginia University.
Part of this letter is also quoted in Ambler, *Pierpont*, p. 350.

Prospects, which was brought out in 1872. Nothing need be said of this pamphlet, for dozens of similar ones can be found in nearly any chamber of commerce. It did, however, substantiate in a tangible way the ideas he had outlined to Mrs. Pierpont.

At the end of March, Strother resigned from the *Herald.* The newspaper was barely making its way. Competition from half a dozen other sheets, several of which were dailies, was keen, and the mortality rate among Charleston newspapers at this time was especially high. Walker computed his share in the profits of three months, which amounted to only $144. Although Porte Crayon left him, Walker was able to retain Emily Strother, who became his bride the following month. The match seemed like a promising one, but Walker's energy often outreached his ability, and the millions which he so ardently desired were not forthcoming until the following decade.[7] His period of editorship at an end, Strother returned to Berkeley Springs. The rewards of the Kanawha had proved to be as elusive as those of the Ohio in 1838 or the James in 1865, but he had his collection of West Virginia impressions and a more immediate awareness of the virtues as well as the limitations of the state.

Before he left Charleston, Strother received a letter from the new editor of *Harper's Monthly,* H. M. Alden, who invited him to submit further articles and thereby patched up the quarrel resulting from the initial refusal to publish the Watkins Glen piece. Strother accepted the offer after an exchange of several letters. His subject was already at hand—a travel series based upon a tour through the West Virginia mountains. Now, at the age of fifty-five, he wished to relinquish forever the world of practical affairs and to devote himself solely to literature. Although he did not feel old, he was beginning to find that men he regarded as "old bogies" were actually five or ten years younger than he. In April, he took possession of his upstairs

7. Strother gave as a wedding gift to Emily the three hundred dollars he had received from his article on Watkin's Glen. This gift was ironically appropriate, when one considers that the commercial cast of the article matches the mood of Walker's later career. The marriage ended in divorce after eight children.

study at Berkeley Springs "with a sense of pleasure at the quiet-
ness and seclusion it offered." He still had to struggle with his
old enemy, indolence, but he had a new ally, necessity.

Strother did not at once begin work on his series, *The
Mountains*. Other pressing matters distracted him. His older
son, who already showed signs of becoming an artist, was taken
ill and wasted away before his eyes during the summer. Davy's
death on August 25, 1871, was a blow from which Strother never
recovered. Until the end of his life, he recorded this unhappy
anniversary in his journals. The only reference which he made
to a life after death was in connection with Davy: "Even when
dead and buried out of our sight, we *hope* to see them again."
Meanwhile, the world had not forgotten Porte Crayon. John S.
Hart, who was preparing a handbook of American literature,
obtained from Strother a long autobiographical sketch, which
was published along with accounts of other important American
writers.[8] The preparation of this occupied part of his time;
other interruptions, not the least of which was his activity in
dissuading a local segment of the Republican Party from running
him for the state senate, prevented his immediate return to
writing. By October, however, he was ready to begin his new
series, which occupied him for a year and a half.

The Mountains consists of ten articles published in *Harper's
Monthly* between April, 1872, and September, 1875. The subject, a tour by nine people into the remoter portions of the
West Virginia mountains, was based upon travels made nearly
two decades before, probably in 1854.[9] Lawrence Laureate replaces the familiar Porte Crayon as the protagonist; he is diffi-
dent in personality, jaded in taste, and the "author of the greatest
book of the age—not yet out."[10] His antagonist is Major Martial,
a grizzled and worldly veteran of the Mexican War who engages

8. John S. Hart, *A Manual of American Literature* (Philadelphia, 1873),
pp. 457-59. Because Strother wrote it, this sketch of his life is by far the
most accurate one; the narrative, however, is embellished with romantic colora-
tion.

9. Strother's daily journals, kept from 1861 to 1888, prove that he made no
tour of the West Virginia mountains between these dates. Among his papers
is a sketch of the Blackwater Falls, dated 1854.

10. This and the following characterizations are from "The Mountains,
First Paper," *Harper's New Monthly Magazine*, XLIV (April, 1872), 661.

Laureate in a spirited competition for the love of a beautiful young widow with the unlikely name of Rhoda Dendron. Richard Rattlebrain, whose name reveals the man, is a Virginia blood of more nerve than sense who "enjoys city sausages without suspicion of dogs and cats." Augustus Cockney is a dry-goods clerk from New York City who is wholly at a loss in the wilderness; encumbered by all kinds of store-bought equipment, he looks like "a cross between an English groom and an Italian brigand." The sportsmen are accompanied as far as Moorefield by Mr. and Mrs. Meadows and their daughter Lily of the South Branch Valley, by Prue Primrose, a New England schoolteacher, and by Rhoda herself. In the course of the narrative, which by virtue of its sentimental subplot and its extreme length is the closest thing to a novel which Strother ever wrote, the vivid delineation of mountain landscape and life overshadows everything else. So absorbed was Strother in the traveling that he often forgot to develop his characters and his plot.

The Mountains was the first important presentation of West Virginia in literature and Strother was the state's first local colorist. Of especial interest is the manner in which he adapted his technique to the new locale. As we have seen, his reputation as a writer had been largely founded upon his descriptions of Virginia. Now he wished to focus upon the glories of West Virginia. The South Branch Valley, therefore, thirty miles west of the Shenandoah, is represented as the most verdant region of the Virginias. It is "the garden spot of Virginia" where the inhabitants "have all the homogeneousness of an island community, preserving the simplicity of ancestral manners."[11] South Branchers are unquestionably "the best riders in Virginia," and their profuse hospitality reminds the author of "the English squirearchy of past centuries." Such superlatives show his subtle rejection of the Old Dominion as clearly as they define the virtues of the Mountain State. True patrician nobility is to be found not in the Tidewater or the Shenandoah Valley but in its final outpost, the South Branch Valley of the Potomac. As

11. *Ibid.*, p. 663. The other references to the South Branch Valley are found in *ibid.*, pp. 669-72.

might be surmised, *The Mountains* has found few admirers in Old Virginia.

The total time for the trip is about four weeks.[12] After leaving Petersburg, the four sportsmen find themselves in the midst of the mountains, which are by far the most striking feature of West Virginia. They are impressed by the succession of cliffs and precipices on every side, and the mountain folk seem to have similar rock-like qualities. The party stops overnight with a family that is self-sufficient except for the lack of an iron furnace. Such people have about them the best of everything the land affords and are never compelled to live in the presence of their superiors. The mountaineer knows freedom in ways impossible for the dweller on the plain, for he is not hedged about with the "slopshops of civilization at hand to furnish him ready made clothing, manners, and opinions."[13] At the same time, Strother knew that self-reliance was doomed to fall before the encroaching railroads. As Laureate says, " I was anxious to get into the mountains before the steam horses and bill-posters of our progressive civilization had defiled the temples of Nature, and in time for trout."[14] One wood-drawing entitled "The Van of Civilization" is a grim vision of the future—mighty peaks emblazoned with advertisements of corn plasters and flea powders.[15]

Passing Seneca Rocks, the travelers press on to the Gandy, "the ultima thule of Anglo-Saxon civilization,"[16] a region so remote that even missionaries and newspapers are rarities. At Hetterick's cabin, the missus owns a weathered hymnal but no Bible. Ironically she says, "I've hearn tell as how they sends shiploads of them Bibles to the heathen, but us poor lonesome Christians in the mountains gets none, we don't." Although a member of no church and without religious instruction, her practical morality is as pure as if she had all her life "enjoyed

12. Laureate says he and his companions spent thirty days in the wilderness: "The Mountains, Ninth Paper," *Harper's New Monthly Magazine,* XLIX (July, 1874), 166. However, my count, using the narrative, is twenty-three days.

13. "The Mountains, Second Paper," *Harper's New Monthly Magazine,* XLIV (May, 1872), p. 802.

14. "The Mountains, First Paper," *Harper's,* XLIV, 671.

15. *Ibid.*

16. "The Mountains, Fourth Paper," *Harper's New Monthly Magazine,* XLV (August, 1872), 358.

the advantage of a five thousand dollar pew under the ministry of Rev. Dr. Plumpcushion in the great and enlightened city of Hubbabub."[17] In the remote passes of the mountains all is not sublime, and sometimes the natural formations suggest not the handiwork of God but the monstrous heavings of chance and chaos. Sometimes the travelers stumble upon a clearing of rude and dirty shacks, called by the natives "an improvement." Strother's portrait of West Virginia is far from idealized, for against the background of splendid scenes and generous natives is the occasional ugliness of nature and man.

The Mountains concludes in the Moorefield Valley with a tournament in which rustic knights compete against each other for the greatest number of "counts"—spearing a ring with a lance while galloping at full speed. These tournaments, which were one of the more obvious evidences of *Ivanhoe's* popularity in the South, were common in Virginia both before and after the Civil War and revealed the Southerner's devotion to horses and chivalry. At the tournament, Laureate, disguised as the Black Knight, defeats Major Martial and wins the heart of Rhoda, who is more impressed by his riding than his poetry. Masculinity and sensibility prevail over masculinity alone, and on this theme the series ends. However, the scene has a satirical motive which would be plain enough to Virginia readers of that time. When Southern knighthood was in flower before the war, the most famous tournament rider was Turner Ashby, who during the war as a Confederate general became known as "the centaur of the South." At tournaments Ashby often rode disguised as Hiawatha.[18] Because of the almost reverential regard for Ashby by Virginians, Strother entered Dick Rattlebrain in the tournament as Hiawatha and subjected him to a ridiculous fall from his horse after a splendid beginning. The implication is clear: the author took this opportunity to reveal his own opinion of the grand chevalier of the Confederacy. He had known Ashby too well before the war to have any patience with the mythmakers. The tournament scene in the final installment of *The*

17. *Ibid.,* p. 354.
18. Grace W. Landrum, "Sir Walter Scott and His Literary Rivals in the Old South," *American Literature,* II (January, 1931), 263.

Mountains is by no means an unqualified commitment to the forms of Southern chivalry.

The Mountains is not the best example of Strother's work. Much of the material was somewhat stale, and the narrative is too repetitious. His journals tell us that he had hoped to produce a quality of drawing which would rival Doré's, but they also tell us that some of the articles were prepared in less than a week's time. Moreover, Strother used short cuts in preparing the blocks: photographing large drawings, reducing them to block size, and tracing them on the blocks so that he would not have to rework them. A fear of poverty motivated this work more than a love of creativity. Under such pressing circumstances, it is not surprising that *The Mountains* failed to add anything to Strother's reputation or to demonstrate any noticeable improvement in his craft. Perhaps his own estimate of the series is as accurate as any: "To advance in literature I must do something different from my last. My Mountain series smacks too strongly of twenty years ago, so says the editor and the critics. My own judgment condemns the pictures as lacking in zest and originality." Yet if he had not improved, he still had not failed. The social historian can find in *The Mountains* a realistic document about life in the Alleghenies, and the literary historian a work which is as close to the requirements for local color as West Virginia can offer. In what was the nadir of the state's literary development, Strother alone dramatized the mountains and their people. He hoped that his efforts would be the beginning of a native literature emanating from West Virginia. Selected to write an article about the state for William Cullen Bryant's *Picturesque America,* Strother challenged the American artist to explore and to exploit the wild natural beauty of its mountains: "Will not some one of our famous masters of landscape who have buried the Hudson and the White Hills under mountains of canvas, and venturesomely plucked the mighty hearts out of the distant Andes and Rocky Mountains, condescend to accept the challenge from the virgin wilderness of West Virginia?"[19] None did. Although Melville Davisson Post and Margaret Prescott Montague made efforts to portray West

19. "In West Virginia," in *Picturesque America* (New York, 1872), II, 377.

Virginia in literature, Strother was the first to do so and remains the best. *The Mountains* was also his last ambitious literary and pictorial work.

Since his boyhood, Strother's imagination had fed upon the Far West, which represented for him the raw energy of America unhampered by the bondage of tradition. Financial considerations and other responsibilities had prevented him from gratifying his curiosity, even when his former commander, General John Pope, had invited him to join an excursion across the plains from Leavenworth in 1872.[20] However, when H. T. Williams, the editor of *Horticulturist,* a magazine to which Strother had been for some years contributing literary scraps, invited him to accompany a party of journalists and editors to the Rocky Mountains during the summer of 1873, Strother at once accepted.[21] Many of the cities en route had promised entertainment without charge, so the costs would be kept to a minimum. The tour, which lasted about a month, passed through the principal cities of the West as far as Salt Lake City and extended Strother's familiarity with the American scene. Although he did not utilize his Western experiences for literary articles—writers had already combed the area for *Harper's*—his journals contain some valuable insights and impressions.[22]

The excursionists started from Harpers Ferry, traveled by rail to Staunton, White Sulphur Springs, and Cincinnati, stopped for a day in St. Louis, and then turned south to Texas. Strother found Dallas composed of "eating houses, drinking saloons, gambling houses, groceries—circus bills for picture galleries." He was gratified to find that college men worked as hotel por-

20. Letter from John Pope to David Strother, June 22, 1872. In the possession of the author.

21. The artistic and literary excursion was not a new experience for Strother. In June, 1858, he accompanied Thomas Rossiter, Thomas Hicks, John Durand, Brantz Mayer, and many others on an excursion sponsored by the Baltimore and Ohio Railroad from Baltimore to Wheeling. For particulars, see Strother, "Artist's Excursion on the Baltimore and Ohio Railroad," *Harper's New Monthly Magazine,* XIX (June, 1859), 1-19, and John Durand, "An Excursion on the Baltimore and Ohio Railroad," *The Crayon,* V (July, 1858), 208-10.

22. " 'Porte Crayon' in the Rocky Mountains," an edition of the portion of Strother's journals including the Rocky Mountain excursion, appeared in *Colorado Magazine,* XXXVII (April, 1960), 108-21.

ters and waiters; in Texas, at least, they had to earn their keep. If the place had a major fault it was "the way they killed people about here." The prairies of the Indian Territory and Kansas defied his power of description. At one time the party's railroad car was filled with thousands of grasshoppers escaping a sweeping prairie fire; in the buffalo country heaps of skeletons surrounded every depot, awaiting shipment East to be ground into fertilizer. Indian shanties fringed the railroad near the settlements, curiously incongruous with advertisements for "Woodward's ague cure." For the first time in his life Strother ate at a table with a Negro, "a man and a citizen." At Salinas, he noted with amusement the keen competition between two rival hotel keepers, one of whom advertised pointedly, "Beware of Railroad Hotels, come to a white man's hotel. Don't go to that Bug Hole."

For Strother, the Rocky Mountains were the climax of the trip. He ascended Gray's Peak "without fatigue" and was impressed by the panorama which stretched a hundred miles in all directions, "the line of the plains rising to the eastward like the sea." In Denver, he was delighted with the discovery that the Lees of Colorado were Chinese coolies and heard some fine tall tales and rustic anecdotes, samples of the miner's brand of humor. One of them is nearly identical to a dialogue used by Mark Twain in *The Adventures of Huckleberry Finn,* written twelve years later:

Loafer: "Gimme a chaw of tobaccer, will ye?"
(Miner hands out his plug. Loafer helps himself.)
Miner: "Well, mister, if ye'll only gimmie that chaw, ye may keep the plug."

Another concerns Sam, a Caribou athlete, who hears of a Central City bully of gigantic proportions and longs for an encounter. He goes to Boulder, where the Centrals are planning to have a spree, and is told by a barkeeper that the bully, a great fiddler, will be along presently. A wagon arrives and among other things a bass fiddle is handed out. After Sam stares in amazement, the barkeeper sees him slinking off. "Hello," he cries, "are you going to leave?" "Look, mister," says Sam, "I like a fa'r fight but I don't kear to fight a fellow that handles a fiddle like that."

At Salt Lake City, the excursionists were met by a delegation of Mormons and entertained with a "tone of entertainment equal to any we might have received in any city west of the Alleghenies." Strother found, however, that the Mormons regarded artists with rude suspicion. The mayor, on being told who Strother was, said, "We are afraid of artists." Strother's complimentary reply was cut short with "We don't want to be flattered either." Here the excursion reached its Westward limit. The return trip was anticlimactic. In Nebraska, Strother met a pathetic group of Pawnee Indians who had just been defeated by the Sioux,[23] and in Chicago he was pleased when a hotel proprietor, recognizing Porte Crayon at his table, said solicitiously, "Do take something more, Sir. You can't keep up and entertain the world on such slim fare." As a result of his Rocky Mountain tour, Strother had extended his travels nearly to the limits of the American scene and had absorbed more during a month than he had in any previous decade. But the very speed which characterized the tour precluded successful sketching. The tempo of America had changed, and Strother's older method of travel and description, dependent more upon the foot and carriage horse, was now a past chapter of history.

If his Western tour widened his knowledge of America, the centennial year, 1876, provided him with several modest opportunities to piece together his own accumulated thoughts and recollections of sixty years. With thousands of other Americans, he took his family to the exposition at Philadelphia. Like America itself, the exposition was vast, exciting, and confusing. The seemingly endless exhibits of art, machinery, natural history, and ethnography seemed a part of some great complex which he could not understand. Usually quick to see through multiplicity to the single principle beneath it, Strother was only frustrated by the reflection of modern America he found at Philadelphia.

23. His impressions of the Pawnees were included in his article, "Sitting Bull—Autobiography of the Famous Indian Chief," *Harper's Weekly,* XX (July 29, 1876), 625-28. Most of the article, however, concerned a sketchbook of drawings said to have been made by Sitting Bull.

"I have thus far enjoyed the Exhibition very much," he wrote in his journal, "but it has been confused and unorganized. I have got but few new ideas; although I have seen and remember much, I have not yet seen with method or regularity." Strother had no way of knowing that his confusion was less in the viewer than in the viewed. Like Henry Adams, Strother was trying to fit together the pieces of an inscrutable puzzle which had no parts. Born during the administration of James Madison, he was much more at home at Independence Hall, where he read an address about his ancestor, Edmund Pendleton, a signer of the Declaration of Independence.[24] Yet even here he met a disturbing reminder of contemporary America: "On entering the room the first person I was accosted by was a venerable long white-haired and bearded man whom I thought was "Walt Whitman" but who turned out to be the omnipresent and irrepressible Col. J. Johnson, the artist . . . . Johnson invited me to meet Walt Whitman at his house in Camden, N. J. He said the poet was anxious to see me. Johnson was taken by several others for Walt and some amusing scenes occurred." Why was Whitman eager to see Strother again? The answer to this would tax the abilities of a Landor. It is regrettable that Strother did not accept the invitation, but comes as no surprise. At the Union League Club, Strother did meet Mark Twain and perhaps exchanged anecdotes, but about the humorist Strother recorded nothing but his name.

The notable and dignified celebration at Independence Hall was in striking contrast to the Fourth of July festivities at Berkeley Springs only a few days later. Early in the morning Strother mounted a wagon containing his son John and dog Zango and addressed an assembly of Sunday-school people, and at noon delivered an oration to the townspeople in the shaded square in front of the hotel. His address was printed, and if no better it is certainly no worse than most speeches given on such occasions.[25] But the fact that Strother was chosen to deliver the most important address in a hundred years of Berkeley

24. Strother's address was later published as "Edmund Pendleton of Virginia," *Pennsylvania Magazine*, III ([No. 3] 1879), 177-79.

25. *Historical Address* [delivered at Berkeley Springs, July 4, 1876] (Washington, 1876).

Springs history was a modest honor which he appreciated. If the nation was gradually forgetting Porte Crayon the writer, his town still respected David Strother the man. Nothing in his career was more appealing than his unaffected transition from the distinguished gathering of American worthies at Philadelphia to the assembled group of fellow townsmen at Berkeley. He took both occasions seriously, but it is a tribute to Berkeley that his greater preparation was for the less impressive audience. Had it not been for the ever-pressing financial obligations, Porte Crayon would have welcomed his disappearance from the public scene and submersion into the secluded and provincial life of his West Virginia village.

In the mid-seventies, the editors at *Harper's,* feeling that Porte Crayon was out of touch with the times, gave him little encouragement and looked to a younger generation of Southern writers for contributions. Early in 1874, Strother wrote in his journal: "The World has probably become sated with my style of goods. The keen edge of novelty has worn off and I have many rivals in art and literature, more than the world has ever known before, so that to make a stir again I must seek new fields." The first literary renaissance of the South was getting under way with the local-color stories of George Washington Cable, Mary N. Murfree, and Joel Chandler Harris, to mention only a few. Strother, as has been remarked, had been writing in the local color vein for over twenty years, if under the guise of the travelogue; he now undertook six articles, all of which were for *Harper's New Monthly Magazine,* but none of which was based on travel.[26] Through them he hoped to regain the popularity he had lost, and he nearly succeeded. Two of them must be rated among the best he ever did: "Confessions of a Candidate" is a skillful satire on politics, and "Old Time Militia Musters" is a broad burlesque of citizen soldiery. After these, his powers faltered and in 1879 he penned his last literary essay.

The Negro question had long interested him, and nothing better showed his adaptability to a changing era than his non-

26. "Our Negro Schools," XLIX (September, 1874), 457-68; "Confessions of a Candidate," LII (February, 1876), 329-46; "The Baby," LII (March, 1876), 538-49; "Boys and Girls," LIV (December, 1876), 19-32; "Old Time Militia Musters," LVII (July, 1878), 212-21; "Home," LVIII (January, 1879), 236-48.

partisan evaluation of that race in "Our Negro Schools." In preparation for this article, he visited the free colored schools in Martinsburg, Charles Town, and Harpers Ferry, and found that the equipment was up-to-date and the standards, at least among the younger students, matched those of white schools. Education had brought improvement in taste and morals but had weakened the Negro's skill and interest in the manual arts. Relations between former master and slave were uniformly good. "It suggests," he wrote as an aside to Northern fanatics, "that after all, the oppression was not so grievous and unmitigated as some have supposed, and the readiness with which the evil has been forgotten . . . is highly creditable to both parties."[27] He was pleased to see that the objectives of Negro education were practical rather than intellectual—the student would not be turned loose into the world with a head full of Latin quotations. Although he knew that education would not alone solve the problems of the Southern Negro, it would give him the training and the confidence to make his way alone. His article concluded with an affirmation of ability rather than privilege as the mark of the coming era: "The Southern country, with all its natural wealth, is now in the market, and in twenty years will belong neither to the speculators, politicians, nor thieves, but to those who may earn it by intelligent and persistent labor."[28] For all this, only a month before the article was published in *Harper's,* a Negro was lynched in Martinsburg. Strother had not known this kind of racial violence before the war.

Politics had long been treated in a peripheral manner in Strother's articles, but "Confessions of a Candidate" summarizes his political philosophy. Colonel Candid is a man of culture and honor who has retired to the little village of Hardscrabble. Having made the error of airing his political views to the editor of the local newspaper, he is waited upon by a delegation of the village bosses, all of them rogues, who request him to run for Congress. Duty-bound, the Colonel accepts and at once notices how the townspeople have changed toward him. Deference gives way to familiarity and to bullying. In short order, he is

27. "Our Negro Schools," *Harper's,* XLIX, 464.
28. *Ibid.,* p. 468.

compelled to contribute to the missionary society, to buy a
spavined horse, and to buy liquor for rascals whom formerly he
would not have allowed in his back door. His opponent is Ely
Squirms, impudent, ignorant, and brilliantly crafty. Squirms
reads the Colonel's campaign address to the illiterate constituents
who cannot read it for themselves: "In a line respectfully al-
luding to 'the masses,' he crimped the paper so as to make it read
'them asses of the Democracy.' The worst of it was, my phrase
was so inappropriate in our sparsely populated region that the
crimped reading seemed the most natural and obvious."[29] At
a public debate on the proposed Hardscrabble and Funksville
Railroad, Squirms wins the crowd by his promises, ignorance and
obsequiousness, while the Colonel without descending to the
level of the crowd logically proves that the railroad would be a
disaster to the community. Of course, Squirms wins the election
and is sent to Congress. Taxes are increased, the railroad is
built, carries one passenger, and is heard of no more. Strother
prefaced his essay with a quotation from "Coriolanus" and concluded it with an allusion from Plutarch: "The Athenian
populace were always jealous of character and ability, fearing to
intrust a strong man with power lest he should grow too strong
for them; preferring to suffer from the dishonesty and incapacity of a weak ruler, whom they might set up and pluck down
at will."[30] Strother felt that the American political system attracted the incompetents rather than the gifted. To his mind,
it was nothing short of miraculous that democracy worked at all.
"Confessions of a Candidate," which Strother regarded as the
most carefully written piece he had ever done, is an effective
blend of amusing satire and artful design. It stands as his political credo.

His next Hardscrabble essay, "Old Time Militia Musters,"
conforms to the more traditional style of Southern humor rather than the newer vein of local color. The quotation from
Dryden that is prefixed to the essay sets the stage:

> The country rings around with loud alarms,
> And now in fields the rude militia swarms; . . .

29. "Confessions of a Candidate," *Harper's,* LII, 340.
30. *Ibid.,* p. 346.

Of seeming arms to make a short assay,
Then hasten to be drunk—the business of the day.[31]

All classes, all ages were recruited for the militia. Officers were elected less for their military capacity than for their ability to whip any other man in the company. Colonel Swingletree is such an officer. On the mustering ground he never succeeds in substituting "right and left wheel" for "gee and haw," and he seldom is able to draw his rusty sword from its scabbard, but he holds his command together by the joint use of two fists and two barrels of raw whiskey. Strother's caricatures of rustic louts trying to tell left from right are equal to the best of Oliver H. Prince or Johnson Hooper.

It is regrettable that Strother did not continue with the Hardscrabble stories, which were successful in evoking the humor of a provincial Virginian town. His next three articles were less fortunate. "The Baby" and "Boys and Girls," companion pieces, are commonplace and sentimental essays which not even Porte Crayon's sketches successfully redeem. While his last *Harper's* article, "Home," is of limited interest, its picture of a couple returning to their home after the war is a pleasant and graceful narrative. With this, a twenty-six year association with Harper and Brothers ended. Fletcher Harper, Strother's friendly sponsor, had died in 1877, Dr. Guernsey had long departed, and H. M. Alden was little interested in Strother's work. "Sophistication" was to be the guiding editorial policy of *Harper's* during the next quarter-century, and its pages had no room for Porte Crayon.

After the break with *Harper's Monthly,* Strother cast about in search of other outlets for his writing. *Lippincott's* took his "A Visit to the Shrines of Virginia," an account of his trip to the Virginia Tidewater in 1849, a subject which was entirely in the spirit of the past, although none the worse for that. Newspapers provided him with a number of opportunities. "Old Fort Frederick" appeared in the *Baltimore Sun and Commerical Advertiser,* but the author was mortified with the paltry sum of seven dollars he received for it, hardly enough to cover his ex-

31. "Old Time Militia Musters," *Harper's,* LVII, 212.

penses. Much more promising was the Philadelphia *Weekly Times,* which was sponsoring a series of articles on Civil War themes, a favorite Strother subject. The *Times* took three of his unillustrated articles, "General Averell's Last Ride," "Banks in Louisiana," and "The Port Hudson Expedition," all written early in 1879. These were his last literary papers; at the age of sixty-three Porte Crayon terminated his literary career.

Chapter XI

Mexico and Beyond, 1879-1888

BY 1875, Strother had paid off his father's debts, some of which extended back forty years, and thereby won what he called "the great financial battle of the last ten years." His struggle for self-respect left him prostrate. A year later, he summarized his financial condition: "I enter my 61st year with 25¢ in my pocket, a thousand dollars in debt, but healthy, honourable, and impudent." Despite his pluck, he knew that unless something turned up he was destined to become the village wastrel he had written about thirty years before. As he looked back on his life, it seemed that his personal values were insufficient to cope with the complexities of the present: "I am beginning to feel that I have outlived my time. The problems of life which seemed clear enough thirty years ago are again becoming confused. My standards don't serve now for the measurement of anything either in the moral or material world . . . . Blundering ignorance and self-stultifying rascality seem to direct the destinies of mankind." Here again was the dilemma of Henry Adams—how to reconcile the absolute values of the past with the relative concepts of the present. Disenchantment with the grosser aspects of American life was overtaking the boundless optimism of the prewar years. The materialism of the Gilded Age baffled Strother, for whom abstractions like justice, honor, duty, and patriotism were sincere and meaningful convictions.

After the inauguration of Rutherford B. Hayes, friends urged Strother to join the ranks of office-seekers in Washington. Although he was loath to do this, necessity compelled him to visit Secretary Evarts of the State Department and to call upon the President, with whom he had campaigned during the Hunter raid in 1864. With greater vivacity than diplomacy, he corrected some of the President's faulty recollections of the campaign, but Hayes was favorably impressed by Porte Crayon.[1] No promises were made about a consular or diplomatic appointment, but General David Hunter, who was a power in Washington's political circles, actively promoted Strother's candidacy during the next two years. His name was submitted to Congress as the proposed consul general to Mexico in 1877 but no action was taken. He was neither disappointed nor surprised. Since the war his name had been mentioned so many times for foreign posts—Sardinia, Buenos Aires, Hong Kong, Rio de Janeiro—that Strother had quite wearied of the subject. He was too proud to beg or beseech. As Washington seemed to have forgotten him, so he forgot Washington. For his friend Dr. Boyd Pendleton, he designed a cottage (which fell down a few years later) and he wrote legal papers for villagers ("I delivered Hammond's papers who promised to pay some time"). Like Colonel Candid, he accepted an invitation to run for the state senate, campaigned for ten days, and spoke at a Sunday School picnic: "As I was at the climax of my address, a jackass responded from an adjoining field with several lusty brays, which amused the audience more than my speech did." The candidate withdrew from the campaign. Once each week he led his side to a noisy victory at the village debating society ("Resolved: that women should preach").

Meanwhile, his financial plight had not improved. His old Baltimore friend, Benjamin F. Latrobe, died before the collected works of Porte Crayon could be prepared for publication and the project died with him. There were many opportunities to write up visits to mines, boom towns, and railroads, but the

1. Shortly after this interview, Hayes wrote to Evarts, "I conceive with General Hunter in thinking favorably of Genl. Strother. Please confer with him about the case of Genl. S." Letter from Hayes to Evarts, August 1, 1877. In the National Archives.

corporate directors of these enterprises had considerably more zeal than money. By late in 1878, Strother's situation had become so perilous that an unexpected knock at the front door became for him the rap of another bill collector. Household expenses were cut to the bleakest minimum. A few genteel boarders, all of them carefully recommended by friends, helped the family through the summer season, and during the winter they lived with Mrs. Strother's mother in Charles Town—a sensible old Virginia lady who had put her money in Baltimore banks during the first year of the Civil War.

But early in 1879, Strother's luck abruptly changed. With surprise, he discovered that President Hayes had again sent his name to the Senate for confirmation as consul general to Mexico. The news was received with mixed sentiments in West Virginia. Many Democrats and former Confederates still thought of Strother as the right-hand man of the devilish General Hunter. Many Republicans protested that he had not been active enough in the political machinery of West Virginia. This excerpt from a letter sent to a West Virginia Congressman by a constituent represents one side of public opinion: "He has not aided the party by his speeches and writings. His time since the war has been occupied with literary pursuits and hunting the deer in the Mountains of West Virginia .... His voice has not been raised, nor his pen wielded in behalf of the Rep. Party."[2] Fortunately, the efforts of men like General Hunter, ex-Governor A. J. Boreman, and Francis H. Pierpont prevailed over those of the party partisans. On April 3, 1879, Strother's appointment was announced, and he was deeply moved when former enemies like C. J. Faulkner and Andrew Hunter stepped forward to offer their hands after nearly two decades of enmity. He did not, however, re-enter public life by preference; necessity drove him from his retirement at Berkeley Springs. To Mrs. Pierpont, he wrote: "I have enjoyed the 13 years of peaceful, half rural life at Berkeley more than I can express. It was the goal I had longed for and dreamed of all through my varied and tempestuous career and my dreams were fully realized .... So

2. Letter from Robert Northcutt to Hon. Stanley Mathews, January 18, 1879. In the National Archives.

contented have I been that nothing but financial necessity could
have induced me to leave it. But I shall go out into the world
again rested and refreshed with those thirteen pleasant years
ever green in my memory."[3] The house at Berkeley Springs was
closed, the key given to a neighbor, and Strother with his wife
and son hurried to New York to board the *Morro Castle,* which
would take them to Cuba on the first lap to Mexico. On
April 23, the steamer left New York. Sitting back to back on
its top deck was an elderly couple. Mrs. Strother looked homeward at the receding shoreline while her husband looked sea-
ward toward the unknown—Mexico.

On May 16, 1879, Strother arrived in Mexico City and three
days later assumed his position as consul general, responsible for
the twenty-six other consulates scattered throughout the republic.
Because of the Maximilian affair, many European nations had no
official representatives in Mexico at this time, and the American
officers were called upon to settle affairs relating to many European citizens. But the duties of the consul general were not
heavy, and Strother had plenty of time to himself after he had
transferred the office to his private quarters at No. 7 Calle de
Seminario. He drew a salary amounting to about $175 per
month, exclusive of occasional fees, which was enough for him
to live modestly and even to save small amounts.

Diplomatic relations between the United States and Mexico
were strained, largely because of frequent border disturbances:
on the Rio Grande frontier cattle raids had become an organized
business, border smuggling went unchecked, and filibustering ex-
peditions by both Mexican and American troops often brought
the countries to the verge of formal hostilities.[4] The Mexican
president, Porfirio Diaz, honestly desired peace with the United
States—one of his first official acts had been payment of the
first installment of a long overdue debt—but because his power
was limited in the northern part of his country, he was unable to
satisfy the American demands that the Mexican offenders be

3. Letter from Strother to Mrs. F. H. Pierpont, April 5, 1879. Among the
Pierpont Papers at the library of West Virginia University.
4. Robert D. Gregg, *The Influence of Border Troubles on Relations between
the United States and Mexico, 1876-1910* (Baltimore, 1937).

punished.[5] At the time of Strother's arrival, the tension and tempers were high. As head consul, Strother was less concerned with improving diplomatic relations than with the encouragement of commerical relations and investment in Mexico. More specifically, he was to search out all the possibilities for trade and to publicize them through his reports to the Department of State in Washington. Yet it seems that Strother was entrusted with an authority not customarily given to a consular officer. The American minister, John W. Foster, had long been distrusted by certain members of the State Department, and Strother was requested on several occasions to write reports upon the political conditions of the country. At the end of his tour of duty, he was told by a high-ranking Mexican official that informants in Washington had notified Diaz that the American policy toward Mexico would be largely determined by the dispatches of General Strother. If this be true, it nevertheless came as a complete surprise to Strother and it never interfered with his warm friendship with Minister Foster, who in 1880 was transferred to St. Petersburg. His journals record unusual courtesies and attentions by Diaz, and these may be interpreted as a confirmation of Strother's important role.

Immediately after arriving in Mexico, the consul general began the study of Spanish, which he mastered within a short time. This application to the language was itself unusual in a period when foreign appointees were drawn from the political rolls and often could not speak their own language properly, to say nothing of another. During his six years in office, Strother wrote two hundred and seventy dispatches for the State Department, some of them extensive analyses of climate, railways, health, politics, agriculture, and mining. Sometimes Porte Crayon's humor lights up the dispatches now in the National Archives, as when for example, he requests a new American flag for the consulate window: "Our diminutive bit of bunting flutters like a toy banner or a boy's pocket handkerchief amidst the flowing from the voluminous pavilions surrounding it, some-

5. Pauline S. Relyea, *Diplomatic Relations between the United States and Mexico under Porfirio Diaz, 1876-1910* (Smith College Studies in History, Vol. X, 1924).

what to the mortification of our National Pride."[6] His duties
were often absurd, and his journals record unusual requests. A
young Mexican lady desired to give the American government a
pair of young tigers and applied to the consul general for his
advice; a New York freight agent wrote to inquire whether the
monkeys of Ixtaccilinati fed on wormwood—if they did he could
prove that the Chinese visited Mexico in the sixth century; a
world traveler asked him to find some mules and balloons left
in Mexico twenty-two years before (and Strother privately recorded, "I think his intellect must have escaped in one of his
baloons and never recovered.") He traveled widely in Mexico
and filled his journals with fresh impressions. At some future
day, he promised himself, he would arrange to publish his
Mexican notes.

Strother was by far the most popular American in Mexico.
Even President Diaz called upon the consul general, a visit
transcending the requirements of diplomatic etiquette. Inadequate funds prevented the Strothers from entertaining upon a
grand scale or joining the fast international set, but Strother did
become the close friend of European and Mexican people of all
classes and conditions. Nearly all American travelers to Mexico
sought him out—Joel C. Harris, Thomas Janvier, George Bancroft, General Lee's daughter—but his most memorable acquaintance was General Ulysses S. Grant, who visited Mexico
in 1880 shortly after his world tour. The General, feted all over
the world in an unprecedented style for an American abroad,
was interested in Mexican mining as a possible investment.
Strother, who had been an admirer of Grant since the dark days
of 1864 when he had wrested victory from three years of stale-
mate, was the principal speaker at the banquet held in honor
of the General on his arrival. The two became instant friends.[7]
Strother saw him as the best representative of the modern American—expedient, democratic, modest, and intelligent. "I found
him a ready and intelligent conversationalist, and altogether
unpretending, earnest, and kindly in manner," he wrote. Dur-

6. Diplomatic Report, January 10, 1881. In the National Archives.
7. The Grant-Strother relationship is developed at greater length in Cecil
D. Eby, Jr., " 'Porte Crayon' Meets General Grant," *Illinois Historical Society
Journal,* LII (Summer, 1959), 229-47.

ing one of their conversations the subject of the Civil War was brought up and tactfully managed by both ex-soldiers: "General Grant asked my proper title. I told him it was General. He said he had been calling me Colonel, but would make up for it in future by calling me Lieutenant General. I thanked him and hoped I would never have the opportunity to earn that title in a war at home. He replied, 'I hope so too, sincerely; neither you nor any one else.'" Strother accompanied the Grant party both on its visits to the Mexican War battlefields and to the mines of Pachuca. On these occasions Strother became Grant's Boswell, recording even such minutiae as the hat size of the General. Strother was particularly struck by the delicate sensibility which underlay Grant's single breach of etiquette—a polite but firm refusal to attend a bull fight gotten up in his honor. Often during his Mexican sojourn Grant escaped from state functions to chew his innumerable cigars in the back office of the consulate, where he and Strother discussed their favorite subjects, war and politics. In later years, Strother assembled his notes for a reminiscence of the general he so much admired, but the manuscript was never completed.

By 1883, Strother's position in Mexico had become important only as a source of income, for he was tiring of the country. Deaths and suicides in the diplomatic corps, both American and European, made Mexico "the land of gory tragedy." Yet moods of homesickness were usually dispersed after reading the stacks of West Virginia newspapers in every mail: "Yellow fever, Sunday fanaticism, and Rebel supremacy made me feel glad I was in Mexico." Twice, late in 1881 and early in 1884, Strother returned to West Virginia on leaves of absence, and these trips home proved all too short. He found that most of the old enmity had died; he was again Dave Strother rather than a Virginia Yankee. He overcame his pride for a visit to "The Bower," home of the Dandridges, his cousins and friends from boyhood until the war. This family had supported the Confederacy, their house had been the headquarters of Jeb Stuart, and Strother had not ventured near the place nor talked with its occupants in a quarter-century. The meeting was at first awkwardly strained, but a jolly frankness soon cleared the air. All were touched at the friendship renewed after so many years of bitterness and misunderstanding. The visit to "The Bower" symbolized a new attitude toward Strother—one of reconciliation and good feelings.

The arrival of American engineers and the building of railroads in Mexico brought many changes to the people. The country was in an era of transition which affected its personal mores as well as its public welfare. Strother noted that wooden effigies of the Catholic saints were burned by locomotives for firewood and remarked, "Jesus Christ don't visit this country since the liberals got into power." He recorded an anecdote which further illustrated how Mexican values were breaking down under contact with the Gringos:

A North American railroader entering the office of a Mexican employee saw a very handsome pen knife lying on the desk. "Whose knife?" exclaimed the American with evident admiration. The Mexican with accustomed courtesy replied, "It is mine, and yours if you will deign to accept it." The Northman thanked him and coolly put the knife in his pocket and walked out, leaving the Mexican dumbfounded. Shortly after he bought another knife and laid it on the desk as usual. Another American acquaintance coming in asked with like interest, "Whose knife is this?" "It's mine, by God!" said the Mexican hastily snatching up his knife and thrusting it deep down into his pocket. The Mexicans are evidently becoming Americanized.

The election of Grover Cleveland in 1884 meant, as a matter of course, that Strother would be relieved of his Mexican post. He was unaware that attempts were being made by strangers as well as friends to have him retained. George Peabody, entirely on his own volition, wrote the President as follows:

I have no personal interest whatever in Genl. Strother, having only met him in my recent trip there, but I was much impressed with his usefulness and fitness for the duties of the office.

I came home from Mexico particularly impressed with the importance of having our government represented by such men as General Strother . . . . If it be deemed wise by you I feel certain that the interest of our government will be advanced by retaining Genl. Strother.[8]

With his natural tolerance and his cosmopolitan spirit, Strother had been an ideal consul general, but was not reluctant to be replaced. His six years in Mexico had rounded out his varied career and they had passed agreeably. From his salary and incidental fees he had saved four thousand dollars, which he thought should be enough to support himself during the years remaining. On July 4, 1885, he delivered an Independence Day speech to the American colony and four days later wrote his last consular dispatch and closed his office. On the same day, he left by train for the United States. He thought fondly of returning to literature, but he was without self-deception: "I may spread my wings again for higher flights that I have yet attempted. The longing fancies of an old man—irrealizable." Strother was nearly seventy years old.

Historians of Mexican-American relations are generally agreed that the relationship between the two countries improved markedly after 1880.[9] Doubtless the increased stability of the Mexican government was the principal cause of this. Strother, however, had contributed to the favorable surge in commerce between the two countries. His reports had helped to reassure American businessmen that investments in Mexico would be profitable.[10] Moreover, Strother had been an officer whose intelligence, sympathy, personal honor, and venerable mien had reflected favorably upon the American government. Perhaps John Hay's remark upon Strother's consul service is the best summation: "He is first class, an honor to literature and to the service."[11]

For the three remaining years of his life, Strother and his wife lived during the summers in Berkeley Springs and during the

8. Letter from George Peabody to Grover Cleveland, May 12, 1885. In the National Archives.

9. Gregg, *Border Troubles* pp. 146 ff., and Relyea, *Diplomatic Relations,* pp. 42 ff.

10. Imports increased from 462,384 tons in 1880 to 2,685,780 tons in 1885; three railroads were built which connected the United States and Mexico. Relyea, *Diplomatic Relations,* pp. 51-52.

11. According to James Blaine's secretary, Hay said this to Blaine. Quoted in Strother's Journal, December 3, 1881.

winters with his wife's mother in Charles Town. His literary energy was expended only in long letters to his son John, who was attending Peekskill Military Institute in New York. Despite his many disappointments as a writer, Porte Crayon encouraged John's literary talent and tactfully dissuaded him from entering the military profession:

In a Democratic country like ours, whose whole military establishment is neither as large, nor as well paid as the police force of a large city, where the popular jealousy of strong government enables politician and demagogues to starve out, insult, and bedevil the military profession in every way, the army in time of peace is a service in which a man may spend his life amid more hardship, exposure, and neglect . . . than can be found in almost any other career . . . . Now you seem to have become disgusted with your experiences as a lieutenant, and we hear little of you now about the military department of your school, but we hear of your lonely rambles in the hills, and have poems for criticism, and glimpses of literary aspirations, which indicate nothing of the brutal, practical, patient qualities required for a soldier, but rather the enthusiastic fervor and high wrought imagination which find their natural and noblest expression in the pen of a writer . . . . If I have not diagnosticated your case correctly for the present, I will probably be correct a year or two hence.[12]

Although he wished John to become a writer, Strother wanted him to become a successful one. *"Materialism,"* he told him, "is the ruling power in the world and your career must be in its service. I was educated and served in the court of idealism, whose power is now declining."[13] To assist his son with something more than words, he planned a fresh travel series which would be the work of "Porte Crayon and son."

In the middle of April, 1887, they started together for the Eastern Shore of Virginia, a region still remote from the main thoroughfares of postwar America. The hospitality, ease, and gracefulness of the region recalled the Virginia which Strother had recorded in *Virginia Illustrated* nearly thirty-five years be-

12. Letter from David Strother to John Strother, January 27, 1886. Among the family papers.

13. Letter from David Strother to John Strother, January 1, 1888. Among the family papers.

fore. There was a wealth of colorful material which filled his notebook. In Accomac County the travelers sketched the local characters and dug into the peculiar social history of the region. Wildlife abounded. From a boat they bagged seventy-eight birds in three hours off Hog Island. For three glorious weeks Strother and his son combined work with pleasure, but fatigue broke up the excursion prematurely. This was the last tour of Porte Crayon, and his account of it was never written.

While in Mexico, Strother had been plagued by publishers begging for his book on that country, and after his return to America he still received letters requesting that he write it. On a visit to Harpers in 1885, H. M. Alden unbended to show him great deference and even Thomas Nast came upstairs for an autograph. Strother, however, did little more than review his journals and make endless preparations for writing. Age and idleness were not readily overcome: "The Muses who were the sweethearts of my capricious youth, alternately fondled and disdained, must now be solicitously wooed to become the companions and counselors of age. Furthermore I must leave off coquetting with the nine fair damsels and be content with the smiles of one." While wintering at Charles Town in the winter of 1887, he rented an abandoned law office on the courthouse lawn, furnished it with two chairs, a store-box desk, and a feather duster, and prepared for serious work on his Mexican notes. He wrote his son facetiously: "I burn soft coal and make my own fires, brush up with a bunch of turkey feathers your grandmother gave me, and carry out my ashes in my overcoat (enveloped in a newspaper, of course) being determined to keep independent of those social nuisances, women and niggers, and that no floor sweeping, stove polishing cranks shall profane my temple of the muses, consecrated to literature and dirt."[14] From his window he could look out into the yard of the courthouse or see on the opposite corner the jail from which John Brown had come on the morning of his execution thirty years before. He did a great amount of thinking but little writing. His

14. Letter from David Strother to John Strother, November 24, 1887. Among the family papers.

papers brought back the past vividly, and he had few thoughts to waste upon the future.

Strother showed few signs of advanced years. Although his famous beard was now completely white, he retained his wiry frame and walked with a springy step. Even during the bitter winter of 1887-1888, one of the severest in Virginia history, he seldom failed to take his daily walk along the railroad to the Crane farmhouse. The Cranes were long gone from "Locust Grove" and few of his boyhood friends remained. David E. Henderson was dead and James Ranson, his companion in the jaunt up the Valley of Virginia a half century before, was dying, but Strother refused to fold his hands "and wait for death like the old bogies I see about Charles Town." No fan letter went unanswered, and Porte Crayon retained his sense of humor. Hearing that a volcanic eruption was throwing up water and mud in the heart of Charleston, South Carolina, he wryly remarked, "This may be the remnant of the Secession sentiment in that region." As late as February, 1888, he read two books which represented the dual interests of a lifetime—Sherman on war and Stillman on Ruskin. The first impressed him more, for it embodied his own axiom for life, "action, action, action." One day on the streets of Charles Town, he was deeply moved when a Confederate veteran took his hand and said, "General, you have a splendid intellect, and from what I hear, something that is even better, an excellent heart." This simple remark from a former enemy was better than the praise of the mighty.

On February 27, after a visit to a cousin's house in the country, Strother returned to town, stoked a fire in his office, and spent the whole evening in the dark alone with his thoughts. On the following day, he visited the studio of an art teacher at the female seminary, and from her window noted that the view stretched across the wintry fields toward the gap at Harpers Ferry. This was his last view of the Valley of Virginia (he did not record that John Brown, standing on the scaffold, had also looked across the same fields and had said, "This is a beautiful country. . . .") On March 1, a cold caught at his cousin's house became aggressive. Strother continued to walk to his office, where he stuffed himself with calomel. On March 3, he felt improved but still weak. His last entry in the journal was made on this day:

March 3: Saturday. Bright and cooler. Passed a tolerably comfortable night and becoming restless at six, Madame got me a cup of coffee and later a breakfast of beef tea and crackers. My cold and cough apparently broken up, but I am feeble and without appetite. The Doctor came and prescribed quinine in a liquid as being best, he also advised toddy. A band of itinerant musicians appeared on the street and played along the house. I hoisted the window and threw them a dime, when in response they struck up "Yankee Doodle." I am curious to know if it was intentional—or haphazard. Dined on two plates of chicken broth and toast and afterward went to my office and made a fire and dozed a while. Then got my watch regulated feeling entirely relieved and clear-headed and disposed for exercise.

If he ever solved the mystery of the musicians and their "Yankee Doodle," the information was not recorded. His physical condition rapidly became worse. Porte Crayon died from pneumonia on March 8, 1888.[15] Nearly illegible at the very end of his journal is what seems to be his last communication to the world—"Omar Khayyam-Rubaiyat."

15. Obituaries appeared in many newspapers. See the *New York Times,* March 9, 1888; the *Baltimore Sun,* March 9, 1888; and the *Virginia Free Press* (Charles Town, W. Va.), March 15, 1888. Strother was buried in the Green Hill Cemetery in Martinsburg next to his first wife. The funeral, called by the *Virginia Free Press* "one of the largest ever witnessed in Martinsburg," was held on March 10. Mary H. Strother, who inherited much of her mother's property, died in 1913 and was buried to the left of her husband. John Strother, their son, after a varied career as an engineer, a soldier in the Spanish-American War, and a politician, died in 1923. Four of Porte Crayon's grandchildren are still living: Mr. David H. Strother of Milwaukee, Mrs. Louise Strother Shepard of Falls Church, Va., Mrs. Emily Strother Kreuttner of North Tarrytown, N. Y., and Mr. Charles Porter Strother of Grosse Pointe Park, Mich.

Chapter XII

Evaluation

His Ideas

BORN during the presidency of James Madison, Strother died during the first administration of Grover Cleveland. His seventy-one years spanned a period of incredible change—probably greater than any other such period in history—so that the "hobgoblin" consistency is no more apparent in his life and thought than in the tumultuous period in which he lived. He was roughly contemporaneous with Whitman, Lowell, and Melville, and like them he reflected both hope and despair, both clarity and confusion. Years before the speculations of Henry Adams, Strother emotionally worked out a similar thesis —singleness of moral and social principles was giving way to multiplicity and confusion. In his lifetime, he saw the aristocratic conception of life fall before the democratic, an agrarian way of life replaced by an industrial, and romantic idealism vanish before relativistic realism. Brought up on Scott, he died in the Whitman era, and he was always closer to the former. The Civil War split his life in two and forced him to face both halves. The first part looked backward to the patrician absolutes of the nineteenth century, a simpler world controlled by those men who combined common sense with uncommon dedication. The second part faced the democratic flux of the twentieth century, a world of unceasing and often purposeless change. As a writer, Porte Crayon caught the flavor of the first and was unable to sound the depths of the second. His writings of the

1870's, for example, show little awareness of the dynamic forces at work upon American life after the Civil War. Strother continued to express the past in the manner of his earlier work. His journals, however, record more fully his thoughts and observations about modern America from 1865 to 1888. He was a recorder of intuitive insights rather than a systematic philosopher, and for this reason it is often difficult to formulate with absolute certainty his political and social philosophy. He did not avoid inconsistencies; sometimes, for example, he was skeptical about democratic government, and at other times he was hopeful. Yet certain ideas are repeated more than once in his journals throughout the years, and it is possible to discern the general framework within which his thoughts operated.

Strother believed that emotion was a more trustworthy guide than reason. Man's animal rather than his rational nature motivated him in affairs of life. As a result, Strother was interested in concrete realities and bothered little with abstract intangibles. He grasped the object or the particular case and distrusted the ideal or the general law: "Simple human nature underlies all philosophy, social and moral. Ideas are said to control society but the inherent natures control ideas . . . . Men do what they desire and find good reasons for it afterward. They seize greedily upon ideas and appear to be swept away by them when all the while the motive is found in the simple selfish underlying principle—self-love." He doubted that human nature would ultimately improve, although he admitted that physically constituted externals could be changed. This view, doubtless derived in part from Voltaire, put Strother in the camp of the anti-optimists. Long before the term *relativism* had come into general use, Strother wrote, "There is no positive vice or virtue in human nature, . . . all is relative and mixed." This principle, he claimed, had been the leading philosophic rule of his life. Essentially, it placed ethics outside the requirements of a divine being and within the frame of human possibility. Speculations upon the nature of God were wholly useless, for God's position in the universe was inscrutable to man. Many years before he had read Herbert Spencer, Strother developed a similar notion of the unknowable. John Pendleton Kennedy once tried to interest Strother in spiritualism, but without much success. He refused to speculate upon matters which could never be known: "My belief is that it is not given to man to know these things . . . . They confuse, stultify, and absorb to the detriment of man's practical utility and therefore without pretending to despise or discredit the phenomena, it is nevertheless unwise for a man to trouble himself with such subjects." As a Southerner brought up in a culture not inordinately religion-directed, Strother was perhaps far less disturbed by the conception of a pilotless universe than was the New Englander. Deism had always attracted the enlightened Southerner and doubtless was another factor in Strother's unconcern with supernatural religion. Whereas Henry Adams found that shaking off his religious indoctrination was accompanied by the chills of cosmic doubt, Strother was little concerned about the solution of unsolvable riddles.

The first half of the nineteenth century was the era of reform. Controversies concerning abolitionism, capital punishment, education, the position of the female, the nature of marriage, property rights, and dozens of other questions raged without cessation. Whatever their differences were, both Poe and Strother held one idea in common—a belief in change rather than progress. Poe contended that reformers annihilated the individual by aiding the mass and that reform had no real support in human nature.[1] Strother's conservatism took a similar view. Both looked upon the reformer as a crank whose freakishness could cause more harm than good. The shock of the Civil War was for Strother ample evidence of this. "Perhaps the greatest evils that afflict society," he wrote, "are those produced by the attempts of well-intentioned but ignorant zealots to manage and mend that which they can not control and do not understand."[2] To deal with mankind it was necessary to work within human capacities—however paltry these might be—instead of superimposing ambiguous ideals from outside the human understanding. Doubtless thinking of the troublesome "isms" of his day, Stroth-

1. Ernest Marchand, "Poe as Social Critic," *American Literature,* VI (March, 1934), 28-43.
2. "Personal Recollections of the War, Sixth Paper," *Harper's New Monthly Magazine,* XXXIV (March, 1867), 434.

er wrote in his New England series, "Why should a man carp at the world? Why undertake to tinker at creation? Can he mend it? Some people think they can; I do not."[3] For a man of Strother's realistic temper, Brook Farm was little better than applied lunacy.

Strother's religion was pragmatic. He seemed to have no conception of immortal life, and relying upon his senses rather than ideas, he accepted the wise teachings of the Bible and other religious books without referring them to supernatural agencies. A strong sense of fatalism led him often to express his favorite maxim, "Man proposes, God disposes." Strother believed that religion would be more effective if based upon deeds rather than faith, for theologians too often mistook dogma for morality. Institutionalized Christianity was base and degrading:

Perhaps the world would get on better . . . if the worship demanded was good works and good will to our neighbors rather than servile flattery and silly ceremonies, degrading alike to the worshipper and the worshipped. . . . The God now in vogue is but the image of an Oriental despot, cruel, tyrannical, passionate, vindictive, vain, and vacillating as the worse types of that class are represented. He is supposed to be pleased and influenced by the basest and most fulsome flattery, humiliating genuflections, beggary, lies, shams, and pretences of admiration and devotion . . . . It is time for a new God and new forms.

Part of the extraordinary success of Christianity, Strother thought, lay in its pretending to answer the riddle of the universe; but he believed that man could find enough to do in this life without worrying about the next. At the same time, he was not excited by the controversy between science and religion which shook the metaphysical foundations of the nineteenth century; both were but efforts to rationalize and to justify personal opinions. In his journal he wrote: "Whether the priest or the pedagogue have guessed nearer the truth I don't know or care, for I am sure neither of them know any more about it than I do myself."

3. "A Summer in New England, First Paper," *Harper's New Monthly Magazine*, XXI (June, 1860), 2.

Strother's political ideology was also pragmatic. Government had but little relation to individual happiness, and "opinion is geographical." No matter what party ruled or what philosophy prevailed, power would ultimately fall into the hands of the strong. "In spite of all our efforts at Free Government (so called) we must confess that all power in the end falls into the hands of the able and ambitious." Democracy was a system of checks whereby the weak exercised their control over the strong by delegating power to the unexceptional rather than the exceptional man. Strother doubted that it would last indefinitely. In America, the political system had hacked leadership to an abysmally low level. The process of democratic leveling had eaten like a cancer into the whole national organism until it threatened to destroy the nation upon which it had fed. He anticipated a class struggle in America between the plutocracy and the mob. No victory was really possible, for if the former won we should have despotism, and if the latter won, we should have anarchy.

Against the rampant sectionalism which characterized the first half of the nineteenth century, Strother stood firmly for nationalism. He had been reared as a Virginian with faith in an agrarian economy and an aristocratic society. He transcended these provincial limitations, however, and obtained an appreciation of America as wide, though perhaps not as detailed, as Whitman's. A year after the Civil War Strother wrote: "I abhor the South, I despise the West, I ignore the East, and damn the North. I acknowledge nothing but nationality and the American people, no country but the United States." Although he never learned to admire the values of the New Englander, he nevertheless respected New England energy, persistence, and ingenuity. He saw that the Northern way of life would prevail over the Southern, and was too much the pragmatist to sing psalms over a dead horse. He insisted upon a basic principle of human relationship—tolerance. For this reason, Melville was his favorite American writer:

I am now disposed to let people's harmless little fetishes alone. I take off my hat to an inoffensive belief and with Melville am ready to burn tobacco before the pocket idol of a gentlemanly pagan companion, Queequeg. But when Belshazzer the king sets up a graven

image and with the sound of trumpets . . . commands the world to
bow down, I will not bow . . . . When the dogma becomes ferocious,
arrogant, and tyrannical, I rise against it.

His course in the Civil War, one motivated solely by personal
conviction and public duty, proved that Strother not only
had such principles but also that he was prepared to fight for
them. From first to last, David Strother was an adamantine
individualist whose mind was skeptical and concrete rather than
optimistic and abstract. Endowed with common sense, broaden-
ed by wide reading, and conditioned by an unusually diversified career, he was an outstanding example of the individualistic
Virginian of the John Randolph stamp, but without the graceless
and arrogant qualities.

His Work

As a literary figure, Porte Crayon has been overlooked by
most scholars of American literature.[4] While writers whose
popularity and accomplishments are far less remarkable have
been treated in dissertations, anthologies, and literary histories,
Strother has not yet received the critical attention he deserves.
There are several reasons for this oversight. First of all, his published articles are scattered through fifty volumes of *Harper's
Monthly* (only *Virginia Illustrated* was published in book form),
a situation which makes a reading of his complete works a physical exercise. His writings were never collected, nor was any
bibliographical study ever made. Porte Crayon remains, quite
literally, buried among thousands of pages of *Harper's*. Second-
ly, when studies of regionalism were made, Strother was a writer
who did not easily fit into a particular section. He had described
the United States from New Hampshire to New Orleans, not
merely a restricted area such as Virginia or West Virginia.
"Charles Egbert Craddock" is linked with Tennessee, Grace

4. No general anthology of American literature or literary history has
treated Strother's writings with the exception of John S. Hart, *A Manual of
American Literature* (Philadelphia, 1873), and Edwin A. Alderman *et al., A
Library of Southern Literature,* XI (Atlanta, 1907). There have been a thesis
and a dissertation written about Strother: Sister Joseph Miriam Costello, "The
Life and Works of David Strother—'Porte Crayon'" (St. John's University,
1956), and Cecil D. Eby, Jr., "A Critical Biography of David Hunter Strother,
'Porte Crayon'" (University of Pennsylvania, 1958).

King with Louisiana, Richard Malcolm Johnson with Georgia, and so on, but Strother was for many Virginians a renegade who had repudiated his state and its people. Virginia was more inclined to forget him than to remember him, and West Virginia produced no circle of regionalistic writers into whose company Strother could have been admitted. He was a member of no literary coterie. In Berkeley Springs, he was isolated from other writers and artists and did not have the benefit of their discussion and criticism. Except for Philip P. Kennedy, it is doubtful if any other writer saw one of his manuscripts before it was published. Because of his isolation—perhaps greater than that endured by any other American writer of his age—his work suffered and, worse than this, no group of associates sought to perpetuate his name. A third reason for his neglect is that he wrote almost entirely within a literary genre that has never been accepted without reservation as belonging to belles-lettres. Critical works treating travel literature as literature are virtually nonexistent. While in recent years there has been a revival of interest in American travel narratives, this interest has been demonstrated by the social rather than the literary historian. Nearly all major American writers from Irving to James wrote of their travels, but investigation of such narratives has resulted from an initial interest in their other works. Strother, however, wrote little else. Had he prepared ten novels of Southern life, he would doubtless be rated above John Esten Cooke and William Alexander Caruthers. Instead, he wrote non-fiction and his accomplishments have been forgotten.

Within the past twenty years, there have been signs of a reawakened interest in Porte Crayon. His delineations of real scenes and real characters—which worked to his disadvantage when such pictures were fresh in everyone's mind—have become more valuable with the passing of time. Writers as different as Van Wyck Brooks and Elmer Davis have found that Strother's narratives are delightfully readable,[5] reprints of his articles have appeared in newspapers and periodicals from Massachusetts to

5. Van Wyck Brooks, *The Times of Melville and Whitman* (New York, 1947). Elmer Davis, "Constant Reader," *Harper's Magazine,* CCI (October, 1950), 161-72.

North Carolina,[6] anthologies of American folklore and Civil
War history have included samples of his work,[7] and a collection
of his best writings and illustrations pertaining to the South has
been published.[8] However, the greatest tributes have come
from West Virginia, which recalls Strother as its first and foremost writer. In 1941, the "Porte Crayon Memorial Society" was
formed by a group of West Virginia sportsmen and historians.
These had three objectives: to dedicate a mountain in his honor,
to establish a state park or forest in his memory, and to collect
funds for publishing his collected works in a single volume.[9]
Only the first was successfully accomplished before the Second
World War broke up the Society. On July 5, 1941, Haystack
Knob, a peak some fifteen miles south of the Virginian Canaan
country, was renamed Mount Porte Crayon in honor of David
Strother. Rising 4760 feet in height, Mount Porte Crayon is the
second highest peak in West Virginia and is probably the only
mountain in the United States named for a man of letters.[10]
When one recalls Strother's affection for the Allegheny high-
lands, the monument is strikingly appropriate. He loved mountains, whether the Blue Ridge, Apennines, Alleghenies, or Rock-
ies, and the fact that loyal sportsmen comprised the inner ring
of the Society would have delighted Porte Crayon.

Two major influences were paramount in shaping the literature of David Strother: the romantic tradition of English letters
and the indigenous tradition of early nineteenth-century America,
especially the agrarian culture of Virginia. From the first he

6. Among them, the *Vineyard Gazette* (Edgartown, Mass.), n.d.; *Sunday
Post* (Salisbury, N. C.), August 10, 1952; *Tableland Trails* (Oakland, Md.), I
(Spring, 1953), 14-23. Also, *Virginia Cavalcade,* III (Autumn, 1953), 4-7; III
(Spring, 1954), 23-29; IV (Winter, 1954), 23-29; and IV (Winter, 1954), 32-
37.
7. See "Piloting a Flatboat," an excerpt from "A Winter in the South," in
B. A. Botkin (ed.) *A Treasury of Southern Folklore* (New York, 1949), pp.
429-30; and three excerpts from "Personal Recollections of the War" in Henry
Steele Commager (ed.), *The Blue and the Gray* (Indianapolis, 1950), II, 176-80,
203-6, and 207-12.
8. *The Old South Illustrated* (Chapel Hill, N. C., 1959).
9. From a mimeographed prospectus of the Porte Crayon Memorial Society,
1941.
10. Theodore Winthrop gave his name to a glacier, but Strother's claim
as the only literary man who has a mountain named for him stands un-
challenged to date.

obtained his method; from the second, his materials. Lacking a usable native tradition, American writers prior to the Civil War turned to English models, imitating and adapting them to convey American themes. For Strother, the writers of greatest importance during his formative years were Scott and Byron. Scott was read to him as a child, and he was the only writer whom Strother consistently reread. The moonlit scene at the wizard's tomb in *The Lay of the Last Minstrel* was Strother's favorite passage in literature. According to Professor Hubbell, Scott—by far the most popular writer in the South—taught his readers loyalty, self-sacrifice, chivalry, honor, courage, and hospitality.[11] Without exception, these qualities were ones most pronounced in David Strother. If Scott did not cause the so-called chivalric tradition of the South, he nevertheless confirmed its values and gave it literary sanction. The mountainous border country in his novels was readily transferred to Strother's Virginia, and the sturdy yeomanry and handsome nobility were as easily found in the Blue Ridge country as in the Scottish lowlands. Scott's formula, consisting of regionalism, romantic landscape description, and a sense of the past, was the same which Strother, by accident or design, used extensively in his own work. Irving had first analyzed the formula and used it, Kennedy shortly thereafter employed it, and finally Strother found it serviceable. The secondary characteristics of Scott's writing, according to Professor Orians,[12] are portrayal of local and national legends, stress upon dialect and regional characteristics, the glamor of the remote and the strange, depiction of humble people, and antiquarianism in defining an older culture and tradition. Each of these could become the subject for an essay on Strother's literature, but examples of each must suffice here for purposes of illustration. He imbued the Shenandoah Valley with synthetic and oral legends; he transcribed the dialect and individual character of the Virginia Negro and mountaineer; he found in natural formations like Weyer's Cave and Seneca

11. Jay B. Hubbell, *The South in American Literature, 1607-1900* (Durham, N. C., 1954), pp. 188-93.

12. G. Harrison Orians, "The Rise of Romanticism, 1805-1855," in *Transitions in American Literary History*, ed. Harry H. Clark (Durham, N. C., 1953).

Rocks the equivalents of Europe's catacombs and cathedrals; in such personalities as Tim Longbow and Little Mice he delineated the common man with understanding and warmth; and throughout his work, particularly the earlier articles, he defined the tradition of Virginia's past. Scott was an independent writer with a practical outlook upon his work and the world, and Strother was struck with correspondences between their lives:

I am struck with the similarity of our leading views and experiences. Scott never seemed to be sure of his own talent and issued every work with a certain dread of failure and then judged his success by the ledgers of his publishers. He avoided literary coteries and took his place among men in the current world, avoiding thereby exaggerated ideas of the importance of his literary occupation and thus understanding the character and disposition of the popular reader. He responded to no criticisms, abuse, or parodies, maintaining his personal dignity and letting his works fight their own battles.

While Scott was the spokesman for tradition and social responsibility, Byron was the advocate of revolt and egoism. Strother admired the latter's dramatic individualism, aristocratic bearing, and exaggerated gestures. Byron, who was infinitely more popular in the South than in the North, moved John Randolph of Roanoke to say, "No poet in our language . . . has the same power over my feelings as Byron."[13] The poet was admired for his melancholy, his analysis of sentiment, his public notoriety, his apparent carelessness (bookishness was anathema to the Southerner), and his scorn of public opinion. The Southern hero, whether political like John Randolph or military like Jeb Stuart, often had a Byronic cast, and Strother greatly admired the poet. Particularly during his flamboyant youth, Strother took lessons from Byron. He, too, reveled in solitary brooding moments, enjoyed defying the populace, and developed an impromptu style of writing. The Byronic hero became as much a part of Strother's myth of himself as the gentleman out of Scott.

13. Quoted in Grace Landrum, "Sir Walter Scott and His Literary Rivals in the Old South," *American Literature,* II (January, 1931), 269.

The problem of treating the indigenous influences upon Strother's work is more difficult, because the forces were multifarious, conflicting, and less tangible. One of the most obvious is literary nationalism. Strother reached maturity during the era when American writers and artists were discovering in American scenes the raw materials for a native literature and art. While most agreed that America lacked epical depth, which was dependent upon noble traditions and great men, nearly all were unanimous in their view that the natural beauty of the American continent equaled anything in Europe. To deepen the national tradition, many writers employed the historical romance and the Indian tale, but these conformed not to the present but to the past. The landscape and the countryside were vastly more interesting to the public and rewarding for the writer. A writer in *The Knickerbocker Magazine* for 1838 called for a fuller rendering of nature: "We have sublimities of nature, and by seizing upon these, our poets might be immortal . . . . How rarely are they sung."[14] It was national pride in American scenery which provided inspiration for the Hudson River school of painters, and the celebration of nature in literature reached its apex in Thoreau. Magazine editors encouraged literary exploitation of hinterland American scenes, and it was found that if the provincial character was not the subject for epics, he was nevertheless interesting, individualized, and amusing. Before a national literature was possible, it was necessary to have a dozen or more regional literatures from which to draw. Strother played a significant part in depicting native scenes and people with realism, skill, and understanding. In his search for localities uncharted on the literary map, he was as much a nationalist as his better known contemporaries, the genre and landscape painters and the nature poets and historical novelists.

If a pigeonhole is required for Strother, perhaps "Southern Knickerbocker" is best, inasmuch as he shared many things with the New York school, differing from it largely through writing from the perspective of Southern culture. Nor were his ties with the Knickerbockers merely literary. First as a student and

14. Quoted in Benjamin T. Spencer, "A National Literature, 1837-1855," *American Literature,* VIII (May, 1936), 132.

then as a draftsman, he knew and admired the Kembles and the Pauldings; he absorbed their interest in social conviviality, the theatre, magazines, and oral wit. After Virginia had seceded, Strother thought for a time of moving to Cold Spring on the Hudson, but he knew that the ties of blood were stronger than those of intellect. Ease rather than intensity, amusement rather than instruction, was the dominant mood of Knickerbocker literature. For such men, literature was not the dedicated activity it was in New England; they rather thought of reading as a necessary adornment to a man's cultivation. Their outlook was Chesterfieldian. The accomplishments of their circle required the continued inspiration of fellow raconteurs, independent means, and a close association with editors of magazines and newspapers. When Strother returned to Berkeley Springs in the 1850's, he cut himself off from kindred spirits and was compelled to develop without their assistance. But his literary theory remained very close to that of the Knickerbockers: "shifting patterns, gay and grave, satirical and sentimental, imitative and original, fatuous and sophisticated."[15] Uppermost always were the principles of moral utility and gentility. Feeling was more important than thinking; common sense rather than uncommon sense was the desideratum. Strother, having acquired their outlook and methods during his New York years, proceeded to make his way alone and to find his materials in the South.

The often-remarked parallels between Irving and Strother require discussion. Porte Crayon was the country-cousin of Geoffrey Crayon, but Irving's influence upon Strother was indirect and inadvertent. Only once or twice in his journals did Strother mention Irving's name or work, and the most evaluative reference, "a weak simplicity," was far from flattering. It is difficult to believe that he set out to imitate Irving, but there were similarities between the two men. Both felt that writing was an affair of the heart rather than the head; both believed that manner was more important than matter; both were better at conveying detail than at conceiving grand design. Their minds were receptive rather than creative. "He has never invented an

15. Kendall Taft, *The Minor Knickerbockers* (New York, 1947), p. lxxxvi.

incident,"[16] a critic wrote of Irving, and the assertion is equally true of Strother. Neither was particularly concerned about obtaining new effects, wishing to write of what had been seen or heard, not what had been imagined. Both relied upon caricature rather than characterization. However, there were differences as well, the most noticeable of which was in their attitude toward America. Strother largely acepted America for what it was and devoted his career to its realistic delineation. He found it infinitely more exciting than Europe, and he minutely analyzed its political, economic, and social structure. On the other hand, Irving was happiest when in the storied grandeur of Europe. He shied away from the rawness and coarseness of the United States, and was largely oblivious to the principal issues of his day. Although both Irving and Strother were gentlemen writers who eschewed ignoble and indecorous materials for their literature, Strother more nearly approximated Whitman's interest in the varied facets of American life.

In the ante-bellum South there were at least two well-demarcated literary traditions: the genteel tradition of the historical novelists, essayists, and poets, and the indigenous tradition of the frontier humorists. The first were widely read, cosmopolitan, and serious men and women who were conscious of literary style; the second were men, predominantly lawyers or journalists, who wished to capture the raucous and provincial humor of their regions without concern for literary effects. Only rarely did a writer span both traditions, but Strother was one of these. He had the polish and seriousness of Simms and Cooke, but he also had the lively interest in incongruities and hyperbole of Longstreet and Hooper. Undoubtedly, the best parts of Strother's narratives are those in the frontier vein, scenes rich with local color, ludicrous situations, eccentric caricatures, and rustic anecdotes. These savor of the best oral tales of the old South, tales current since Strother's boyhood in the Virginia back-country. Like the Southwestern humorists, Strother enjoyed masculine tales treating situations without psychological refinement. Physical discomfiture, cockfighting, hunting, fishing, riding, drinking

16. Stanley Williams, *The Life of Washington Irving* (New York, 1935), II, 276.

can be found in the work of Porte Crayon along with—sometimes on the same page as—reflective and sentimental passages owing more to the sophisticated Southern tradition. He was familiar with the writings of Hamilton C. Jones, Johnson Hooper, Mark Twain, and others of the indigenous school, yet he did not regard them as serious writers of any more than ephemeral interest. In this he was entirely mistaken, for their work is infinitely more virile than that of the romancers. Strother's writing is a link between the two traditions of Southern literature, but it is best when it falls within the style and mood of the humorists.

To overlook Strother's pronounced consciousness of Virginia —particularly evident in his early writing—is to ignore one of the most important influences on him. "The Virginian," wrote Nathaniel Beverley Tucker, "is a Virginian everywhere. In the wilds of the West, on the sands of Florida, on the shores of the Pacific—everywhere his heart turns to Virginia."[17] Strother, too, saw the world through Virginia-tinted glasses. He gauged Europe, New England, and the Deep South by the measure of his criterion, Virginia. Though he took an active part in the publicizing and development of West Virginia after the war, he was uncomfortable west of the Alleghenies. Within a twenty-five-mile radius of Martinsburg he was born, lived, and died. He adapted to other places, but was at home nowhere else. To George William Bagby and David Hunter Strother belong the credit of first describing the Old Dominion with careful realism; and Strother influenced Bagby rather than the reverse. Before these men began writing in the 1850's, Virginia literature had been almost exclusively devoted to the grand tradition of the plantation aristocracy. Kennedy, Caruthers, and Cooke turned to the past for their inspiration, but Strother had pictured Virginia as it was—its natural scenery, its anachronistic characters, its provincial crotchets, and even its absorbing decadence. He respected its history and traditions, but he never permitted his fancy to take improbable flights in buzzard-less skies. To Strother belongs the credit for taking Virginia literature out of the manor house and into the inn yards, for introducing the three-dimensional Negro, and for demonstrating that homely

17. Quoted in Hubbell, *South in Literature*, p. 428.

details among the common people could be more absorbing than the incredibly romanticized deeds of the First Families. Certainly, the single thread which draws together every writer of the Old Dominion from Robert Beverley to Ellen Glasgow is respect for and love of Virginia's rural culture. Strother, too, shared this feeling, and his last writings, instead of reaching out to embrace the industrialism of the century, turned back to the familiar agrarian and small-town scenes he had known as a boy—the militia muster, the stump politician, old-fashioned hospitality. Porte Crayon's earliest and his last writings were Virginia illustrated.

The Man

"I feel like a bubble floating on a restless current of events, a feather caught up in a whirlwind," Strother wrote toward the end of his life. The analogy, fitting for many men of the nineteenth century, particularly suited David Strother, who was carried by circumstance from one situation to another. He was a multi-sided paradox: a dreamer and a doer, an aesthete and a man of affairs, an aristocrat and a democrat, a Southerner and a Unionist—the list could be expanded. But it allows one generalization. He never found a panacea which answered dogmatically all the queries of life. In a more stable era, he might have become an artist or a writer exclusively, but like a Renaissance man, he found that his talents could be employed in several areas —as an artist, a writer, a soldier, a journalist, and a diplomat. His was an age in which versatility enhanced the man, but while he was competent in many careers, he never became the master of one. In nineteenth-century America there were better writers, better artists, and better soldiers than Strother, but it is doubtful whether any other man served so well in all three roles. It is even more doubtful whether our era of hyper-specialization will ever produce again a Latin-quoting general of the army who has mastered the art of painting only to become a well-known writer.

By birth, training, temperament, and preference, David Strother was a gentleman, old (Virginia) style. This required intellectual cultivation, good family, social conviviality, public re-

sponsibility, and, above all else, a respect and preference for the
leisurely way of life. "I am resolved wholly to minde my business here, and next after my penne, to have som good book
alwayes in store, being in solitude the best and choicest company. Besides among these cristall rivers and odoriferous woods
I doe escape much expense, envye, contempte, vanity, and vex-
ation of mind."[18] This utterance, which except for its archaic
orthography could have been taken from Strother's journal, was
that of a first gentleman of Virginia, Secretary Pory, in 1619,
more than 250 years before. It summarized the Virginian's easy
adaptation to pastoral life, garden and family, and literary pursuits, all of which characterized Strother's final phase at Berkeley
Springs. Such a philosophy called for the art of living rather
than the skill of getting, and it went counter to the principal
ideologies of nineteenth-century America. One thinks of Washington at Mt. Vernon, Jefferson at Monticello, and more humbly,
Strother at Berkeley, as embodiments of the Virginia ideal. All
were aware of public responsibilities at critical times, but all returned at the first opportunity to their rural seats. John Esten
Cooke said that "literature and gardening are the really philosophical pursuits of life."[19] Here was at least one postwar sentiment of his cousin's with which Morgan County's contributor to *Horticulturist* magazine would have agreed.

Strother's personal integrity was easily one of his most pronounced characteristics, and this was never more evident than
when the principal actors in the American drama revealed so
little of it. In New Orleans during Banks's occupation, in Richmond under Pierpont, and in Mexico as consul general, the
opportunities for acquiring surreptitious wealth were on every
side, but not even Strother's detractors ever accused him of dishonesty. Honor was for him no abstraction but a personal conviction. He did not need Shakespeare's assistance in writing
while at New Orleans, "If a man sells an estate, a house, a horse,
or any visible property and afterwards repents of his bargain, he
may repurchase his property. But having once sold his honour

18. Quoted in Matthew P. Andrews, *Virginia, the Old Dominion* (New York, 1937), p. 141.
19. Quoted in Hubbell, *South in Literature,* p. 518.

he cannot buy it back." From a "head-devil" youth, Strother developed into an unusually responsible man. Once he refused to participate in a public debate, an intellectual exercise which he dearly loved, because the subject was: "Resolved, it is sometimes permissible to lie." However valid the arguments might be, Strother would not tolerate a public airing of them. But despite this careful sense of patrician responsibility, he was no prig who refused to face the unpleasant realities. In both war and peace, he had seen the depths of human nature and faced them squarely. With brave honesty, he had often plunged into his own psyche, but he separated those things which were private from those which were public.

Although dignified, Strother was never dull. He met story with story, and even within a month of his death penned an impromptu verse to an admiring young female cousin. He always stole the thunder of the Negro violinists at Virginia dances by his rousing rendition of "The Chickasaw Nation," and even when seventy years old Strother at the piano was apt to call in the servants from the kitchen (when his wife was out) for a dancing spree. He was the only man in the Kanawha Valley who could recite (and did) Hopkinson's "Battle of the Kegs," and he knew the expurgated lines. His amusing, uncondescending, and tactful letters to his son John, filled with humorous advice ("Don't attempt to ascend Parnassus before breakfast without a lunch in your pocket and when you do start, don't stop at the snow line and lay down to take a nap."[20]), show little sign that their writer was a man of advanced years. David Strother himself was as natural, as unpretentious, and as warmly human as "Porte Crayon."

Loyalty is a more difficult virtue than honesty, and it was strongly rooted in Strother's character. He believed that a man must stand by his family, his friends, and his nation at all costs. As we have seen, he readily forgave his enemies, saved their homes, and interceded for their lives. Although his financial situation was precariously near disaster in the late seventies, he adopted Rebecca Crane, the daughter of a destitute kinsman,

20. Letter from David Strother to John Strother, March 22, 1886. In the possession of D. H. Strother II.

educated her, and gave her all the advantages offered to his own son. When General Hunter was reviled by his officers, Strother as a distant cousin and subordinate officer would tolerate no criticism within his hearing, although inwardly he agreed that the accusations were warrantable. This was not obsequiousness. Strother sincerely believed that loyalty to one's commander, if that commander were acting according to his principles, was the essence of military discipline. The list of Strother's attractive qualities could be enlarged almost indefinitely; deprecations would prove to be a more difficult enterprise. Misunderstood by many in his day and neglected by most in this, David Hunter Strother's life was an enactment of his family motto, *Prius mori quam fallere fidem.*

Appendix A

Published and Unpublished Writings of
David Hunter Strother

Articles

Gazette (Martinsburg, Va.):
"Pen and Ink Sketches of an Artist."
No. 1, February 18, 1841.
No. 2, February 25, 1841.
No. 3, May 20, 1841.
No. 4, July 8, 1841.
No. 5, July 15, 1841.
No. 6, September 30, 1841.
No. 7, March 10, 1842.
No. 8, April 7, 1842.
No. 9, April 21, 1842.
No. 10, September 29, 1842.
No. 11, October 6, 1842.
No. 12, October 13, 1842.
No. 13, February 23, 1843.

Harper's New Monthly Magazine:
"The Virginian Canaan," VIII (December, 1853), 18-36.
"Virginia Illustrated."
First Paper, X (December, 1854), 1-25.
Second Paper, X (February, 1855), 289-310.
Third Paper, XI (August, 1855), 289-311.
Fourth Paper, XII (January, 1856), 158-78.
Fifth Paper, XIII (August, 1856), 303-23.

"The Bear and the Basketmaker," XIII (June, 1856), 18-25.
"The Dismal Swamp," XIII (September, 1856), 441-55.
"North Carolina Illustrated."
    "The Fisheries," XIV (March, 1857), 433-50.
    "The Piny Woods," XIV (May, 1857), 741-55.
    "Guilford," XV (July, 1857), 154-64.
    "The Gold Region," XV (August, 1857), 289-300.
"A Winter in the South."
    First Paper, XV (September, 1857), 433-51.
    Second Paper, XV (October, 1857), 594-606.
    Third Paper, XV (November, 1857), 721-40.
    Fourth Paper, XVI (January, 1858), 167-83.
    Fifth Paper, XVI (May, 1858), 721-36.
    Sixth Paper, XVII (August, 1858), 289-305.
    Seventh Paper, XVIII (December, 1858), 1-17.
"A Reminiscence of Rome," XV (November, 1857), 740-45.
"Artist's Excursion on the Baltimore and Ohio Railroad," XIX
    (June, 1859), 1-19.
"Rural Pictures," XX (January, 1860), 166-80.
"A Summer in New England."
    First Paper, XXI (June, 1860), 1-19.
    Second Paper, XXI (September, 1860), 442-61.
    Third Paper, XXI (November, 1860), 745-63.
    Fourth Paper, XXII (May, 1861), 721-41.
    Fifth Paper, XXIII (July, 1861), 145-63.
"Personal Recollections of the War by a Virginian."
    First Paper, XXXIII (June, 1866), 1-25.
    Second Paper, XXXIII (July, 1866), 137-60.
    Third Paper, XXXIII (September, 1866), 409-28.
    Fourth Paper, XXXIII (October, 1866), 545-67.
    Fifth Paper, XXXIV (January, 1867), 172-91.
    Sixth Paper, XXXIV (March, 1867), 423-49.
    Seventh Paper, XXXIV (May, 1867), 714-34.
    Eighth Paper, XXXV (August, 1867), 273-95.
    Ninth Paper, XXXV (November, 1867), 704-28.
    Tenth Paper, XXXVI (February, 1868), 273-91.
    Eleventh Paper, XXXVI (April, 1868), 567-82.
"An Excursion to Watkin's Glen," XLIII (June, 1871), 32-49.
"The Mountains."
    First Paper, XLIV (April, 1872), 659-75.
    Second Paper, XLIV (May, 1872), 801-15.

Third Paper, XLV (June, 1872), 21-34.
Fourth Paper, XLV (August, 1872), 347-61.
Fifth Paper, XLV (September, 1872), 502-16.
Sixth Paper, XLV (November, 1872), 801-15.
Seventh Paper, XLVI (April, 1873), 669-80.
Eighth Paper, XLVII (November, 1873), 821-32.
Ninth Paper, XLIX (July, 1874), 156-67.
Tenth Paper, LI (September, 1875), 475-85.
"Our Negro Schools," XLIX (September, 1874), 457-68.
"Confessions of a Candidate," LII (February, 1876), 329-46.
"The Baby," LII (March, 1876), 538-49.
"Boys and Girls," LIV (December, 1876), 19-32.
"Old Time Militia Musters," LVII (July, 1878), 212-221.
"Home," LVIII (January, 1879), 236-48.

Harper's Weekly:
"The Jamestown Celebration," I (June 27, 1857), 404-6.
"The Late Invasion at Harper's Ferry," III (November 5, 1859), 712-14.
"The Trial of the Conspirators," III (November 12, 1859), 729-30.
"Narrative of an Eye-Witness," V (May 11, 1861), 292.
"Sitting Bull—Autobiography of the Famous Indian Chief," XX (July 29, 1876), 625-28.

Riverside Magazine:
"The Little Broom," I (December, 1867), 566-69.
"The Young Virginians."
    Chapter One, II (February, 1868), 53-60.
    Chapter Two, II (March, 1868), 122-29.
    Chapter Three, II (May, 1868), 215-20.
    Chapter Four, II (June, 1868), 261-67.
    Chapter Five, II (August, 1868), 371-78.
    Chapter Six, III (April, 1869), 171-77.
    Chapter Seven, III (May, 1869), 202-8.
    Chapter Eight, III (September, 1869), 405-11.
    Chapter Nine, IV (April, 1870), 153-59.
    Chapter Ten, IV (June, 1870), 254-61.
    Chapter Eleven, IV (August, 1870), 348-53.
    Chapter Twelve, IV (December, 1870), 563-69.

Philadelphia Weekly Times:
"General Averell's Last Ride," January 18, 1879.

"Banks in Louisiana," March 29, 1879.
"The Port Hudson Expedition," April 5, 1879.

Miscellaneous:

"In West Virginia," in *Picturesque America,* ed. William Cullen
Bryant, I (New York, 1872), 377-93.
"Notes from My Garden," *Horticulturist,* XXVIII (March,
1873), 76-78.
"Old Fort Frederick," *Baltimore Sun,* December 6, 1878.
"Edmund Pendleton of Virginia," *Pennsylvania Magazine,* III
(Number 3, 1879), 177-79.
"A Visit to the Shrines of Old Virginia," *Lippincott's Magazine,*
XXIII (April, 1879), 393-407.
"A Schatterndorf Episode," *Cosmopolitan,* IX (May, 1890), 94-
112.
"John Brown's Death and Last Words," in Boyd Stutler, "An
Eyewitness Describes the Hanging of John Brown," *Ameri-
can Heritage,* VI (February, 1955), 4-9.
"The Horse Jockey," *Magazine of the Jefferson County Historical
Society,* XXI (December, 1955), 29-31.

Books and Pamphlets

Virginia Illustrated. New York: Harper & Bros., 1857. Second
edition, 1871.
The Capital of West Virginia and the Great Kanawha Valley.
Charleston, W.Va.: *Journal* Publishing Co., 1872.
Historical Address [delivered at Berkeley Springs, W.Va., July 4,
1876]. Washington: M'Gill, 1876.

Anthologies Containing Reprints
from the Works Listed Above

Alderman, Edwin A., *et al. A Library of Southern Literature.*
Atlanta: Martin & Hoyt, 1907.
Botkin, B. A. *A Treasury of Southern Folklore.* New York: Crown
Publishers, 1949.
Commager, Henry Steele (ed.). *The Blue and the Gray: The
Story of the Civil War as Told by Participants.* Indianapolis:
Bobbs-Merrill Co., 1950.
DePuy, W. H. (ed.). *University of Literature.* New York: Barcus,
1896.
Eby, Cecil D., Jr. (ed.). *The Old South Illustrated.* Chapel Hill,
N. C.: University of North Carolina Press, 1959.

Turner, Ella May. *Stories and Verse of West Virginia.* Hagerstown, Md.: Diamond Printing Co., 1923.

Published Consular Reports

Commercial Relations of the United States. Washington: Department of State.

"Climate and Health of the City of Mexico," III (January, 1881), 16-21.

"Industrial Progress in Mexico," VII (May, 1881), 648-52.

"National Progress in Mexico," XVII (March, 1882), 434-38.

"Quicksilver in Mexico," XVII (March, 1882), 447-48.

"Living in the City of Mexico," XX (June, 1882), 223-31.

"Paper and Paper Plants of Mexico," XXVII (January, 1883), 58-60.

"Church and State in Mexico," XXVII (January, 1883), 87-91.

"The Currency of Mexico," XXXVI (December, 1883), 282-92.

"Commerce and Industries of Mexico," XLI (May, 1884), 368-93.

"City and State of Mexico," XLIII (July, 1884), 412-17.

Unpublished Writings

Autobiographical Sketch. In the possession of D. H. Strother II, Milwaukee.

Biography of John Strother. Among the family papers.

Consular Dispatches to the Secretary of State, 1879-1885. National Archives, Washington, D. C.

Valley Tour Notes [1835]. Among the family papers.

Appendix B

Journals, Correspondence and Sketchbook of
David Hunter Strother

Journals

Literary Journals:

Journal [A], *1838-1852*. Biographical material; miscellaneous
poems; miscellaneous sketches; Baltimore notes; unfinished
short story; Mexican War ballad; "The Horse Jockey"; notes
on Washington and Tidewater; checklist of paintings, 1836-
1852. In the possession of D. H. Strother II, Milwaukee.

Journal [B], *1847 and Later*. Description of portion of European
tour, rewritten from letters; original versions of Third,
Fourth and Fifth Papers of "Virginia Illustrated"; copy of
review from London *Spectator;* notes on John Brown raid;
sketches for "Our Negro Schools"; notes for "Confessions of
a Candidate"; 101 verses of the *Rubaiyat.* In the possession
of D. H. Strother II, Milwaukee.

Journal [C], *1868, Earlier and Later*. Notes on tour through
"Dismal Swamp" and North Carolina, 1856; notes on Catacombs of the Piazza Barberini; notes on the identity of Ney
and Rudolph; verses on children; subjects for lectures. In
the possession of D. H. Strother II, Milwaukee.

Journal [D], *1860-1872, Miscellaneous*. Random remarks; notes
on Berkeley Springs Hotel; business accounts. In the Handley
Library, Winchester, Va.

*Daily Journals, Nearly Consecutive from July 9, 1861, to March 3,
1888*. Thirty-two volumes. In the possession of D. H. Strother
II, Milwaukee.

Correspondence

Letters from David Hunter Strother to:

Hansom Pigman.

    [1838] October 13. In the Simon Gratz Collection of the Historical Society of Pennsylvania, Philadelphia.

John Strother.

    1841 September 7; September [?]; October 10. In the possession of D. H. Strother II, Milwaukee.

    1842 November 2; November 5. D. H. Strother II.

John Pendleton Kennedy.

    1851 July 10. Among the John Pendleton Kennedy Papers at the Peabody Institute, Baltimore.

    1852 March 31. Peabody Institute.

    1862 August 9; October 29. Peabody Institute.

    1863 March 7. Peabody Institute.

    1864 March 29; April 14. Peabody Institute.

    1865 June 9. Peabody Institute.

John Esten Cooke.

    1851 December [?]. Among the John Esten Cooke Papers in the library of Duke University.

    1855 May 23. Duke University.

Charles J. Faulkner.

    1855 September 21; October 15. Among the Alexander P. Boteler Papers in the library of Duke University.

Alexander P. Boteler.

    1855 October 28. Among the Alexander P. Boteler Papers in the library of Duke University.

    1857 June 6. In the New York Public Library.

    1859 June 15. Among the Alexander P. Boteler Papers in the library of Duke University.

Brantz Mayer.

    1857 April 11. In the Mayer-Rossel Collection of the Maryland Historical Society, Baltimore.

Ben Perley Poore.

    1858 March 25. In the possession of Cecil D. Eby, Jr., Lexington, Va.

Mary E. Hunter Strother.

    1861 September 27. In the possession of D. H. Strother II, Milwaukee.

N. P. Banks.
>   1861   November 22.   Among the N. P. Banks Papers at the Essex Institute, Salem, Mass.
>
>   1862   January 23.   Essex Institute.
>
>   1871   April 7.   Essex Institute.

Waitman T. Willey.
>   1862   February 22.   Among the Waitman T. Willey Papers at the library of West Virginia University.

F. H. Pierpont.
>   1862   June 25.   Published in the *Calendar of Virginia State Papers and Other Manuscripts,* XI, 380-81.
>
>   1865   July 19.   Among the F. H. Pierpont Papers at the library of West Virginia University.
>
>   1879   April 5.   West Virginia University.

H. J. Samuels.
>   1862   July 9.   In the West Virginia Archives, Charleston.

A. J. Boreman.
>   1864   July 8.   In the West Virginia Archives, Charleston.
>
>   1865   October 14.   West Virginia Archives.

E. H. Goss.
>   1866   October 9.   In the possession of Cecil D. Eby Jr., Lexington, Va.

Judge Hall.
>   1868   May 7.   In the West Virginia Archives, Charleston.

The Editors of *Horticulturist.*
>   1871   January [?].   *Horticulturist,* XXVI, 11.

Mrs. F. H. Pierpont.
>   1871   February 4.   Among the F. H. Pierpont Papers at the library of West Virginia University.
>
>   1879   March 4.   West Virginia University.

Fitz-John Porter.
>   1878   July 4.   Published in *Harper's New Monthly Magazine,* LVII (January, 1879), 306-7.

G. N. Galloway.
>   1878   December 26.   In the possession of Cecil D. Eby, Jr., Lexington, Va.

A. K. McClure.
>   1879   March 3.   In the Simon Gratz Collection of the Historical Society of Pennsylvania, Philadelphia.

J. Marshall McCue.
>1887 December 7. Published in *Tyler's Quarterly*, XI
>(April, 1930), 223-24.

Danske Dandridge.
>1887 June 27. Among the Danske Dandridge Papers at the
>library of Duke University.

John Strother II.
>1885 September 22; October 8; October 22. In the possession
>of D. H. Strother II, Milwaukee. December 7;
>December 19. In the West Virginia Archives,
>Charleston.
>
>1886 January 5. West Virginia Archives. January 27;
>February 1; March 10; March 22; April 17; May
>12; May 26; June 9; September 23; October 10;
>October 21; October 29; November 7; November
>19; December 3. D. H. Strother II.
>
>1887 May 14; June 1; June 15; June 30; July 14; July 23;
>August 3, August 13; August 26; September 10;
>September 22; October 7; October 21; November
>4; November 15; November 20; November 24;
>December 6; December 17. D. H. Strother II.
>
>1888 January 1; January 24; February 10. D. H. Strother II.

Letters to David Hunter Strother from:

Maria Rossi.
>1843 July 22. In the possession of D. H. Strother II,
>Milwaukee.

John Pendleton Kennedy.
>1851 March 8; July 13. Among the John Pendleton Ken-
>nedy Papers at the Peabody Institute, Baltimore.
>
>1864 February 22; April 2. In the possession of Boyd
>Stutler, Charleston, W. Va.

John Esten Cooke.
>1854 December 5. Among the John Esten Cooke Papers in
>the library of Duke University.

A. V. Tidball.
>1855 September 4; September 7. Among the Alexander P.
>Boteler Papers in the library of Duke University.

Henry Augustus Wise.
>1857 August 16. In the possession of Boyd Stutler, Charles-
>ton, W. Va.

Mary E. Hunter Strother.

    1863 Febraury 22. In the possession of Boyd Stutler, Charleston, W. Va.

David E. Henderson.

    1859 October 19; October 22. In the Negro Collection at the library of Atlanta University.

John Pope.

    1872 June 22. In the possession of Cecil D. Eby, Jr., Lexington, Va.

John Brisben Walker.

    1888 January 20. In the West Virginia Archives, Charleston.

Other Relevant Correspondence:

John Strother to John Pendleton Kennedy.

    1813 March 16; June 3. Among the John Pendleton Kennedy Papers at the Peabody Institute, Baltimore.

John Strother to the Governor of Virginia.

    1813 April 8. Published in the *Calendar of Virginia State Papers and Other Manuscripts,* X, 223.

John Strother to Henry Boteler.

    1836 January 1. Among the Alexander P. Boteler Papers in the library of Duke University.

John Strother to his daughter, Emily.

    1843 April 20. In the possession of Boyd Stutler, Charleston, W. Va.

William G. Simms to John Pendleton Kennedy.

    1852 February 17. Among the John Pendleton Kennedy Papers at the Peabody Institute, Baltimore.

John Esten Cooke to John R. Cooke.

    1850 August 4. Among the John Esten Cooke Papers in the Library of Congress.

W. H. Pratt to John Bragg.

    1852 July 24. Among the John Bragg Papers in the Southern Historical Collection at the library of the University of North Carolina.

John Esten Cooke to Hamilton Sands.

    1852 August 31. Among the John Esten Cooke Papers in the Library of Congress.

Washington Irving to John Pendleton Kennedy.

    1853   April 24.   Among the John Pendleton Kennedy Papers at the Peabody Institute, Baltimore.

    1854   August 31.   Peabody Institute.

Henry P. Cooke to John Esten Cooke.

    1854   February 13.   Among the John Esten Cooke Papers at the library of Duke University.

Andrew Kennedy to John Esten Cooke.

    [1861] Among the John Esten Cooke Papers at the library of Duke University.

William Seward to John Pendleton Kennedy.

    1862   August 20.   Among the John Pendleton Kennedy Papers at the Peabody Institute, Baltimore.

Edwin Stanton to John Pendleton Kennedy.

    1862   August 24.   Among the John Pendleton Kennedy Papers at the Peabody Institute, Baltimore.

[George] Duyckinck to John Esten Cooke.

    1863(?) February 19.   Among the John Esten Cooke Papers in the Library of Congress.

Philip P. Kennedy to John Pendleton Kennedy.

    1864   January 30; April 17.   Among the John Pendleton Kennedy Papers at the Peabody Institute, Baltimore.

B. H. Bunley to F. H. Pierpont.

    1866   August 10.   Among the F. H. Pierpont Papers at the library of West Virginia University.

Rutherford Hayes to William H. Evarts.

    1877   August 1.   In the National Archives, Washington, D. C.

Robert Nortcutt to Stanley Mathews.

    1879   January 18.   In the National Archives, Washington, D. C.

James L. Randolph to James G. Blaine.

    1881   April 28.   In the National Archives, Washington, D. C.

John W. Foster to James G. Blaine.

    1881   May 27.   In the National Archives, Washington, D. C.

George F. Peabody to Grover Cleveland.

    1885   May 12.   In the National Archives, Washington, D. C.

Mary E. Hunter Strother to Miss Porter.

    1900   December 24.   In the West Virginia Archives, Charleston.

J. McCarthy Duckwall to T. Marshall Hunter.
    1940 March 12. In the possession of T. Marshall Hunter,
        Pottsville, Penn.

Sketchbook

European Sketchbook. Contains forty-five drawings. In the possession of Mrs. Louise Strother Shepard, Falls Church, Va.

Bibliography

In addition to the journals, correspondence, and published and unpublished writings of David Hunter Strother listed in appendixes.

Books

Adkins, Nelson F. *Fitz-Greene Halleck: An Early Knickerbocker Wit and Poet.* New Haven: Yale University Press, 1930.

Aler, F. Vernon. *History of Martinsburg.* Hagerstown, Md.: Mail Publishing Co., 1888.

Allen, Hervey. *Israfel: The Life and Times of Edgar Allan Poe.* New York: Farrar & Rinehart, 1934.

Allen, John D. *Philip Pendleton Cooke.* Chapel Hill, N. C.: University of North Carolina Press, 1942.

Ambler, Charles H. *Francis H. Pierpont.* Chapel Hill, N. C.: University of North Carolina Press, 1937.

————. *Sectionalism in Virginia from 1776 to 1861.* Chicago: University of Chicago Press, 1910.

————. *West Virginia, the Mountain State.* New York: Prentice Hall, 1947.

————. *West Virginia Stories and Biographies.* New York: Rand McNally & Co., 1937.

Andrews, Matthew P. *Virginia, the Old Dominion.* New York: Doubleday, 1937.

————. *The Women of the South in War Times.* Baltimore: Norman, Remington Co., 1923.

Appleton's Cyclopedia of American Biography, ed. James G. Wilson and John Fiske. New York: D. Appleton & Co., 1888.

Atkinson, George W., and Alvaro Gibbens. _Prominent Men of West Virginia._ Wheeling, W. Va.: W. L. Callin, 1890.

Avirett, James. _The Memoirs of General Turner Ashby and His Compeers._ Baltimore: Shelby and Dulany, 1867.

Bagby, George W. _The Old Virginia Gentleman and Other Sketches,_ ed. Thomas Nelson Page. New York: Scribners & Sons, 1910.

[Bailey, Robert]. _The Life and Adventures of Robert Bailey._ Richmond: J. G. Cochran, 1882.

Battles and Leaders of the Civil War. Vol. II. New York: Century Co., 1887.

Baur, John. _American Painting in the Nineteenth Century._ New York: Frederick A. Praeger, 1953.

Bayard, Ferdinand M. _Travels of a Frenchman in Maryland and Virginia with a Description of Philadelphia and Baltimore in 1791._ Translated and edited by Ben C. McCary. Ann Arbor, Mich.: Edwards Bros., 1950.

Baylor, George. _Bull Run to Bull Run, or Four Years in the Army of Northern Virginia._ Richmond: B. F. Johnson, 1900.

Beaty, John O. _John Esten Cooke, Virginian._ New York: Columbia University Press, 1922.

Beebe, Lucius, and Charles Clegg. _The American West._ New York: E. P. Dutton & Co., 1955.

Beers, Henry A. _Nathaniel Parker Willis._ Boston: Houghton Mifflin Co., 1885.

A Bibliography of Virginia. Compiled by Earl G. Swem. Richmond: Superintendent of Public Printing, 1916.

A Bibliography of West Virginia. Compiled by Innis C. Davis. Charleston: Department of Archives and History, 1939.

Biographical and Historical Catalogue of Washington and Jefferson College, 1802-1902. Philadelphia: George Buchanan & Co., 1902.

Biographical Dictionary of America, ed. Rossiter Johnson. Boston: American Biographical Society, 1906.

Blair, Walter. _Native American Humor, 1800-1900._ New York: American Book Co., 1937.

[Bliss, Alexander, and John P. Kennedy]. _Autograph Leaves of Our Country's Authors._ Baltimore: Cushing & Bailey, 1864.

Bosworth, A[lbert] S. _A History of Randolph County, West Virginia._ Elkins, W. Va.: Privately printed, 1916 (?).

Bowen, Ele. _Ramblings in the Path of the Steam Horse._ Philadelphia: Wm. Brownell and Wm. White Smith, 1855.

Branch, E. Douglas. *The Sentimental Years, 1836-1860.* New York: Appleton-Century-Crofts, 1934.

Brooks, Van Wyck. *The Times of Melville and Whitman.* New York: E. P. Dutton & Co., 1947.

Brown, Herbert Ross. *The Sentimental Novel in America, 1780-1860.* Durham, N. C.: Duke University Press, 1940.

Brown, Stuart E. *Annals of the Blackwater and the Land of Canaan.* Berryville, Va.: Chesapeake Book Co., 1959.

Bryan, Daniel. *The Mountain Muse.* Harrisonburg, Va.: Davidson & Bowine, 1813.

Burke, William. *The Virginia Mineral Springs.* Second edition. Richmond: Ritchie & Dunnavant, 1853.

Burton, William (ed.). *Cyclopaedia of Wit and Humor.* New York: D. Appleton & Co., 1858.

Burke, W. J., and Will D. Howe. *American Authors and Books, 1640-1940.* New York: Grammercy Publishing Co., 1943.

Bushong, Millard K. *A History of Jefferson County, West Virginia.* Charles Town, W. Va.: Jefferson Publishing Co., 1941.

Calendar of Virginia State Papers and Other Manuscripts, ed. H. W. Flournoy. Richmond: 1875-92.

Callahan, James Morton. *Semi-Centennial History of West Virginia.* Semi-Centennial Commission, 1913.

Catalogue of Paintings, Engravings, etc., of the Picture Gallery of the Maryland Historical Society. Baltimore: John D. Tay, 1848.

Catalogue of Paintings, Engravings, etc., of the Picture Gallery of the Maryland Historical Society. Second annual exhibition. Baltimore: John D. Tay, 1849.

Catalogue of Paintings, Engravings, etc., of the Picture Gallery of the Maryland Historical Society. Sixth annual exhibition. Baltimore: John D. Tay, 1858.

Chapman, John Gadsby. *The American Drawing Book: A Manual for the Amateur.* New York: A. S. Barnes, 1870.

Clark, Eliot. *History of the National Academy of Design.* New York: Columbia University Press, 1954.

Conley, Phil. *West Virginia Encyclopedia.* Charleston, W. Va.: West Virginia Publishing Co., 1929.

Cooke, John Esten. *Ellie: or the Human Comedy.* With illustrations after designs by Strother. Richmond: A. Morris, 1855.

Couper, William. *History of the Shenadoah Valley.* Vol. II. New York: Lewis Historical Publishing Co., 1952.

————. *One Hundred Years at V.M.I.* 3 vols. Richmond: Garrett & Massie, 1939.

Cullum, George W. *Biographical Register of the Officers and Graduates of the U.S. Military Academy.* New York: D. Van Nostrand Co., 1868.

Crozier, William A. (ed.). *The Buckners of Virginia and the Allied Families of Strother and Ashby.* New York: Privately printed, 1907.

Dayton, Abram C. *Last Days of Knickerbocker Life in New York.* New York: G. P. Putnam's Sons, 1897.

Davis, J. Lee. *Bits of History and Legends Around and About the Natural Bridge of Virginia.* Lynchburg, Va.: Privately printed, 1949.

Dictionary of American Biography. New York: Scribners & Sons, 1936.

Dictionary of American History. New York: Scribners & Sons, 1940.

DuBellet, Louise Pecquet. *Some Prominent Virginia Families.* Vol. IV. Lynchburg, Va.: J. C. Bell Co., 1907.

Dunlap, William. *A History of the Rise and Progress of the Arts of Design in the United States.* Boston: C. E. Goodspeed, 1918.

Dupont, H. A. *The Campaign of 1864 in the Valley of Virginia.* New York: National Americana Society, 1925.

Elliott, Charles W. *Winfield Scott, the Soldier and the Man.* New York: Macmillan Co., 1937.

Evans, Willis F. *History of Berkeley County, West Virginia.* Privately printed, 1928.

Fiske, John. *The Mississippi Valley in the Civil War.* Boston: Houghton Mifflin Co., 1900.

————. *Old Virginia and Her Neighbors.* Boston: Houghton Mifflin Co., 1898.

Fitzpatrick, John C. (ed.). *The Writings of George Washington.* Vol. II. Washington, D. C.: Government Printing Office, 1931.

Flinn, Frank M. *Campaigning with Banks in Louisiana, '63 and '64.* Lynn, Mass.: Thomas P. Nichols, 1887.

Foster, John W. *Diplomatic Memoirs.* Vol. I. Boston and New York: Houghton Mifflin Co., 1909.

Freeman, Douglas S. *Lee's Lieutenants: A Study in Command.* Vol. II. New York: Scribners & Sons, 1943.

Gardiner, Mabel H., and Ann H. Gardiner. *Chronicles of Old Berkeley.* Durham, N. C.: The Seeman Press, 1938.

Gibbes, Robert. *A Memoir of James DeVeaux of Charleston, S. C.* Columbia, S. C.: Privately printed, 1846.

Goodrich, S. G. *Recollections of a Lifetime.* 2 vols. New York: Miller, Orton, & Co., 1857.

Gregg, Robert D. *The Influence of Border Troubles on Relations between the United States and Mexico, 1876-1910.* ("The Johns Hopkins University Studies in History and Political Science," Series LV, No. 3.) Baltimore: Johns Hopkins Press, 1937.

Groce, George C., and David H. Wallace. *The New York Historical Society's Dictionary of Artists in America.* New Haven: Yale University Press, 1957.

Gutheim, Frederick. *The Potomac.* New York: Rinehart and Co., 1949.

Gwathmey, Edward M. *John Pendleton Kennedy.* New York: Nelson, 1931.

[Halpine, Charles G.] "Miles O'Reilley." *Baked Meats of the Funeral.* New York: Carleton, 1866.

Harper, J. Henry. *The House of Harper.* New York: Harper & Bros., 1912.

Harrington, Fred H. *Fighting Politician: Major General N. P. Banks.* Philadelphia: University of Pennsylvania Press, 1948.

Hart, Freeman H. *The Valley of Virginia in the American Revolution.* Chapel Hill: University of North Carolina Press, 1942.

Hart, John S. *A Manual of American Literature.* Philadelphia: Eldredge & Bro., 1874.

Hepworth, George. *The Whip, Hoe, and Sword, or the Gulf Department in '63.* Boston: Walker, Wise, & Co., 1864.

Historical Hand-Atlas. Special Berkeley and Jefferson County edition. Chicago: H. H. Hardesty & Co., 1883.

Hubbell, Jay B. *The South in American Literature, 1607-1900.* Durham, N. C.: Duke University Press, 1954.

———. *Virginia Life in Fiction.* Privately printed, 1922.

Hunter, Katherine M. *Pavilion vs. Pavilion, or Polk's Choice.* Privately printed, 1953.

Illustrated Life of General Winfield Scott, Commander-in-Chief of the Army in Mexico. Illustrated by Strother. New York: A. S. Barnes, 1847.

Kennedy, John Pendleton. *The Border States: Their Power and Duty.* Philadelphia: J. B. Lippincott Co., 1861.

———. *Defence of the Whigs.* New York: Harper & Bros., 1844.

————. *Swallow Barn: A Sojourn in the Old Dominion.* With twenty illustrations by Strother. New York: G. P. Putnam's Sons, 1852.

————. *Swallow Barn.* Edited with an introduction by Jay B. Hubbell. New York: Harcourt, Brace & Co., 1929.

[Kennedy, Philip Pendleton] "The Clerke of Oxenford." *The Blackwater Chronicle: A Narrative of an Expedition into the Land of Canaan in Randolph County, Virginia . . . .* With illustrations from life by Strother. New York: Redfield, 1853.

————. *Narrative of an Expedition of Five Americans.* English edition of *The Blackwater Chronicle . . . .* London: James Blackwood, n.d.

Kercheval, Samuel. *A History of the Valley of Virginia.* Strasburg, Va: Shenandoah Publishing Co., 1925.

King, Joseph L. *Dr. George William Bagby: A Study of Virginia Literature, 1850-1880.* New York: Columbia University Press, 1927.

Lang, Theodore. *Loyal West Virginia from 1861 to 1865.* Baltimore: Deutsch Publishing Co., 1895.

Larkin, Oliver W. *Art and Life in America.* New York: Rinehart & Co., 1949.

Lewis, Virgil A. *History of West Virginia.* Philadelphia: Hubberd Bros., 1889.

Linton, W. J. *The History of Wood-Engraving in America.* London: George Bell, 1882.

Lord, Walter (ed.). *The Fremantle. Diary.* Boston: Little, Brown, & Co., 1954.

Mabee, Carleton. *The American Leonardo: A Life of Samuel F. B. Morse.* New York: Alfred A. Knopf, 1943.

McDonald, Mrs. Cornelia. *A Diary with Reminiscences of the. War and Refugee Life in the Shenandoah Valley, 1860-1865..* Annotated and supplemented by Hunter McDonald. Nashville, Tenn.: Privately printed, 1934.

Morse, Edward Lind. *Samuel F. B. Morse: His Letters and Journals.* 2 vols. Boston: Houghton Mifflin Co., 1914.

Miller, F. T. (ed.). *The Photographic History of the Civil War.* Vol. X. New York: Review of Reviews Co., 1911.

Miller, Thomas C., and Hu Maxwell. *West Virginia and Its People.* Vol. III. New York: Lewis Historical Publishing Co., 1913.

Milne, Gordon. *George Williams Curtis and the Genteel Tradition.* Bloomington, Ind.: Indiana University Press, 1956.

Moormann, John. *The Virginia Springs with Their Analysis.* Philadelphia: Lindsay & Blackiston, 1847.

Morton, Frederick. *The Story of Winchester in Virginia.* Strasburg, Va.: Shenandoah Publishing House, 1925.

Mott, Frank Luther. *A History of American Magazines.* Vol. II. Cambridge, Mass.: Harvard University Press, 1938.

National Academy of Design Exhibition Record, 1823-1860. Vol. II. New York: New York Historical Society, 1943.

National Cyclopedia of American Biography. New York: James T. White & Co., 1907.

Newman, Carol M. *Virginia Literature.* ("University of Virginia Studies in Southern Literature," No. 3.) Pulaski, Va.: B. D. Smith & Bros., 1903.

Norris, J. E. (ed.). *History of the Lower Shenandoah Valley.* Chicago: A. Warner & Co., 1890.

O'Ferrall, Charles T. O. *Forty Years of Active Service.* New York: Neale Publishing Co., 1904.

Orians, Harrison. "The Rise of Romanticism, 1805-1855," in *Transitions in American Literary History,* ed. Harry H. Clark. Durham, N. C.: Duke University Press, 1953.

Paine, Gregory. *Southern Prose Writers.* New York: American Book Co., 1947.

[Paulding, James K.] *Letters from the South during an Excursion in the Summer of 1816.* Vol. I. New York: James Eastburn and Co., 1817.

Percy, Alfred. *Piedmont Apocalypse.* Madison Heights, Va.: Percy Press, 1949.

Pochmann, Henry (ed.). *Washington Irving: Representative Selections.* New York: American Book Co., 1934.

Pond, George E. *The Shenandoah Valley in 1864.* New York: Scribners & Sons, 1883.

Preston, Elizabeth. *The Life and Letters of Margaret Junkin Preston.* Boston: Houghton, Mifflin Co., 1903.

Quaife, Milo M. (ed.). *The Diary of James K. Polk.* Vol. IV. Chicago: A. C. McClung, 1910.

Quinn, Arthur H. (ed.). *The Literature of the American People.* New York: Appleton-Century-Crofts, 1951.

Redpath, James. *The Public Life of Captain John Brown.* Boston: Thayer & Eldridge, 1860.

Relyea, Pauline S. *Diplomatic Relations between the United States and Mexico under Porfirio Diaz, 1876-1910.* ("Smith College

Studies in History," Vol. X.) Northhampton, Mass.: Smith College, 1924.

Reniers, Percival. *The Springs of Virginia.* Chapel Hill, N. C.: University of North Carolina Press, 1941.

Richards, William C. (ed.). *Georgia Illustrated in a Series of Views.* Penfield, Ga.: Privately printed, 1842.

Richardson, Edgar P. *Painting in America.* New York: Thomas Y. Crowell, 1956.

Rusk, Fern Helen. *George Caleb Bingham, the Missouri Artist.* Jefferson City, Mo.: The Hugh Stephens Co., 1917.

Scharf, J. Thomas. *The Chronicles of Baltimore.* Baltimore: Turnbull Bros., 1874.

———— and Thomas Wescott. *History of Philadelphia, 1609-1884.* Vol. II. Philadelphia: L. H. Everts & Co., 1884.

Simms, William G. *The Life of Captain John Smith.* Sixth edition. Boston: John Philbrick, 1855.

Sioussat, Annie L. *Old Baltimore.* New York: Macmillan Co., 1931.

Siviter, Anna Pierpont. *Recollections of War and Peace, 1861-1868.* New York: G. P. Putnam's Sons, 1938.

Smith, Joseph. *History of Jefferson College.* Pittsburg: J. T. Shryock, 1857.

Spiller, Robert. *The American in England.* New York: Henry Holt & Co., 1926.

————, Willard Thorp, Thomas H. Johnson, and Henry S. Canby (eds.). *Literary History of the United States.* 3 vols. New York: Macmillan Co., 1948.

Stevens, William Oliver. *The Shenandoah and Its Byways.* New York: Dodd, Mead & Co., 1941.

Stewart, A. M. *Camp, March, and Battlefield, or Three Years and a Half with the Army of the Potomac.* Philadelphia: James B. Rodgers, 1865.

Stewart, Andrew. *The Annual Address to the Franklin and Philo Societies of Jefferson College, Canonsburg, Pa., September 24, 1835.* Privately printed, n.d.

Stewart, Randall. *Nathaniel Hawthorne: A Biography.* New Haven: Yale University Press, 1948.

Swem, E. G. *Virginia Historical Index.* Roanoke, Va.: Stone Co., 1934.

Taft, Kendall B. *Minor Knickerbockers.* New York: American Book Co., 1947.

Trollope, Frances. *Domestic Manners of the Americans,* ed. Donald Smalley. New York: Alfred A. Knopf, 1949.

Tuckerman, Henry. *Book of the Artists.* New York: G. P. Putnam's Sons, 1871.

————. *The Life of John Pendleton Kennedy.* New York: G. P. Putnam's Sons, 1867.

United States Congress, House of Representatives. *Executive Document No. 1.* (37th Congress, First Session.)

Veech, James. *The Annual Oration before the Alumni of Jefferson College.* Canonsburg, Pa.: Privately printed, 1835.

Villard, Oswald. *John Brown, A Biography Fifty Years After.* Revised edition. New York: Alfred A. Knopf, 1943.

Wade, John Donald. *Augustus Baldwin Longstreet.* New York: Macmillan Co., 1924.

War of the Rebellion: A Compilation of the Official Records of the Union and Confederate Armies. Series I: Vols. V, XII, XV, XIX, XXIX, XXXIII, XXXVII, LII; Series III: Vol V. Washington, D. C.: Government Printing Office, 1880-1901.

West Virginia: A Guide to the Mountain State. (Writers' Program of the Work Projects Administration.) New York: Oxford University Press, 1941.

Williams, Stanley T. *The Life of Washington Irving.* 2 vols. New York: Oxford University Press, 1935.

Wilson, James G. (ed.). *The Memorial History of the City of New York.* Vol. III. New York: New York History Co., 1893.

Wood, Warren. *Representative Authors of West Virginia.* Ravenswood, W. Va.: Worthwhile Book Co., 1926.

Yarborough, Minnie C. (ed.). *The Reminiscences of William C. Preston.* Chapel Hill, N. C.: University of North Carolina Press, 1933.

Young, John R. *Around the World with General Grant.* 2 vols. New York, 1879.

Periodicals

"Advertisment," *Harper's New Monthly Magazine,* III (bound volume).

Ball, Arthur. "George Washington Rested in Wheeling," *West Virginia School Journal,* LXXXIII (February, 1955), 12.

Bowles, Ella Shannon. "Porte Crayon, Berkeley Springs' Able Publicist," *Iron Worker,* XXII (Summer, 1958), 10-11.

Carpenter, Charles. "The Berkeley Springs Home of 'Porte Crayon,'" *West Virginia Review,* XIV (February, 1937), 184-85.

Chapin, James R. "Random Recollections of a Veteran Illustrator," *Quarterly Illustrator* (January, February and March, 1895), p. 107.

Chappelear, Curtis. "Irving's Visit to the Valley," *Magazine of the Jefferson County Historical Society,* I (December, 1935), 21-24.

Coleman, Elizabeth D. "Chimneys without Smoke," *Virginia Cavalcade,* II (Autumn, 1952), 45-47.

Davis, Curtis Carroll. "The First Climber of the Natural Bridge: A Minor American Epic," *Journal of Southern History,* XVI (August, 1950), 277-90.

Davis, Elmer. "Constant Reader," *Harper's Magazine,* CCI (October, 1950), 161-72.

Davis, Rebecca Harding. "By-Paths in the Mountains," *Harper's New Monthly Magazine,* LXI (July, 1880), 167-85.

"Death of John Strother," *Harper's Weekly,* VI (February 15, 1862), 98.

Durand, John. "An Excursion on the Baltimore and Ohio Railroad," *The Crayon,* V (July, 1958), 208-10.

Eby, Cecil D., Jr. "A Critical Biography of David Hunter Strother (Porte Crayon)," *Dissertation Abstracts,* XIX, 808-9.

————. "John Pendleton Kennedy Was Not 'X.M.C.,'" *American Literature,* XXXI (November, 1959), 332-34.

————. "'Porte Crayon' and the Local Color Movement in West Virginia," *West Virginia History,* XX (April, 1959), 151-62.

————. "'Porte Crayon' in the Tidewater," *Virginia Magazine of History and Biography,* LXVII (October, 1959), 438-49.

————. "'Porte Crayon' Meets General Grant," *Journal of the Illinois State Historical Society,* LII (Summer, 1959), 229-47.

————. "'Porte Crayon's' Quarrel with Virginia," *West Virginia History,* XXI (January, 1960), 65-75.

————. "A West Virginian in Europe: The Apprenticeship of 'Porte Crayon,'" *West Virginia History,* XIX (July, 1958), 266-79.

"Fifty Years of *Harper's Magazine,*" *Harper's New Monthly Magazine,* C (May, 1900), 947-62.

Gaines, William H. "Going Underground in Virginia," *Virginia Cavalcade,* III (Spring, 1954), 23-29.

————. "Men against the Swamp," *Virginia Cavalcade,* IV (Winter, 1954), 23-29.

Griffin, Lloyd W. "The John Pendleton Kennedy Manuscripts,"

Maryland Historical Magazine, XLVIII (December, 1953), 327-36.

Hawthorne, Nathaniel. "Chiefly about War Matters," *Atlantic Monthly,* X (July, 1862), 43-61.

Hunter, Andrew. "John Brown's Raid," *Publications of the Southern History Association,* I (July, 1897), 165-73.

Hunter, T. Marshall. "Two Famous Springs of Eastern Virginia," *West Virginia History,* VI (January, 1945), 193-204.

Kouwenhoven, John A. "America on the Move," *Harper's Magazine,* CCI (October, 1950), 94-144.

Landrum, Grace. "Notes on the Reading of the Old South," *American Literature,* III (March, 1931), 60-71.

————. "Sir Walter Scott and His Literary Rivals in the Old South," *American Literature,* II (January, 1931), 256-76.

Marchand, Ernest. "Poe as Social Critic," *American Literature,* VI (March, 1934), 23-43.

Meade, Everard Kidder. "Clarke County Historical Association Collection of Negatives of Portraits," *Virginia Magazine of History and Biography,* L (Spring, 1942), 157.

Nicklin, Calvert. "The Strother Family," *Tyler's Quarterly Historical and Genealogical Magazine,* XI (October, 1929), 113-40; (January, 1930) 182-99; (April, 1930) 251-65.

Orians, G. Harrison. "The Romance Ferment after *Waverly,*" *American Literature,* III (January, 1932), 408-31.

Owen, Thomas M. "William Strother of Virginia and His Descendants," *Publications of the Southern History Association,* II (April, 1898), 27-51.

"A Partial List of Artists Who Worked in Jefferson County," *Magazine of the Jefferson County Historical Society,* VI (December, 1940).

"The Porte Crayon Memorial Society," *The New York Times Book Review* (January 12, 1941), p. 14.

Princeton University Library Chronicle, XII (Summer, 1951), 222.

Rachal, William M. E. "Grandstand of the Blue Ridge," *Virginia Cavalcade,* I (Autumn, 1951), 23-28.

————. "Salt the South Could Not Savor," *Virginia Cavalcade,* III (Autumn, 1953), 4-7.

————. "Treason on Trial," *Virginia Cavalcade,* IV (Winter, 1954), 32-37.

Richards, T. Addison. "The Landscape of the South," *Harper's New Monthly Magazine,* VI (May, 1852), 721-29.

Rutledge, Anna Wells. "Early Art Exhibitions of the Maryland Historical Society," *Maryland Historical Magazine,* XLII (June, 1947), 124-36.

Sanford, Charles L. "The Concept of the Sublime in the Works of Thomas Cole and William Cullen Bryant," *American Literature,* XXVIII (January, 1957), 434-48.

Spencer, Benjamin. "A National Literature, 1837-1855," *American Literature,* VIII (May, 1936), 125-59.

Strother, Henry. "Some Notes on Smith, Strother, Houston, and Jones," *William and Mary Quarterly,* XXII (April, 1914), 276-77.

Taft, Kendall B. "William Cox, Author of *Crayon Sketches,*" *American Literature,* XVI (March, 1944), 11-18.

West, Edward W. "Memoirs," *Illinois State Historical Society Journal,* XXII (July, 1929), 276.

The Western Pennsylvania Historical Magazine, XXIII (December, 1940), 248.

Williams, Stanley T., and Leonard B. Beach (eds.). "Washington Irving's Letters to Mary Kennedy," *American Literature,* VI (March, 1934), 44-65.

Wynne, James. "John Pendleton Kennedy," *Harper's New Monthly Magazine,* XXV (August, 1862), 335-40.

Newspapers

Baltimore Sun. Obituary, March 9, 1888.
Daily Intelligencer. Wheeling, W. Va. 1863.
Daily News. Denver, Colo. 1873.
Enterprise. Bath, Va. 1857.
Gazette. Martinsburg, W. Va. 1811; 1827; 1840-44.
Herald. Charleston, W. Va. 1871.
Herald. Martinsburg, W. Va. Obituary, March 17, 1888.
Independent. Martinsburg, W. Va. Obituary, March 10, 1888.
Jefferson Republican. Ranson, W. Va. 1951.
Journal. Martinsburg, W. Va. 1954-1957.
Leader. Winchester, Va. Obituary, March 16, 1888.
News Leader. Richwood, W. Va. 1955.
New York Times. Obituary, March 9, 1888.
New York Tribune. Obituary, March 9, 1888.
Register. Shepherdstown, W. Va. 1866; 1935.
Spirit of Jefferson. Charles Town, W. Va. 1865.
Sunday Post. Salisbury, N. C. 1952.

Virginia Free Press. Charles Town, W. Va. Obituary, March 15, 1888.
West Virginia Courier. Charleston, W. Va. 1870.
Whig. Richmond, Va. 1864-65.

Manuscript Materials

Berkeley County Court Records. Deed Books, Land Books, and Marriage Records. Martinsburg, W. Va.
Costello, Sister Joseph Miriam. "The Life and Works of David Strother—'Porte Crayon.'" Unpublished Master's thesis, St. John's University, 1956.
Hilleary, Esta. *David English Henderson.* A manuscript prepared for the Jefferson County Historical Society, March 29, 1940. Typescript in the Princeton University Library.
Hunter Family Records. In the library of Princeton University.
Jefferson County Court Records. Deed Books and Will Books. Charles Town, W. Va.
John Pendleton Kennedy Journals, 1851-53. Among the John Pendleton Kennedy Papers at the Peabody Institute, Baltimore.
McVeigh, Donald. "Charles James Faulkner." Unpublished Ph.D. dissertation, West Virginia University, 1954.
Miller, Mrs. J. M. *Old Grave Yards of Jefferson County.* Manuscript, compiled in 1934, in Old Charles Town Library.
Minutes of 1st and 2nd Battalion, 67th Virginia Regiment. Berkeley County Courthouse, Martinsburg, W. Va.
Morgan County Court Records. Birth Records, Deed Books, and Will Books. Berkeley Springs, W. Va.
Strother Family Genealogy from Adam and Eve. Among the Kennison Papers in the Southern Historical Collection at the library of the University of North Carolina.

Reviews of Virginia Illustrated

Athenaeum (November 7, 1857), p. 1389.
Graham's Magazine, LI (September, 1857), 278.
Harper's New Monthly Magazine, XV (August, 1857), 404.
Harper's Weekly, I (July 11, 1857), 438.
Southern Literary Messenger, XXV (August, 1857), 160.

Index

Abbott, Jacob, 69
Adams, Charles Francis, 70
Adams, Henry, 98, 189, 195, 210
Alden, H. M., 74, 180, 193, 205
American Tract Society, 53
Ancora, Pietro, 8-9
Antietam, Battle of, 123-24
Ashby, Turner, 112, 184
Averell, William W., 139, 143, 149, 164

Bagby, George W., 20, 70, 76, 83, 221
Baldwin, Joseph G., 96
Baltimore, Maryland, 48
Bancroft, George, 200
Banks, Nathaniel P., 118-31 *passim*
Bath. *See* Berkeley Springs
Bedinger, Henry, 28, 72
Berkeley Springs, West Virginia, described, 56-58; Irving's visit to, 70-71; mentioned, 62, 114, 118, 132, 162, 168-69, 181, 189, 223
Bishop, John Peale, 153n
Bonaparte, Madame Jerome, 48
Boreman, A. J., 161, 197
Boston, Massachusetts, described by Strother, 98-99
Boteler, Alexander P., 28, 83n, 88-89, 101, 151
Botta, Anna Lynch, 89
Bowen, Ele, 67
Bradley, Arthur G., 83
"Brandon," 61
Brooks, Van Wyck, 80, 214

Brown, John, his raid on Harpers Ferry, 103-6; his trial, 106-7; his execution, 107-9; mentioned, 206
Browne, J. Ross, 69
Bryant, William C., 55, 136, 185
Burke, William, 86
Burnaby, Andrew, 86
Butler, Benjamin F., 127, 129, 153
Byrd, William, 90
Byron, Lord, 30, 42, 45, 217

Canonsburg, Pennsylvania, 13-14
Carlyle, Thomas, 132
Carmi, Illinois, 27
Caruthers, William A., 214, 221
Cass, Lewis, 15-16, 24
Cedar Mountain, Battle of, 122
Century Club, 56
Chapin, James, 25n, 55
Chapman, John Gadsby, plans Strother's European study, 30-31; teaches Strother wood-drawing, 52-53; mentioned, 20, 37, 41, 45, 56, 156
Charleston, West Virginia, 150, 176-80 *passim*
Charles Town, West Virginia, 10, 106, 114, 124, 206
Child, Lydia Maria, 108
Clarksburg, West Virginia, 134
Clemens, Samuel L. *See* Mark Twain
Cleveland, Grover, 202
Cleveland, Ohio, 172
Clevenger, S. V., 38, 39, 45

William and Mary, College of, 60
Williams, H. T., 186
Williamsburg, Virginia, described, 59-61
Willis, N. P., 48
Wilson, Augusta Evans, 73
Winchester, Virginia, 17, 121
Winter in the South, A, 93-97

Wise, Henry Alexander, 105, 109, 112, 162
Wise, Henry Augustus, 85-86
Wood-engraving, the process of, 52-54
Woodstock, Virginia, 141

Young Virginians, The, 170-71, 176